COMPUTERS AND THE SOCIAL SCIENCES

COMPUTERS AND THE SOCIAL SCIENCES

ALAN BRIER
Lecturer in Politics, University of Southampton

and

IAN ROBINSON
Lecturer in Sociology, Brunel University

Columbia University Press
New York, 1974

Alan Brier is Lecturer in Politics at the University of Southampton.
Ian Robinson is Lecturer in Sociology at Brunel University.

Published in Great Britain in 1974 by Hutchinson & Co (Publishers) Ltd
Printed in the United States of America

Library of Congress Cataloging in Publication Data

Brier, Alan.
Computers and the social sciences.

Includes bibliographies.
1. Electronic data processing—Social sciences.
2. Electronic data processing. 3. Computer simulation.
4. FORTRAN (Computer program language) I. Robinson, Ian C., joint author. II. Title.
H61.B645 1974b 300'.28'5 74-12052
ISBN 0-231-03914-X
ISBN 0-231-03915-8 (pbk.)

Contents

Acknowledgments

We must express our gratitude here to the following colleagues and friends who have variously helped to improve this book—
Peter Calvert, Ray Curnow, Tim Harrison, Chris Goodrich, Tony Hill, Peter Hollowell, Robin Lovelock, Mike Rees, Ian Rennie, Andrew Schulkins, David Thomas and John Wise. Mary Brier and Jane Robinson were indispensable at all stages in the writing. David Hancorn, of Burroughs' Machines, kindly tested the FORTRAN examples on a second computer. Any original computation reported was initially undertaken on the ICL 1907 of the University Computing Service, Southampton.

Preface

As is often the case, our interest in computers arose, initially, from necessity. This book was first suggested by our separate experiences of learning to use computers to cope with demands arising from research projects involving data processing at some stage. Learning the necessary techniques and skills in this way, in response to rather narrowly conceived requirements, does, however, leave much to be desired. This is true not least from the point of view of those (fortunately) very patient colleagues whose advice and guidance helped us in the early stages of the process. Later, having achieved some proficiency in persuading others to help us out, we began to explore for ourselves the broader practical and intellectual possibilities of the general purpose computer. At this point, as a consequence of the relative success of our exploratory ventures into computing, we were ourselves cast in the role of adviser on things computing to a small and shifting clientele, and finally felt moved to offer a short course on computer appreciation to postgraduate and final-year political scientists at the University of Southampton where we were then both based. What follows is founded on that course and its successors. Of necessity our individual interests have become more specialised. Alan Brier, who is still at Southampton, and whose honeymoon with the computer proved of longer duration and greater intensity wrote Chapters 2, 3, 6 and 7. Ian Robinson and Alan Brier jointly wrote Chapters 1, 4, 5 and 8.

In many ways, social scientists have computing problems which are similar to those of any other would-be computer user, but our choice of illustrations is intended to stimulate the interest of a social science audience, in the broadest sense. We have tried to meet the need for a treatment which stands somewhere between an introduction for the general reader, of which there are now many available, and the specialist literature of computer science, which is the next step on points of detail for the interested professional reader. It was in this last area that we ourselves experienced the most difficulty in obtaining guidance from appropriate literature.

One main concern in the writing of this book has been to elevate the acquisition of some proficiency in computer usage to the kind of status that statistical analysis, at least at an elementary level, has in a basic training in any empirically-based social science. In the sphere of technique, we hope to have offered a means of shortcutting the rather cumbersome and ad hoc learning process which we were obliged to undertake ourselves in applying computers to our own research. This book is intended to serve both as an introductory text and as a source of reference for understanding problems which may occur during the next stage of learning computing skills by practice. Our other interest is, in the strict sense, methodological. For better or worse, the advent of computers is demonstrably changing the face of some disciplines in the social sciences, both by facilitating existing lines of enquiry and by opening up wholly new possibilities for investigation. Our further and parallel concern is to illustrate and review in the following chapters some ways in which this process is taking place.

Alan Brier and Ian Robinson

1 Introduction

Computers and computing are becoming increasingly significant in business, education, and specialist subjects in the social sciences. Not only are computers increasingly used for data processing purposes, but in the wider sense they affect the way we think. In this book we are largely concerned with the technical aspects of computation but also less tangible social and intellectual pressures have played an important part.

We discuss briefly below some aspects of this reciprocity between computing machines and men, before turning to more detailed technical discussions on the construction and use of computers.

The origins of computers

Logic

Before deciding that the projection of computer imagery on to human behaviour is a one-way process, it is as well to acknowledge the deep interdependence of computer technology and more general intellectual processes. It may help to illustrate this idea by reference to the development of computers themselves. The initial impetus for what is now recognised as the main line of development of digital computers came from the enormous computational requirements of new military technology. Computers did not in fact play a part in the Los Alamos project, but military exigencies did stimulate the search for a practical application of the kind of mathematical theory of computation and automata which had already existed for a few years. This theory in turn was an outgrowth of earlier innovations in the application of mathematics to philosophical and logical concerns which had resulted in the growth of mathematical logic and set theory (Korfhage, 1966). In fact, the technology used in the first electronic machines was also available ten or even fifteen years earlier. The earliest attempts at constructing digital computers made use of available electronics for logical devices and for number storage, for example they used electromechanical relays and mercury delay tubes before alighting on the idea of magnetic memory units of the kind discussed in the next chapter. They also drew on the then most obvious logical theory, which was expressed in terms of Boolean algebra and truth functions. The conventional binary notation for truth values was given practical expression in the fundamental building blocks of nascent computers. The application of the binary number system is explained further in the next chapter, for those unfamiliar with the ideas discussed here. For the present, we will illustrate the general point by reference to the principles involved.

The binary digits, 0 and 1, used to represent numbers to a base of two, can be understood more generally as the logical values 'false' and 'true'. Using Boolean notation, two basic logical operations found an expression in computer circuitry. First, the operator 'OR' results in a value of 'true' if either of two arguments is true. Its outcomes can be represented as the truth table:

A ∪ B		Result
0	0	0
1	0	1
0	1	1
1	1	1

Second, the operator 'AND' has the effect shown in the next table.

A ∩ B		Result
0	0	0
1	0	0
0	1	0
1	1	1

Binary addition requires the same values as the logical 'OR' operator, except that $1+1=0$, and a value of 1 is 'carried' to the next digit place to the left.

We now now show how the basic logic circuit for adding binary digits together was originally conceived. Three elements are needed,

(1) The OR circuit

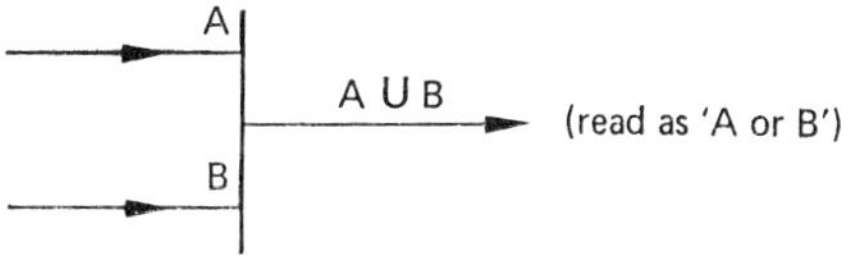

(2) The A N D gate

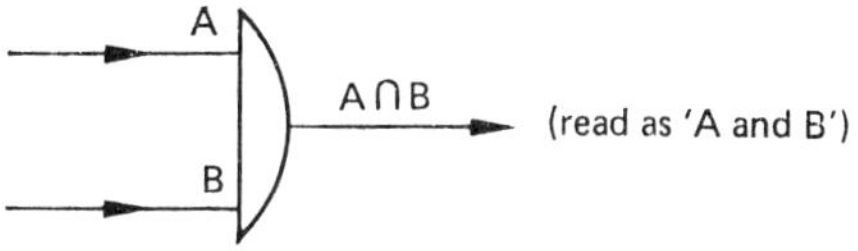

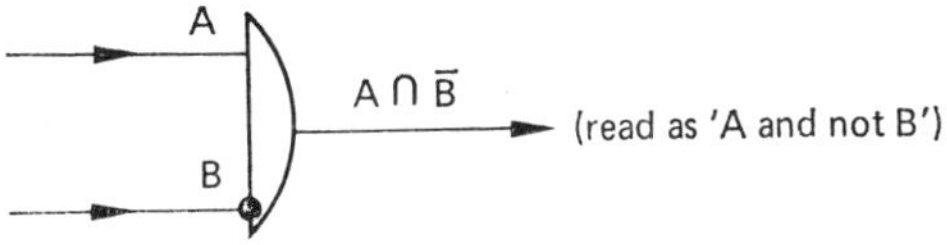

In the last $\bar{B}$ is read as 'not B' and is the opposite of the value of B. From these elements a 'half-adder' can be assembled, to produce a value for the sum of two digits, plus a carry digit. When a signal is applied to A or B, the result is simply the sum of the two signals. Signals applied to A and B together must set the carry mechanism and not transmit a sum signal.

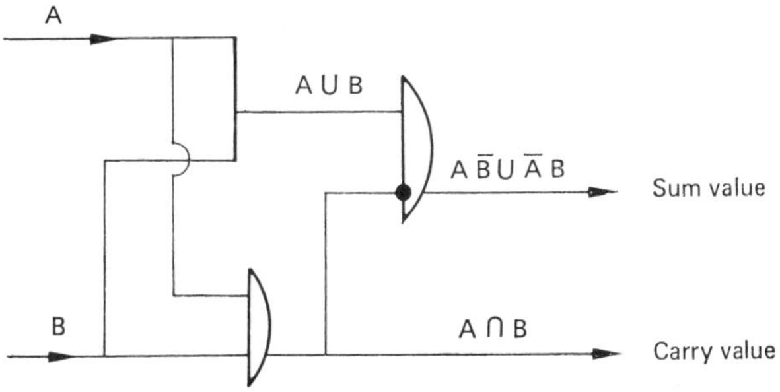

The result of (A∩B) is fed to the carry value, and is inhibited at the modified AND gate, so that a signal is produced as the sum only when

$$(A \cup B) \cap (\overline{A \cap B}) \equiv (A \cap \bar{B}) \cup (B \cap \bar{A})$$

which is the desired behaviour for binary addition.

History

Accounts of computer history frequently begin with Charles Babbage's technically over-ambitious proposal in 1833 for a general purpose 'analytical engine'. This developed his special purpose 'differential engine' of 1812 which was designed, with some British government support, for the production of mathematical tables. He also conceived of the use of the punched cards used to control the Jacquard loom as a medium for the input of data and sequences of instructions. Punched card technology was later developed for use in the 1890 United States census, after which it acquired its now familiar association with the name of George Hollerith. It was eventually adapted by Howard Aiken at Harvard, in collaboration with IBM, for inclusion in the electromechanical Automatic Sequence Controlled Calculator (ASCC—the 'Mark I'). Completed in 1944, this was very much a realisation of Babbage's conception, although the similarity was not discovered by Aiken until he had been working for three years on the project.

Fully electronic machines were completed soon afterwards from several virtually independent projects. Eckert and Mauchly's *Electronic Numerical Integrator and Calculator* (ENIAC) was completed in 1946 at the Moore School of Electrical Engineering of the University of Pennsylvania, and was intended primarily for use on ordinance tables. This might have been regarded as the first fully electronic computer had it not been discovered later that Konrad Zuse, working in Germany, had already designed a successful stored program machine, the Z3, by 1941. He used the binary principle, borrowing from Leibniz, and floating point arithmetic, and later constructed the first general purpose programming language which he called Plankalkul. All of this work, however, passed unnoticed by others in the field. ENIAC required programming by means of a wired plug-board, with dial settings for constants. A further group, including John von Neumann, whose initial impetus was his consultancy to the Los Alamos project on the atomic bomb, proposed the EDVAC (Electronic Direct Variable

Automatic Calculator). This used the binary principle and held a stored program in its memory, but before it was finally constructed a team led by M. V. Wilkes at Cambridge University had produced its EDSAC (Electronic Delay Storage Automatic Calculator). This was the first computer to embody the principles of accumulator registers and program and data storage which are described in later chapters of this book. Serious commercial production of digital computers began in 1951 with the Univac, followed by the IBM 701. Magnetic core memory was first incorporated on a large scale into the Whirlwind I computer at M.I.T. in 1953, and subsequently established itself in commercial models (Bernstein, 1965; Rogers, 1970; Hollingdale and Toothill, 1965).

The intellectual impact of computers

Three areas are especially interesting when we consider the extent of the impact of this new technology on the social sciences. These are, first, some of the more pertinent intellectual issues raised by available computing techniques, which we discuss in this section. Second, the significance of the psychology of the computer aficionado and the computer 'knocker', and thirdly the societal consequences of the exponential growth of computing. The inter-linking element in these three areas is as much the psychology, as the epistemology, of computing. It is at this level, of perceptions as much as methods, that some of the primary imbalances and deficiencies as well as the strengths of computation lie.

The most obvious impact has been in methodology. The results are not just that numbers are added or subtracted more quickly by machine thus reducing the social scientist's need for manual calculations. A major effect at a more general level can be seen in the channelling of intellectual activities as a result of the availability of certain computing techniques. It is, for instance, improbable that econometrics would have developed as it has done without the advent of mechanised regression techniques, or certain areas of psychology progressed without automated factor analytic routines. Thus, although we think of research methods as a means to an intellectual end already conceived, it appears that of itself a technique may come to achieve a more dominant position. This is not a new phenomenon of course. In the physical sciences, new or changed techniques have resulted in an historical change of intellectual direction. The introduction of the microscope is a good case in point. Similarly, not only is computation a useful addition to the social scientist's technical armoury, but a temptation to engage in certain types of research at the expense of others. Moreover, it provides a kind of technological backcloth against which social scientists operate. This can be seen even amongst those who profess a reluctance to tangle with the new technology directly. For instance, authors may refer through analogies to the computer's size, power or sophistication in making other and apparently unrelated points.

A simple analysis based on technological or economic determinism is inappropriate. We prefer an interpretation similar to the position of the critic Raymond Williams (Williams, 1961) that the components of our general culture take the form of dominant images drawn from stages in economic and technological history. The electronic computer provides a highly significant example as both an embodiment of advanced intellectual images in our society, and a notable source and reinforcement of these images. We are dealing, then, not with a mere research tool, but with a machine which is closely related to some of our most influential intellectual formulae.

Further the use of computers tends to give a spurious methodological unity to issues and problems which are theoretically diverse. In terms of the 'law of the instrument', that given a hammer everything tends to become a nail, given a computer everything tends to become programmable. This may be particularly true for the unskilled user of computer programs and sophisticated statistical analysis, for whom availability, rather than relevance, could be the main criterion of use. In this context it is worth noting the currency that linear additive models have gained in multivariate statistical analysis. These aspects are discussed further in Chapter 4.

In other complex applications, such as those associated with the machine translation of languages, or with advanced simulation models, the effects are at the same time more difficult to assess, and arguably more potent. The computer is here used to attempt a sophisticated analysis and re-ordering of the data which would be impossible by any other technique. In the case of simulation models, this approximates to an experimental situation, especially where the results are inherently unpredictable. Machine translation, with its associated problems of producing a meaningful grammatical structure, has emphasised the potentialities and some of the problems of computation. It would obviously be of great advantage, both to program the computer in standard English, and to be able automatically to translate languages. This involves automatically recognising the meaning of words and the structure of sentences.

At present, these possibilities are some distance away, although individual translation and linguistic analysis programs provide a working basis for development. Many scholars would suggest, however, that the attempt to mechanise the translation process is a destructive one. For example, we may recall Pascal's distinction between the conceptual mind (ésprit de finesse) which works with wholes precariously and intuitively, and the geometric mind, which abstracts the definable unit (Bowles, 1967, page 232). The geometric mind is seen here as essentially alien to the humanities in general whose subject matter is, by implication, amenable only to individual qualitative analysis. This point seems overstated in relation to the possible benefits which might follow from a limited intrusion of quantitative methods. At a minimum, a number of computer produced concordances have proved their worth, as have machine techniques on questions of authorship. Other scholars have used computation in more complex ways, as in stylistic analysis. However, whatever the techniques employed, they are only as effective as the men who produce and use them.

Finally, these general applications raise some interesting points in relation to major philosophical controversies in the social sciences. It may be for example that the subjectivist-objectivist debate could become irrelevant (Diesing, 1966). The experimental methods of simulation and the modelling involved in linguistic analysis, could deal with everything that the subjectivist holds unique in individual behaviour. At the same time the modelling methods used need not fall prey to criticism from objectivists. If the example of the controversy between learning theory versus games theory is taken, then the choice between these two theories might be made on empirical and not philosophical grounds. Thus, in the long run, the introduction of computer modelling could render sterile some apparently intractable philosophical problems.

The psychological impact of computers

The personification of the qualities of the computer, and individuals' modes of adaptation to these qualities have considerable significance for the way in which computers are used. Bobrow and Schartz (1968, page 2) suggest three perceptions of computers are relevant. First, some conceive of computers as Merlins, expounding the view that bigger computers and better facilities could by their very presence solve our problems. Secondly, some envisage the computer as a Frankenstein's monster threatening to take over jobs and posing a real danger to personal integrity. Third, there are those who view computers as autonomous social forces. According to this perception, the computer assumes an unpredictable but major influence on social and intellectual life.

Amongst those who actually use computers, variations on these general themes operate. Cline (1968) has suggested a number of particular ways in which individuals use the technology of computers. The entrepreneur, for example, has the skills to generate expensive projects, large teams of assistants and massive increases in facilities to give a new and seemingly better rationale to his work. The researcher then may become distanced from the ongoing project, dependent on his staff for expertise. The dependent user is in a different category. Possibly arising from the ranks of the entrepreneur's staff, he takes on the computer single-handed. He is dependent on a series of packaged programs in a particular installation, although he might have some knowledge of a computer language. A move to another institution in this situation is catastrophic, for a new series of computer programs have to be learned, starting from scratch. The co-opted applied mathematician is somebody who gradually abandons substantive research in favour of the elegance of programming the computer itself. Coming into computation at a later stage in his career, he gradually loosens his ties with his former mathematical colleagues and becomes totally immersed in his new setting. The scorner is the fourth of Cline's categories. He believes that any problem capable of computer treatment is not worthy of serious consideration. Indeed he might go so far as to tackle problems out of the empirical field altogether, at the very least working on macro-research, or in the philosophical aspects of his subject. These four stereotypes echo some of the stages through which many computer users may pass at some time. They tend to reflect the fact that computation becomes more than just one amongst many methodological techniques which social scientists may encounter.

The social impact of computers

Of course more general issues are raised by the social consequences of computers and computing, for the consumers as much as for the producers of the new technology. These consumers may be only remotely concerned or aware at present of the probable impact. There appear to be two easily recognisable views about how consumers may be affected.

The negative view has been emphasised recently by the *Data Bank Society* (Warner and Stone, 1970) in which the unfettered growth of computers is seen as resulting in disastrous social and individual consequences. Rose (1969) spells out some of the negative implications of this view in a more concise way. He suggests five major problems that would arise from the pervasive spread of computers. First, there would tend to be *over-systematisation* of records and individuals' activities. The logically detailed and clear instructions needed to program computers would reduce areas of human activity to a more mechanised level. Second, there would be a growth of *impersonality* in relationships because of the replacement of some personal forms of communication by the machine. Here Rose quotes an early example of a Billy Graham evangelistic crusade replying to letters by stereotyped replies, based on certain keywords in the letters. Third, there would be a growth of the possibilities for *centralised control* resulting from the introduction of data banks, with quick and easy interrogation of these data banks for personal information. In this case there would be very little in an individual's private life that was not stored in some data bank, with relatively simple access to those with possible sinister political motives. Fourth, with the expertise needed to create and program computers and the latter's enormous social implications, a *new élite* would develop. This technically sophisticated élite, Rose suggests, might potentially possess power divorced from responsibility or from any form of democratic control. Fifth there would be a '*technological*' drift resulting from the previous four problem areas. That is, that society would tend to be increasingly ordered by technological and rational criteria, and values, implicitly adopted from the use of computers. These five negative consequences of the widespread use of computers synthesise some of the more detailed criticisms which have been voiced. These predictions of the future present a terrifying picture of the possibilities that await us (or which in some cases already threaten to undermine the established social order). However, it is instructive to compare these prophecies with, for example, those that were current with the rapid extension of bureaucracies (Burnham, 1960), or the extension of communications (Kornhauser, 1960), all of which could have been foreseen to have similar consequences. Over-systematisation, impersonality, centralised control, a new élite, and a version of 'technological' (perhaps bureaucratic) drift, could be as applicable to a heavily bureaucratised society, as to a heavily computerised one. However, the pervasiveness and sophistication of this new phenomenon have added an extra dimension to these issues.

The alternative and positive view of computers is expounded by many computer professionals and others and has become more prevalent with the advent of larger computers and the growth of interactive computing. For example, a recent article by Cornock (1972) suggests that much of the 'man in the street's' concern about computers, privacy, and the dangers of the new technology can be accounted for by substantial information gaps about the reality of computing. There is, he stipulates, a kind of 'cultural lag' between the growth of any radically new technology and its social acceptance and absorption. However, as interactive computing grows, not only will knowledge of the system itself increase, but learning through and about computers will take on a new dimension. The concept of a 'computer utility' (Gruenberger, 1968) embodies the view that from the marrying of computers and communications much more flexible systems will result. Broadly the approach of those who on balance believe in the benefits of computers suggests that the direction of advances is controllable; that questions of privacy and liberty have both political and technical solutions; and that questions of inhumanity and impersonality are not real issues. They emphasise the enormous advantages that the human brain will continue to have over the most advanced computers, while the latter, in performing routine tasks, liberate the human mind for creative purposes.

Of course, these two positions represent extremes of a spectrum but do underline the tendency for polarisation of views. However, both rely heavily on extrapolation from tendencies in the present, to certainties in the future. This in itself is a not uncommon practice, but leads often to a false antithesis, about which little can be done, except to swap prejudices. Ultimately, the extent of either the fears or the hopes about the use of computers will be proven by events. To exercise some control over these events there is a widespread need for the dissemination of information about what a computer is, and what computing does.

In the next seven chapters we explore some of the areas of computation most relevant to the social sciences. The discussion is intended to be technically informative in a general sense about computers and of interest to those who are considering using a computer, whilst not we hope neglecting their wider intellectual and social implications. In Chapter 2 we chart some of the main features of a computing installation, and the ways in which the hardware —the machinery of computers—can specifically influence the user. In Chapter 3 we consider the software—anything other than the machines themselves, particularly computer programs—involved in computing. This introduces some basic concepts of computer programming, and reviews a number of the major programming languages and their potential for the social scientist. Chapter 4 is a look at some of the commonly used computer data processing techniques. We discuss practical considerations affecting the user, and the ways in which data processing can be made easier and more effective. In this chapter we concentrate on the handling of numeric data. Chapter 5 is a review of information storage and retrieval, and text handling. We explore the basic process of information storage, search procedures, content analysis and give a brief introduction to linguistic analysis and machine translation. Chapter 6 surveys simulation procedures in the social sciences and the way they can be, and are being, used as methods of experimentation. Chapter 7 is an introduction to the most widely used of programming languages, FORTRAN. In Chapter 8 we return to the future of computing systems and consider more fully the problems presented by the growth of the use of computing in the area of individual social and political privacy.

References

J. Bernstein (1965) *The Analytical Engine*, London, Secker and Warburg.

D. B. Bobrow and J. L. Schwarz (Editors) (1968) *Computers and the Policy-Making Community—Applications to International Relations*, Englewood Cliffs, N. J., Prentice-Hall.

E. A. Bowles (Editor) (1967) *Computers in Humanistic Research*, Englewood Cliffs, N.J., Prentice-Hall.

J. Burnham (1960) *The Managerial Revolution*, Bloomington, Indiana University Press (other editions available).

H. F. Cline (1968) 'Computer Instruction for Scholars in the Humanities' in *Computers and the Humanities*, **III**, pages 31–40.

S. Cornock (1972) 'The Cultural Impact of Interactive Computing' in '*On-Line 1972*', Conference Proceedings, **1**, pages 93–112, London, Brunel University.

P. Diesing (1966) 'Objectivism versus Subjectivism in the Social Sciences' in *Philosophy of Science, 33*, pages 124–133.

F. Gruenberger (Editor) (1968) *Computers and Communications—Towards a Computer Utility*, Englewood Cliffs, N.J., Prentice-Hall.

S. H. Hollingdale and E. C. Toothill (1965) *Electronic Computers*, Harmondsworth, Penguin.

R. R. Korfhage (1966) *Logic and Algorithms, with Applications to the Computer and Information Sciences*, New York, John Wiley.

W. Kornhauser (1960) *The Politics of Mass Society*, London, Routledge and Kegan Paul.

W. Rogers (1970) *Think: A Biography of Watsons and IBM*, London, Weidenfeld and Nicolson.

M. Rose (1969) *Computers, Managers and Society*, Harmondsworth, Penguin.

M. Warner and M. Stone (1970) *The Data Bank Society*, London, George Allen and Unwin.

R. Williams (1961) *The Long Revolution*, London, Chatto and Windus.

Further reading

On the inter-relations of technology and more general intellectual life we have found:

C. E. Ayres (1962) *The Theory of Economic Progress* (2nd Edition), New York, Schocken Books, and

R. H. Davis (1972) 'The Computer Revolution and the Spirit of Man' in *Perspectives on Electronic Data Processing*, J. D. J. Holmes and E. M. Awad (Editors), pages 180–186, Englewood Cliffs, N.J., Prentice-Hall of considerable interest.

See also A. G. Oettinger (1966) 'The Uses of Computers in Science' in *Information*, San Francisco and London, W. H. Freeman and C. Wrigley (1962) 'The University Computing Centre' in H. Borko

(Editor) *Computer Applications in the Behavioural Sciences*, Englewood Cliffs, N.J., Prentice-Hall.

Two edited collections of essays, about the role of computers, present useful introductions.

Z. W. Pylyshyn (Editor) (1970) *Perspectives on the Computer Revolution*, Englewood Cliffs, N.J., Prentice-Hall.

I. Taviss (Editor) (1970) *The Computer Impact*, Englewood Cliffs, N.J., Prentice-Hall.

2 Development and design

We have already made a brief mention of the common distinction between computer hardware and software. These terms conventionally differentiate considerations relating to the design and operation of the machines themselves in physical terms, from the province of communicating human intentions to the machine by way of instructions, whose existence in the computer is less tangible. This distinction forms the basis for the organisation of our general introduction to computation in this and the subsequent chapter.

Analogue, digital and hybrid computers

In common with most other writers in the field, we use the term 'computer' in this book to refer to the large-scale general purpose electronic digital computers which most readers are likely to encounter in the course of meeting their computational and research needs. All of the concepts and applications to be discussed in this and subsequent chapters are based upon the availability of this kind of general purpose computing facility, which can be readily adapted to the user's requirements by the provision of a program of instructions, and which requires no special engineering insights for its successful use.

It is as well to remember, however, that there is another entire family of computing machines, of a wider range of sizes and complexity, which are based on analogue as opposed to digital principles. This analogue/digital distinction provides us with a convenient starting point for our outline of the basic features of computer construction. For most users interested in the application rather than the design of computers, and this we assume includes almost all social scientists, a very cursory knowledge of machine engineering is quite sufficient at the present stage of the development of computation, but still very useful at times to an intelligent appreciation of the problems which sometimes arise.

In an analogue computer, quantities involved in a calculation are represented in the machine as physical quantities of voltages in circuits, which may vary as continuously as the reliability of the electrical components and measuring instruments in use will permit. A digital machine, by contrast, represents quantities as integral numbers of electrical pulses, and as a result cannot provide more than a close approximation to continuous changes of value. The difference is often conveyed by reference to two rather earlier computing aids, the slide rule and the abacus or counting frame. On the face of a slide rule, numbers are represented physically by lengths of a marked scale which are proportional to their common logarithms. The principle of operation is then very simple. The addition or subtraction of two lengths, by moving the sliding scale against the fixed one, enables the results of multiplication or division to be read off directly. Since the variations possible are continuous, although the accuracy of the instrument depends on its overall length and the accuracy of its markings, the slide rule is a familiar embodiment of the analogue principle in calculation. The abacus permits values to change only incrementally, by the addition of digits of fixed value, and provides a simple example of the digital storage and manipulation of numbers.

Electronic analogue computers, then, are used essentially to simulate the behaviour of theoretical systems or models of the real world. Within a very considerable range of size and complexity of engineering, they provide facilities for the physical representation of system entities by means of actual electronic circuits, which are connected in different ways by the experimenter to suit his requirements. The greater range of purely analogue devices is possible because, unlike digital computers, they require essentially no basic and irreducible minimum of equipment in their construction. They may vary from a few circuits, permanently connected to simulate a particular kind of system and specifically built for this purpose, to quite large arrays of electronics which can be adapted in a variety of ways to different problems.

The basic devices used are high gain amplifiers which ideally will produce exactly magnified images of input voltages. Analogue computing machines are manufactured which contain anything between a basic 50 to 100 amplifiers, to systems using in excess of 500. These can be manufactured to fulfil various functions. For example, circuits can be designed to reverse the sign or polarity of a voltage, or to output a signal equal to the sum of two or more input voltages. Amplifiers also exist which produce signal values equal to the integral with respect to time of the input voltage. The combination of elements of these various kinds produces at desired points in a circuit voltage values which can be interpreted as solutions for linear differential equations with constant coefficients. Additional non-linear elements include devices for multiplication, division, finding square roots and other mathematical functions of input voltage values.

These values, at various points in a simulated system, can be measured and recorded in a variety of ways, either temporarily, for example by voltage meters or oscilloscopes, or permanently as recorded traces or signals. Clearly, the accuracy of the whole process will depend on the accuracy with which devices can be manufactured to measure output values, and on the reliability with which electrical components perform the functions for which they are designed. On both levels, the degree of accuracy possible from purely analogue computing devices is rather strikingly lower than that which is possible using digital design techniques. In the latter, there is at least no theoretical limit to the number of digits with which a number can be represented, whereas the analogue computer is subject to the errors inherent in its actual construction. Such a difficulty would not normally inconvenience most social scientists, given the degree of precision of most of our concepts of system specification and behaviour. There have also been developments in hybridisation, using digital techniques wherever increased accuracy is needed, while attempting to retain the basic analogue facility of continuously varying quantities. Such developments exploit the accuracy available from digital techniques, and the much faster performance of functions such as integration and differentiation available by analogue methods.

More significant restrictions may be experienced in setting up analogue computers to solve particular problems, and in the kind of problem to which they are suited. True analogue machines are basically limited to the integration of functions with time as the independent variable. This restricts their most effective use to applications in which what is needed is virtually a simulator of a time based system, whether the base used is actual clock time or some suitably re-scaled time period. But, as a very simple illustration, a model which included a variable representing the actual size of a population is clearly capable of providing, by differentiation of the voltage corresponding to this variable, a value for the current rate of change (R) of the population (P) is obtained as

$$R=\frac{dP}{dt}$$

If the rate of change is itself constructed as a function of various other inputs, some generated within the simulated system and some perhaps set by the experimenter, passing the voltage corresponding to this rate through an integrator produces the value of the population. The effects of variation of values at any point in the system can be studied as continuous variations at any other point at which values are measured. This very trivial application can be illustrated as follows:

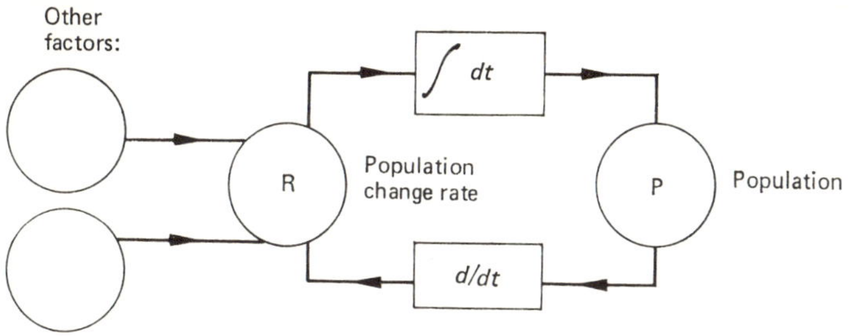

The circles would correspond in practice to potentiometers with or without voltage measuring instruments, and the rectangular boxes to circuits designed to integrate or differentiate with respect to time.

The restriction to time integrals arises out of the basic electronics of analogue computing and its avoidance calls for some ingenuity in the specification of the differential equations of a system (Wass and Garner, 1965; pages 4–5). It is, for example, sometimes possible to substitute derivations with respect to time in equations which contain derivatives with respect to other variables. It is also often possible to operate analogue computers to a time scale either faster or slower than real-time with a consequent broadening of the range of problems to which they can usefully be applied.

Again, this particular problem is overcome in so-called hybrid applications by the inclusion of some digital equipment in the system, and such combinations are then capable of solving a much wider range of problems.

The major difficulty for a user to overcome lies in the manner in which pure analogue computers must be instructed to perform calculations. In some cases, potentiometers can be set by hand to supply initial values appropriate to the problem in hand, or to change parameters in a simulation. The connections between available computing elements needed in setting up the computer to solve a problem may be made through a fixed or detachable plug-board with a series of leads and plugs. The process is sometimes calling 'patching' and the panel a 'patch-board'. At a higher cost, connections and settings can be made automatically, using coded punched tape as a means of conveying instructions to the machine. It is, however, necessary to reduce the problem in hand either to a set of differential equations or a physical simulation of a theoretical system which uses the range of components available.

Finally, analogue devices may, in some cases, be available in a rather more complex hybrid installation, in which the operation of a main digital computer in respect of analogue components is similar to its relationship to any physical system to which it is connected for metering and control. In these circumstances hybridisation consists of the connection of a large general purpose digital computer to any required analogue computer by means of digital-analogue and analogue-digital devices. These configurations are termed 'bilateral' by the authors of one widely used introduction to 'true' hybrid computation, distinguishing them from systems in which the conversion process operates in one direction only, which they term 'unilateral' hybridisation (Bekey and Karplus, 1968; pages

6–11). The user may write instructions to the digital computer, often in extended forms of the computer instruction languages described in the next chapter, and call in the course of his program for certain functions to be performed in the connected analogue circuits. Several manufacturers and many computing centres now offer the basic facilities for mixed digital and analogue computing in terms of a widely used computing language such as FORTRAN, which greatly increases the convenience of setting up simulations and recording and analysis of data from the analogue computer (see, for example, Hambury, 1969; Bekey and Karplus, 1968; Chapter 7).

Although very little used at present in social science, analogue computing techniques may eventually prove very useful in investigating the properties of theoretical systems in a way which is possibly less expensive and conceptually simpler than the programming of a large digital computer to deal with the same problems. One very important feature is the relative ease of modelling systems and subsystems which is implicit in the idea of their actual physical representation as electronic circuits. This makes them particularly attractive, for example, in examining the sensitivity of the highly aggregated world system specification which we discuss below in Chapter 6 (Forrester, 1971) to variations in subsystem behaviour. Refinement of a digital computer simulation to permit a degree of disaggregation of the model eventually presents quite large problems of programming, when the capacity of digital facilities becomes overloaded. But as a glance at any introduction to the subject will suggest, to achieve a reasonable degree of proficiency is likely to require kinds of training and knowledge that are at present very rare in the social sciences (Key, 1965; Wass and Garner 1965). Hybrid systems where the analogue computer is used under the control of a digital machine are more convenient, and the principles of their use are similar to those to be described in the rest of this book.

Mini-computers and micro-computers

A further category of computing equipment which is sometimes overlooked in introductory texts is that of the small mini-computer (Schoeffler and Temple, 1972). These are essentially digital machines, but of a much simpler kind, in use if not always in design, than the larger and more expensive variety. The range of these terms is difficult to define exactly, and an exact classification is of little importance. It is, however, often forgotten in organising data collection and analysis that there is a wide range of machines extending from little more than programmable desk calculators with a few memory locations, to quite powerful small computers. These can operate alone or as communications terminals for networks under the control of a large central computer. Our purpose in mentioning such machines here is to point out that smaller scale and vastly cheaper equipment can often meet at least the statistical needs of a researcher as adequately as the largest configurations. Some of these machines also fall into the category of 'intelligent' computer terminals, which we discuss later.

This range of computation machines shares the ability of larger digital computers to store numbers and manipulate them subject to a series of instructions written by the user. As an illustration of the simpler kind of micro-computer, the Olivetti Programma range of desk-top and office computers achieves a considerable degree of flexibility of application with a very limited capacity to store numbers and instructions and a simple language from which programs of 120 to 150 instruction steps can be constructed. The speed of operation and capacity of accuracy in calculation of this type of machine is, of course, very much less than that of fully-fledged digital computers, but their convenience is such that at least one recent introduction to computing for business students has been based upon the Programma 101 programming language (Smith *et al.*, 1969). Programs of instructions, and data for calculations can be stored and input to this machine from magnetic cards, which serve in this case as a kind of auxiliary memory storage. The use of additional input and output devices, such as printers and paper tape punches and readers, greatly extends the data-handling capacity of a micro-computer, to the extent that some of them can be used as control units for data transmission to larger computers, as well as free-standing units. This kind of small digital computer can be conveniently applied to relatively simple numerical calculations on relatively small quantities of data, when the use of more expensive facilities may be uneconomic. Micro-computers are becoming available which effectively span the gap between programmable desk calculators and the smaller general purpose computers. In some new machines not much larger than the more familiar desk calculator, it is possible to use a version of one of the general purpose programming languages widely available on large scale computers. It seems likely that this increased flexibility will result in much wider use of small digital machines to complement the enormous power of large installations which raise greater problems of economic use. The range and availability of computing equipment at this end of the scale of capacity and price is also increasing rapidly.

Smaller computers, such as Computer Technology Ltd.'s Modular One or Digital Corporation's PDP's, can provide many of the facilities for instruction by users which are described in the next chapter, and need not be restricted to a special code unique to their particular series of equipment. The data storage capacity of these machines may very well not be sufficient for the kind of social science data processing operations described later in Chapter 4, but their relative economy and convenience of use make them an attractive alternative to large scale installations for many research applications as well as to teaching uses. The Modular One series is in fact composed of basic modules which can be combined in a variety of ways to create a wide range of computing capacities. These and other smaller systems are also found frequently as satellite computers in much larger systems, in which they serve very large central computers by collecting jobs together and transmitting information.

Digital systems—fundamentals

In contrast to analogue devices, digital computers use integral numbers of electronic pulses to represent any kind of information, and are programmed by the input of a series of separate instructions. They require a central pulse generator and other circuitry to enable them to carry out transfers of information between various temporary storage locations. These basic functions are discharged by a central processor unit the size of which is incapable of reduction below a certain minimum, but does not increase rapidly with increases in the overall capacity of a computing system. The basic pulse or cycle time of the digital computer determines the speed of information transfers and ultimately the rate at which calculations can be performed. On the latest machines, this time period is measured in hundreds of nanoseconds, a unit of one thousand-millionth of a second whose ratio to one second is of the order of the ratio of one second to thirty-three years. The cycle time does not represent the average time for an instruction to be carried out, for example an information transfer from one location to another. The time for this kind of operation depends upon the complexity of the instruction and is subject to the physical limitation of the speed at which the electrical pulses can travel the required distances inside the machine. This is, of course, one reason for the search for ways of miniaturising computer components which has produced spectacular results in terms of performance times.

In distinguishing basic functions in a notionally typical digital computer it is helpful to draw a diagram such as Fig. 2.1. While

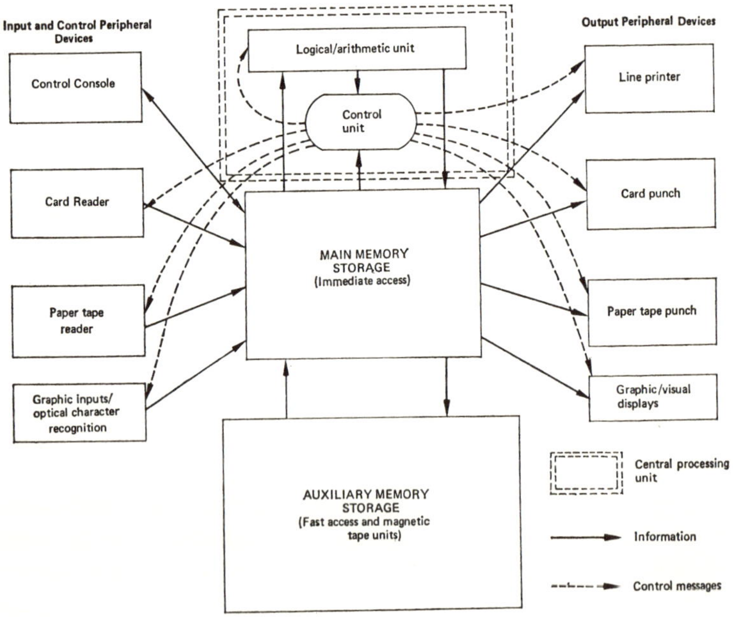

Fig. 2.1 Basic digital computer block diagram

stressing that this is at best an over-simplification of certain large scale systems in which several such units may be linked to form a functional whole, or multiple processors are used in intercommunication, such a diagram does serve to introduce certain fundamental concepts. The extent to which this approach over-simplifies real installations is becoming a matter of decreasing concern to the user who is not a professional computer scientist.

It has become customary to distinguish phases in the exploding technology of computer construction as three 'generations', defined in terms of the hardware itself, with some unresolved discussion about whether a fourth generation might not already have appeared, characterised by advanced software and system design. The first generation of digital computers used the available electronic technology of thermionic valves (vacuum tubes) which in the late 1940's were sufficiently unreliable as to cast doubt upon the general commercial viability of this type of computer. Power consumption caused cooling problems and restricted the size of a feasible design. The development in the mid-1950's of the planar silicon transistor permitted a great reduction in circuit size and electrical consumption, while the introduction of printed circuits made for ease and economy in construction.

The newer technology of monolithic integrated circuits has made it possible to manufacture very small logic circuits which are as reliable as a single transistor.

The extraordinary changes in computer technology from the earliest days are summed up by the rates at which circuits have become smaller and speeds have increased to reduce the unit costs of computing operations. Expressed as the number of logic circuits which can be contained in a cubic inch, the size reduction is exponential, and there has been a log exponential reduction in unit costs, by a factor of 10 every 5 years since 1955 (Martin and Norman, 1970, pages 10–11). Similar factors apply to speeds of operation and improvements in storage capacity.

The earliest digital computers could add numbers at only a few pairs of digits per second, while more than 10 million additions per second are now possible. These phenomenal increases in speed are only possible when all mechanical parts are eliminated, so that input and output for human use must necessarily be vastly slower by comparison. A modest machine operates at 10000 times the speed of hand calculation.

Main storage concepts

The main memory storage of the computer can be thought of as composed of a large number of locations, each of which has a label or *address* attached to it so that its contents can be retrieved by the central processor whenever they are needed. This level of storage is organised into suitable units which represent the minimum *addressable* unit of stores of a particular machine, and an attempt is made in its design to provide the greatest degree of control, and consequent economy of use, over the hardware which is consistent with the economic provision of the necessary circuitry. The cost of such storage is generally quite high, so that its use must justify the expense. Space must not be wasted by the provision of too large a minimum addressable unit, but at the same time too many control circuits to address very small units would also prove wasteful. Main storage, as its name suggests, is used for the temporary storage of information which the processor may need very quickly in the course of a job, and since it is directly accessed by the control unit, the time involved in retrieval or recording of information must be suitably related to the very fast speed of the processor itself. There must be no appreciable time lapse while a search takes place for a particular piece of information, and this is met by allowing locations to be addressed directly at random, and not in any fixed sequence.

One of the most reliable and widely used methods of digital storage for immediate random access has been by means of arrays of small ferrite cores whose magnetic polarity is used to represent values of 0 or 1. Different methods of reading from and writing to this kind of memory exist (Renwick and Cole; 1971) but the basic principle, of switching the polarity of a ring-like ferro-ceramic core by passing electric pulses along the wires on which it is threaded, remains the same. And despite the increasing use of alternative storage methods which are faster in use, smaller or easier to manufacture, the name 'core-storage' or simply 'core' to refer to the main immediate-access memory of the computer remains in common use. Other methods of realising storage units which will have the desired properties include the use of plated wires or flat thin film with similar magnetic properties to the magnetic core arrays. Further devices coming into use exploit the technology of metal oxide semiconductors (MOS) and the creation of whole circuit units of tiny silicone chips by large scale integration methods (LSI) which are likely to bring the distinction between the computing circuitry and the main memory to an end except as a functional concept. It is beginning to be possible to construct storage devices from similar circuits to those used elsewhere in the central processor, since the relative costs of storage and other processing circuitry are beginning to change in favour of such methods. Some new machines use very fast monolithic memories in some modules and slower core storage as a kind of auxiliary storage.

Another functional distinction we have drawn here for conceptual clarity is also disappearing, in two ways. First, the development of the mass storage devices we have described already, with access times which are becoming faster, means that most large computers use a hierarchy of storage devices with differing operating speeds. Some of these devices may well be regarded effectively as part of the main rather than the auxiliary memory, in terms of Fig. 2.1. Very fast central processor speeds make it increasingly likely that a hierarchy of interlinked storage devices and even subordinate and slower processors will be used to maintain an economic workload.

The distinction between various levels of storage device is also being removed, from the point of view of the user, by software methods. The main operating program which runs a large computer can so organise the storage units at its disposal that the capacity of the machine, to the user, becomes enormously enlarged. The concept which IBM in a recent release of such a system now call *virtual storage* enables a user to proceed as though the main memory included all the available storage peripherals, and the allocation of storage to the user's program becomes a matter for the operating system to control. This represents a considerable step forward in ease of use for the non-specialist (Wilkes, 1968; Chapter 4).

Number systems

As we have already noted, digital computers store numbers as finite sequences of digits. The methods of storage in common use, and the way in which logical operations are performed on stored information, are of some importance to users concerned with the applications reviewed later in this book. While many of the details of any manufacturer's particular methods of realising these principles are of little relevance to a researcher whose computational goals are limited to the performance of calculations, the general problems and concepts of digital computation are fundamental to an intelligent appreciation of computer applications.

To explain these general concepts, it is convenient to begin with the representation of numbers, and then consider the representation of alphabetic characters. The basis for the various number systems and codings used in computing, some of which we will mention later, is the binary system, which represents numbers using powers of two. For everyday purposes, we are used to manipulating numbers in a form which uses ten separate digits to represent values. Starting from a 'decimal point' which notionally separates the integer part of a number from its fractional part, successive digits reading towards the left represent their own value multiplied by successive increasing powers of ten, beginning from 10^0, which by mathematical convention is 1. Similarly, digits to the right of the decimal point represent their own value, multiplied by diminishing powers of ten, beginning from 10^{-1} or 0·1. This is, in fact, a number system which uses a base of ten.

The binary system uses a base of 2, and requires only two digits to express a value, that is 0 and 1. In a similar way to the decimal point in the representation of decimal numbers, binary notation inserts its binary point, if necessary, between the digits representing powers of 2^0 and 2^{-1}. In general, we can represent numbers to any base or *radix* r by an appropriate number of distinct characters to represent digits, and evaluation of a digit in terms of a power of r corresponding to its position relative to the *radix point*.

In the table below, the decimal number 196·641 is expressed in both binary and octal or base 8 notations, to illustrate how this process works in two of the number systems frequently encountered in computation.

Decimal (base 10)							
Digit position values	10^2	10^1	10	·	10^{-1}	10^{-2}	10^{-3}
	1	9	6	·	6	4	1
Octal (base 8)							
Digit position values	8^2	8^1	8	·	8^{-1}	8^{-2}	8^{-3}
	3	0	4	·	5	1	0

Binary (base 2)
Digit position values

2^7	2^6	2^5	2^4	2^3	2^2	2^1	2	·	2^{-1}	2^{-2}	2^{-3}	2^{-4}	2^{-5}	2^{-6}
1	1	0	0	0	1	0	0	·	1	0	1	0	0	1

Conversion between binary and octal representation is simply achieved by the separate evaluation of successive groups of three binary digits. To convert decimal integers to binary, they can be divided by two for each binary place until the answer to the division process is zero. The remainder at each stage becomes a binary digit, placed to the left of its predecessor. A further number system sometimes encountered in computing is called hexadecimal, and uses a base of sixteen, with additional single symbols to represent the digits 10 to 16. This achieves a more compact storage of numerical values.

Binary numbers are represented in computers by storage devices which can take one of two states at any point in time, and are capable of transmission in an appropriate sequence in terms of the presence or absence of an electrical pulse of a certain magnitude during a specific time interval. The length of such a sequence is clearly to be measured by the number of binary digits in the number to be stored or transmitted. At the simplest level, a binary number can be thought of as stored by a set of switches, each representing a particular power of two, and each set on or off, according to whether the binary digit for the power is to be set as 1 or 0. The binary number illustrated above can, then, be given direct physical representation in electronic terms.

Here we have a further means of characterising the size and capacity of a digital computer. The term 'binary digit' is conventionally abbreviated to *bit*. The accuracy of a particular machine is then expressed in terms of the number of bits which make up the minimum addressable unit in the main storage unit, and the number of bits employed in arithmetic and other operations on stored values. The smallest addressable unit is usually termed a *word* but sometimes words may be broken down if required into smaller units usually termed *bytes*. Whatever the terminology, the storage capacity provided is expressed as the number of bits in a single storage address. The number of units provided by a module of main storage is conventionally expressed as a multiple of 1024, or 2^{10}, which is shortened to the symbol K for convenience. We can thus refer to the class of machines mentioned earlier as mini-computers as having, typically, a word length of between eight and sixteen bits, and providing between 1 and 8K of store as a main memory unit. A clear dividing line for a class of smaller capacity machines cannot be absolutely drawn, but equipment of this specification clearly differs substantially from a large general purpose computing installation providing perhaps 256K of storage in up to 60-bit words. On the other hand, the actual physical size of a computer clearly depends upon the kind of storage and circuit technology employed in its construction, and not upon these considerations of operating capacity. The type, design and construction of machines do substantially affect the operating philosophy of a computing centre, and the availability of different modes of communicating with the resources at hand, but need not detain us at this stage.

Number representation

The main principle of number representation is thus to provide a finite number of bits, and this determines the ultimate accuracy of calculations. For example, if all numbers are held in a form in which the binary point is always at the same bit of a word, which can be called fixed-point representation, a 20-bit word can hold at most an integer value of $2^{20}-1$. A real number, with an integer and a fractional part, will have its accuracy determined in a similar way by the number of bits allocated to each part. In practice, one bit must be used for the sign of the number, so that our notional 20-bit word could hold only integers in the range $\pm 2^{19}-1$ or the binary numbers:

Sign bit																				
0	1	1	1	1	1	1	1	1	1	1	1	1	1	1	1	1	1	1	1	$\equiv +[2^{19}-1]$
1	1	1	1	1	1	1	1	1	1	1	1	1	1	1	1	1	1	1	1	$\equiv -[2^{19}-1]$

Negative numbers are often expressed in what is called radix complement form, in the case of binary numbers, twos' complement. Each digit of the number is subtracted from one less than the radix or base of 2, and one is added to the result. In this way the smallest negative value capable of expression in 20-bits becomes

Sign bit

1	0	0	0	0	0	0	0	0	0	0	0	0	0	0	0	0	0	0	0	or -2^{19}

The great convenience of this representation is that negative and positive numbers can be added together directly without need for special attention to the sign of the numbers. Readers can check that the binary addition of the largest positive and negative numbers shown does in fact produce the correct two's complement representation of minus one. Fractional numbers can be similarly represented if the binary point is always between the same two bits of a word, and larger numbers can be stored by allocating more than one word to a single value.

In a similar way instruction codes and the addresses of elements in the main storage are fitted into fixed numbers of bits, so that there is, for example, an upper limit to the number of storage addresses which a given length of instruction can cover. All computing elements are eventually binary in form, and separate circuits must be provided for addition, multiplication and division of binary numbers. The conversion of numbers to the decimal form usually preferred by users for the input and output of data is managed by some variant of binary coded decimal notation, or BCD, of which the simplest represents each decimal digit by four bits, corresponding to the values 8, 4, 2 and 1.

In data transmission, an error check is often added in the form of an additional *parity bit* which is switched so that in a correctly transmitted value the number of bits set is always odd, or even, these alternatives being termed *odd and even parity modes*. The purpose is to introduce a check on the coding and attempt to reduce errors due to faulty machine operation. An alternative system using binary digits to code values of 2, 4, 2 and 1 ingeniously provides for radix complementing by complementing each binary digit of a coded decimal digit, and bit-codes of 0, 1, 2, 3 and 6 gives a built-in parity check by having 2 bits set for every possible code (that is, 01, 02, 03, 13, 14, 23, etc.).

BCD codings for the value 9

Bit values	*Code*
8, 4, 2, 1	1 0 0 1
2, 4, 2, 1	1 1 1 1
0, 1, 2, 3, 6	0 0 1 1

Similar schemes, applied to hexadecimal (base 16) notation achieve a further reduction in the number of characters needed to transmit or store numerical values, and may be preferred for this reason. The use of less orthodox methods of number representation can also help to reduce the time taken for computer arithmetic, bringing it closer to the theoretical maximum for a given arithmetic circuit design (Winograd, 1968).

The *fixed point* storage method is clearly capable of no great accuracy unless the number of bits allocated to a single number is very large. An alternative is to represent numbers in the general *floating point* form

$$n = a \times r^b$$

where r is any suitable radix. If r and the form of a are always the same, any real number can be represented by a and b. In a computer, the radix is likely to be 2, and the argument a is in this case usually normalised within the range $1{\cdot}0 > a \geqslant 0{\cdot}5$ or $-1{\cdot}0 \leqslant a < 0{\cdot}5$.

The separate values a and b are allocated a certain number of bits each, and usually more than one computer word is allocated to the storage of a floating-point number. One such scheme is illustrated below. The signed binary fraction a (the mantissa) extends over a total of 37 bits and the exponent takes 9 bits from a pair of 24-bit words of storage.

Floating point representation

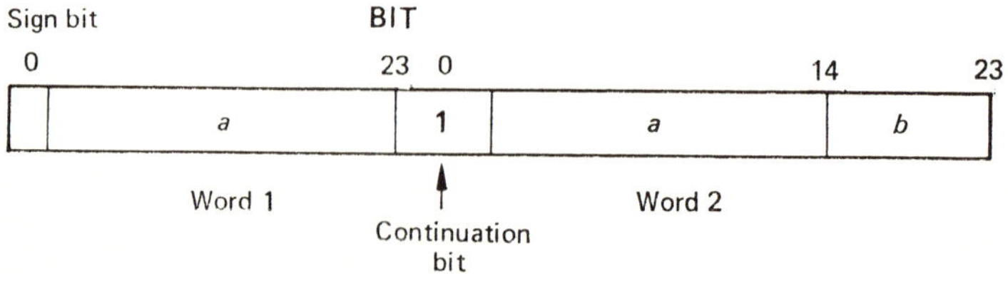

To avoid negative exponents, the value of the maximum permitted positive exponent is added to all exponent values.

Computer arithmetic

In considering arithmetic on fixed and floating point numbers, it is more convenient to use decimal illustrations, although, of course, the principles are the same in binary arithmetic. We will use the familiar fixed point notation for decimal numbers involving fractions, and suppress the base in floating point form,

so that 0·09 is expressed as 0·9 E−01
and 9·0 as 0·9 E 01

Fixed point notation is generally of lower accuracy than floating point, and requires the programmer to know in advance the maximum and possibly minimum sizes of the quantities he is handling, which is not often feasible. But when all numbers are in fixed point form, arithmetic on them is relatively straightforward. Two conditions can, however, give trouble. A series of repeated additions or a large multiplication, which in practice is the same thing, can cause the generation of a number too large for the number of bits available. This condition is called *overflow*.

It is also possible that by dividing a small value by a very large one that the result becomes too small to be registered by the available fixed-point accuracy. For example, 0·01 ÷ 10000 is indistinguishable from zero to less than six decimal places. This condition is termed *underflow*. Both conditions can be recognised by the computer, and would result in incorrect results if ignored in the course of a program.

Arithmetic on floating-point numbers involves more stages, and therefore tends to take longer in a computer. For this reason, unless special hardware is provided in the arithmetic unit, it may be avoided where possible in the interests of efficient use of resources. Computing efficiency measured in time and hardware costs of operations usually involves some compromise between different kinds of advantage, and an avoidance of those operations which take longer to carry out. Some illustrations of different methods of achieving the same result are given in further chapters.

Addition and subtraction in floating point form requires the equalisation of exponents as a first stage, followed by conversion of the results to the standard form of floating point storage. And, since computers operate in a fixed word length, arithmetic overflow to the left must be followed by a shift of all values to the right, truncation of the right-hand end of the previous value and an increase of one in the exponent. Truncation may also occur when equalising exponents. Thus

0·900 E02 + 0·123 E01 must first be expressed as
0·900 E02 + 0·012 E02
and 0·900 E02 + 0·123 E02 must become 0·102 E03

The accuracy is, of course, in practice considerably greater than the three decimal figures of the mantissa shown here. The floating point storage scheme illustrated earlier, giving 37 bits to the mantissa, provides an approximate equivalent to an accuracy of eleven decimal places. Most computers allow the allocation of more units of storage for double-length working, giving greater precision if it is needed.

Multiplication and division in floating point form consists of the simpler process of the separate calculation of products or quotients of the mantissae, and addition or subtraction of the exponent values, all followed by re-expression of the result in the normalised form. Before this process begins, a check must be made that no argument is zero. If, to avoid negative exponents, the standard form uses an exponent value of, say, $50+e$, then the exponent of the result of a multiplication must be reduced by 50 to give the correct answer in this notation. In the case of division, 50 must be added to the resultant sum of exponents. Division raises the additional complication of possible overflow if the mantissa of the divisor is smaller than that of the dividend. For example:

$$\frac{0{\cdot}999}{0{\cdot}125}$$

causes generation of too large a value. For this reason, the divisor must be shifted one place to the right before the division begins.

Some consequences for the user

A programmer using, for example, the FORTRAN language as described in Chapter 7 need not concern himself with the mechanics of these operations, apart from ensuring that division by zero is never attempted in his program. But systems which use floating point arithmetic do raise two kinds of problems which we can deal with most conveniently here.

The first concerns the effects of rounding errors which occur as a result of the arithmetic method used. Any introduction to the branch of mathematics known as numerical analysis begins with the problem of the propagation throughout a long calculation of errors due to the use of a finite number of digits to represent fractions with only a given degree of accuracy. For example, the maximum error in the result of arithmetic operations on two operands can be shown to be equal to the sum of the maximum errors in the operands. Such rounding errors are cumulative, and depend upon the interaction of the inherent accuracy of the machine itself and the method of computation chosen (Noble, 1964, pages 1–11; Tompkins and Wilson, 1969; pages 1–23). That is to say, it is possible to choose computational methods and formulae which minimise these cumulative errors. For this reason, if for no other, the use of a computer to carry out complicated calculations without a clear understanding of the numerical method used in the process is to be strongly discouraged. Knowledge of this kind helps to prevent the acceptance of spurious results.

As an illustration, it is clear that the decimal value 0·1 has no exact binary equivalent. If this approximation is added to itself a number of times, the error becomes larger, but may be decreased, for example, by dividing successive sums by 10 instead of using 0·1 directly as an incremental value in a computational formula.

It is only possible here to hint at the nature of the subject area, but to illustrate the difference such considerations can make in practice, we will examine alternative procedures for the accumulation of sums of squares and products as part of the calculation of means, standard deviations and correlation coefficients (Nealy, 1966). The quantities to be calculated are

$$\bar{x} = \frac{1}{K} \sum_{i=1}^{K} x_i$$

and

$$s_x = \sum_{i=1}^{K} (x_1 - \bar{x})^2$$

The conventional 'desk calculator' method first finds $\sum_{i=1}^{K} x_i$ and $\sum_{i=1}^{K} x_i^2$ and uses the expanded formula $s_x = \sum x_i^2 - \dfrac{(\sum x_i)^2}{n}$

This is only as accurate as the grand total term $\sum x_i$, and this can become rather inaccurate if its accumulation involves the addition of large numbers stored in floating point form, for reasons already illustrated above. An alternative method of calculation uses the relationship of each succeeding term of the data to its predecessor, and directly accumulates the mean and corrected sum of squares on one reading of the data values. The mean can be evaluated from the relationship

$$\bar{x}_k = \bar{x}_{k-1} + \frac{1}{K}(x_k - \bar{x}_{k-1}) \qquad \text{(a)}$$

The equivalence of this to the familiar definition of the arithmetic mean can be shown in the following stages:

$$\frac{1}{K}\sum_{i=1}^{K} x_i = \frac{1}{K}\sum_{i=1}^{K-1} x_i + \frac{1}{K}x_k \qquad \text{(b)}$$

$$= \frac{K-1}{K(K-1)}\sum_{i=1}^{K-1} x_i + \frac{1}{K}x_k$$

(a) follows directly by re-arrangement of (b).
By a similar process the corrected sum of squares can be accumulated using the relationship

$$S_k = S_{k-1} + d_k^2 - \frac{1}{K}d_k^2 \qquad \text{(c)}$$

where d_k is defined as $x_k - \bar{x}_{k-1}$

Another consequence of the number storage systems discussed here lies in the floating point equivalent of zero. A user can, of course, set a value to zero, but if a test for a floating point zero is needed in the course of a program, for example to check the value of a divisor before attempting a division, it cannot be assumed that a series of calculations which in their decimal form ought to reduce to a zero answer will necessarily do so in their binary floating point equivalent. In addition, the effects of rounding during arithmetic operations may result in a very small non-zero result where absolute zero is expected. For this reason, in FORTRAN and other programming languages which use floating point methods, a test for a zero value is treated as a test for an acceptable degree of approximation to zero, say 10^{-6}, which lies within the range of the machine in question. It cannot, in fact, be assumed that the result of the following value assignment in FORTRAN

$$X=10{\cdot}3*5{\cdot}0-51{\cdot}5$$

is necessarily floating point zero in its computer representation.

The second possible source of error which may be mentioned in this context lies in the inherent inaccuracy of the data compared with the machine. There is a serious temptation when using a computer to report results to a larger degree of numerical accuracy than is appropriate to often very imperfectly measured data values. Errors in computed values can also be propagated by measurement errors in data, and in ways which again depend upon the general formula employed. For example, one widely used application of the Newton-Raphson iteration formula (Noble, pages 26–30; Tompkins and Wilson, pages 49–52) applied to the calculation of the square roots of a number which is measured with an error of d can return an answer with an overall error of approximately $d/2$.

The conclusion to be drawn here is that some knowledge at least of the possible sources of error in a particular computer application is essential to avoid misinterpretation of results. Most errors which do occur are likely to result from the user's program rather than the hardware, but it is as well to remember that there can be an interaction between the two sources.

Alphabetic character representation

Alphabetic and other characters can be represented in a similar way to numerical values, by using suitable binary codes. Letters can be given numerical codes for internal use by the computer, so that A might be represented as 1 and Z as 26. Groups of characters can be stored as numbers to a scale which corresponds to the number of bits allocated to each letter. Using a scale of 32, corresponding to an allocation of 5 bits per character, the word CAT can be held as a binary equivalent of

$$3\times 32^2+1\times 32+20=3124$$

In this way strings of characters become very large integer numbers when coded for the computer, and with a knowledge of the internal code values of a particular computer it is possible to treat character-handling problems as arithmetic operations. Individual letters in a string can be assessed by shifting the contents of a storage cell to the left or right as needed. Using our hypothetical 5-bit scheme, the word CAT would appear in binary as

| 0 0 0 1 1 | 0 0 0 0 1 | 1 0 1 0 0 |

shifting 5 bits to the right, the letter A could be retrieved as the value 1, located now in the right-most five bits.

Auxiliary storage

To return to the block diagram of computer functions earlier in this chapter, we now turn to the area of auxiliary storage and peripheral devices for input and output. As we noted earlier, the dividing line between main and auxiliary or 'backing' store becomes blurred in some large systems, and the devices commonly included in the range of this term vary considerably in their speed and convenience of operation. Strictly, backing storage is provided by units which are not essential to the main processor, but are used to extend its capacity by providing areas in which data or sections of a program not currently required can be temporarily stored for later use. Backing store devices work at a slower speed than the processor itself, but compensate by providing many more storage locations in a cheaper way than existing main memory technology. Despite the recent extension of the idea of a 'virtual memory', originally implemented in Burroughs' computers, in which the machine itself handles the allocation of all available storage units automatically, it is usually necessary for programmers to arrange this allocation themselves. And since the requirements of social science data processing often exceed what can be provided in main storage alone, it is useful to have some awareness of the principles involved. Instructions to read from and write to various backing store devices are available in the main programming languages, but may be defined differently for the systems provided by different manufacturers. Example 5 in Chapter 7 shows a straightforward use of magnetic tape as a storage medium. Applications may require only temporary use of a larger store, or it may be that a more permanent method of holding coded values is needed. Typically, decisions will have to be made which involve reaching a compromise between efficient use of the available computer hardware and convenience for the user.

For this, two main types of unit can be distinguished; those which permit only sequential transfers of information, and those in which access to stored information is more nearly random. In the latter category are a wide range of magnetic disc and drum devices which use varying numbers of read and write heads to access magnetisable surfaces which are kept in constant rapid rotation. The principle is not dissimilar from that used in a tape-recorder, except that storage is achieved by setting the polarity of patterns of dots which represent binary digits, according to an appropriate digital code. The time taken to read from or write to a particular area of the disc or drum surface depends upon the time taken for that area to approach the nearest read or write head, by which the value needed can be transferred. If the rotating disc or drum is not to be removable from the unit, it can be made quite large and can have a large number of heads suspended at fixed points above its surfaces. Mass storage devices of this kind of construction can characteristically store several millions of characters and provide average access times which at best begin to approach those of main memories. They can be used for permanent data storage only if they can be devoted to one user for a suitable period, but their speed of operation makes them very useful as temporary support to a program which requires a lot of storage space. Also in very common use are stores which use exchangeable disc packs with several discs mounted on the same spindle. The heads on this kind of device must move to locate information on the rotating discs, and are many fewer in number than are possible on fixed heads units. As a result, the convenience of random access combined with the possibility of permanently storing information in a removable disc pack is achieved at the price of a generally slower rate of operation. Moving head units can offer average access-times of between 30 and 60 milliseconds (millionths of a second), but the latest fixed-head devices can reduce this by a factor of 10 or more.

Magnetic disc or drum devices of any kind are still a much more expensive form of auxiliary storage than the very widely used medium of magnetic tape. This is employed in a variety of ways, including standard cassette form, but the greatest capacity is achieved by the 2400 ft used on the large tape drives which are found in most computing centres of any size. These represent the cheapest method for the more or less permanent storage of data in machine-readable form. Any magnetic storage medium is potentially unstable, and is vulnerable to dust or imperfections in the oxide coating, so that duplicates should always be kept to maintain reasonable security, but with reasonable precautions magnetic tape reels are most convenient for storing and transporting information.

The standard reel can hold nearly 8 million characters, depending upon the density of writing, but the cheapness and generally higher capacity of the medium is accompanied by much slower speeds for information transfers. If tapes are to be exchanged with users of different computing centres, it is important to know the density of recording the data on a particular reel and the way in which information is structured. The main sources of this information are the different manufacturers' hardware manuals, but fortunately certain standards are observed.

The other disadvantage of magnetic tape is that values can be accessed only in sequence. The process of backspacing involves stopping and reversing the tape, with consequent time lapses during which no information can be transferred, and to minimise the delay it is necessary to read or write in blocks of data values rather than single quantities. So it becomes important to know the block structure of the information on a particular tape before it can be retrieved in an intelligible form. For these reasons, when there are faster alternatives available, the main use of magnetic tape is likely to be for input and output of large amounts of data, and for the storage of data and programs, rather than as backing-store during the working of a program. Data preparation machines which enable an operator to code values directly on to tape are now coming into widespread use, so that magnetic tape may soon come to be regarded as a fast input and output medium rather than auxiliary storage.

Whether serial or random access backing storage is used, the structure of the information stored and its sequence of retrieval, within the constraints noted, are ultimately under the control of the user, who must try to make the most efficient use he can of the hardware at his disposal.

The control console

Primary communication between the machine operator and a computer is usually achieved by a console typewriter and display device, which usually includes a means of printing messages. Very commonly used is some variant of the standard teletype, which resembles a typewriter with a number of extra character keys, and a button for transmitting each line after it has been typed. Teletype units are cheap and robust, but print rather slowly compared with other devices. For this reason, operators may receive their information from a form of visual display instead of a roll of printed paper. Teletypes are, however, also in widespread use for 'interactive' communication between a user and his program inside the machine.

The standard keyboard contains certain mathematical symbols and control characters, both printed and unprinted, in addition to the normal typewriter keyboard with numerical values, but uses only upper case letters in its alphabetic section. It transmits a relatively limited standard character set in one of the current codes for information interchange. Character codes, for example the British Standard Data Code (B.S.D.C.), the American Standard Code for Information Interchange (A.S.C.I.I.) and some manufacturers' extended binary-coded-decimal interchange codes (E.B.C.D.I.C.) are mostly related to an I.S.O. (International Standards Organisation) 7-bit standard (McGregor Ross, 1972). This type of unit also currently contains an attachment for punching and reading paper tape, and can serve as a tape punch when not needed as a peripheral device to the computer.

Basic peripheral units

All input and output functions can be served by peripheral units attached to a main computer, or may be incorporated into satellite equipment which shares the main processor with other slow operating data handling stations. The basic devices found in almost all installations are those which use or produce 'hard copy' of some form. Punched cards or paper tape of the kind illustrated in Fig. 2.2 are almost universally used as cheap forms of computer input which can be prepared and edited on machinery which does not need to

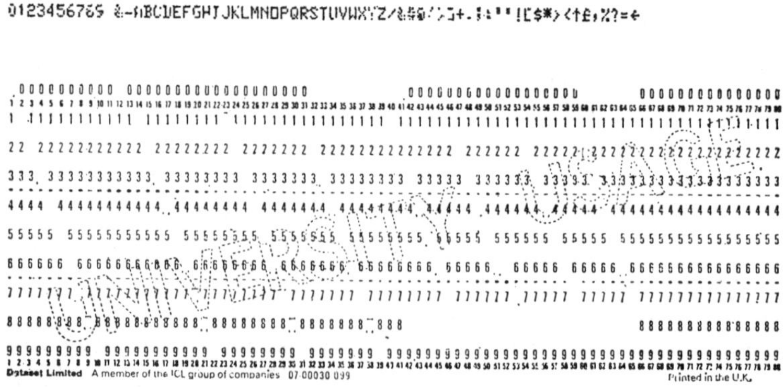

In a card code of this kind, single punches and combinations of two or three position punches are used to convey one character per column. The interpretation at the top of the cardwas printed by the machine used for punching

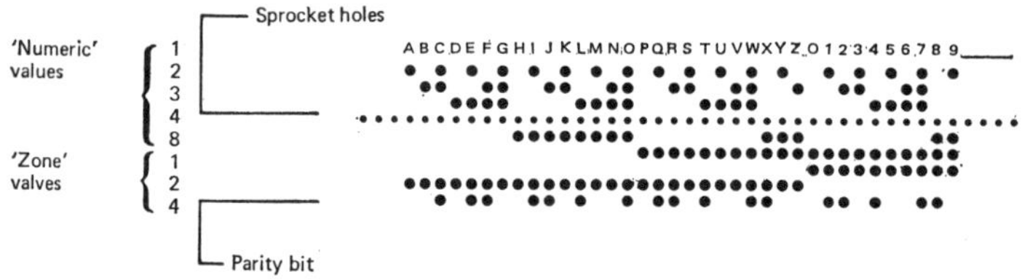

This shows an eight-track tape code, in which combinations of 'zone' and 'numeric' binary values express characters, and the parity is even. The number of possible combinations is the product of the maximum 'zone' and 'numeric' values, although not all are used.

Fig. 2.2 Examples of punched card and paper tape codes.

be connected to the main computer. Output of results can also be obtained from card or tape punches for storage or re-processing. Processing rates on input or output tend to be slow compared with reading from or writing to magnetic tape. Card readers vary in speed between 300 to 1200 or more cards per minute, and punches can output up to 300 cards per minute. Paper tape punching is a simpler and so faster process, but there is little to choose between the two media at input time. However, the obvious difference in bulk between a tape reel and a tray of cards must be set against the relatively greater robustness and ease of editing of cards, and the interpretation of codings which can be printed on the face of a punched card. Paper tape must be rewound after each use, and tears easily, although stronger reinforced or mylar tapes can be used at a greater cost. However, the bit coding of the type illustrated shows how 8-track tape can cover a much wider set of characters, and the inclusion of a parity track can help to eliminate coding errors. Punched cards are sometimes coded in a binary form in which each hole is used as a separate bit. In this case, more information can be held on a single card, but visual interpretation becomes difficult. Character coding of the kind illustrated is usually preferred.

A range of sorting, counting and reproducing equipment is usually available to carry out operations on punched cards for which use a computer would be wasteful. The cards generally in use were originally designed for electro-mechanical tabulating equipment which pre-dates the electronic computer but can still perform many useful jobs. Programming of these machines is typically achieved by means of a plug-board similar to those used on analogue computers (Claffey, 1967). They provide a cheap if relatively slow way of producing tabulations, for example, of social survey data.

Other similar forms of input which are found less frequently in academic installations include punched cards containing magnetic tape or microfilm apertures, which can combine the information compaction of these media with the durability and convenience of an interpreted card, and edge-punched cards which resemble a paper tape with an additional wide margin to carry printed messages. The smaller IBM System 3 computers make use of 90 'column' punched cards which are actually smaller than the standard 80 column card illustrated, but still carry a readable interpretation of their punching. Punch-coded media are durable and cheap for use in exchanging data and programs between installations and users, provided that a standard code is used to avoid the minor problems of incompatibilities between machinery.

The other almost universal form of hard-copy output is obtained from a fast line-printer. Listings with widths of up to 160 characters can be obtained on continuous stationery, printed as a succession of lines at fixed intervals. Speeds as fast as 2500 lines per minute can be achieved with rotating printing barrels and limited sets of characters, while more accurate resolution comes from slower machines using different printing techniques. To achieve rapid printing, text is usually output in upper case characters only, but this is a feature only of present hardware design. Slower printers can easily provide upper and lower case letters, and the simple interchangeable 'golf-ball' type founts used in some office typewriters are also available in similar communications devices. The more recent use of Xerography and infra-red techniques on special papers can produce fast and silent operation, one recent machine almost doubling the speed of the fastest line-printers. Line-printer output is relatively cheap and adequate for most purposes, although it can embarrass by its sheer bulk.

The input peripheral units so far described all require the preparation of machine-readable coded material. The coding process is for most applications an intermediate stage between the collection of data and its analysis by the computer. To some extent, it is possible to eliminate this coding stage by using a document reader which will automatically produce codings from source material, or transmit values direct to a computer if used as input devices. Operating speeds vary enormously, faster input being achieved by the use of specially prepared types of document. The most useful techniques for the social scientist involve sensing pencil marks in specific zones of a document, and the optical recognition of characters, usually from a special type-face. In either case the source document, perhaps a questionnaire form from a survey, can remain as fully intelligible to a human reader as it is to the machine. Given this intelligibility and the saving of the time otherwise spent in punching or other coding work, quite acceptable speeds of data conversion can be achieved without having to use special kinds of stationery, or the magnetic ink characters in use in the banking world for cheque identification. It is possible to present ordinary typewriter characters to some machines now available, which should considerably ease the difficulty of making non-numerical material machine-readable (Schneider, 1971).

Remote access and 'intelligent' terminals

The tele-type described above is also in wide-spread use as a means of communicating with users' programs as they are run by the computer. The differences between this kind of 'interactive' computing and submitting input jobs through a basic peripheral unit such as a card reader, are discussed further in the next chapter. For the present, we can note that these devices are relatively cheap because they simply transmit and receive messages initiated by a user or the computer itself. The main computer to which it is connected must be programmed to recognise 'interrupts' from one of a number of sources in a 'time-sharing' situation, and give the necessary attention when a user types a message and transmits it (Wilkes, 1968; Chapter 5). Direct communication of this kind may, however, be regarded as an unreasonable demand on the time of a large modern central processor, in which case communication terminals are required which can carry out some local processing, calling on the main computer only when this is completed. These terminals may be situated at virtually any distance from the computing centre, and make use of growing facilities for data transmission provided, for example, by the Post Office in Britain. A national network is already in existence which offers several different rates and capacities for information transmission, but many units operate by converting data to audial codes and can send messages over ordinary telephone lines. Apart from problems of reliability which may be greater with different alternatives, the use of terminals is not much affected by the communications arrangements or the distances involved. In fact almost any peripheral device can be used remotely, through a communication line and a suitable modulator-demodulator (abbreviated as 'modem') to handle the signals generated.

Operating speeds for this kind of application depend on the capacity of the line available, which is usually expressed in 'Baud' (after a pioneer of telegraphy) or bits per second. Knowing the number of bits per character, these are readily converted to characters per second, as an estimate of the maximum possible printing speed in direct communication.

At the simplest level, input-only keyboards and even 'touch tone' telephones can be used to send messages over any distance for which normal telephone links are reasonably reliable.

Terminals which are to save input messages and transmit them at a time to suit the work-load of the main computer must clearly have the capacity to hold information in a store and contain suitable logic circuitry to enable them to take appropriate action without the specific intervention of the user. The term 'buffer' is commonly used to describe an area of storage in which information can be accumulated until a large enough quantity is present for an economic transfer to take place from one unit to another. The more storage there is in a data communication unit used as a peripheral device, the more its calls on the central processor can be rationalised to improve the efficiency of the whole operation. 'Buffering' is one way of reducing the delays inherent in the enormous differences in operating speeds between various periphal units and the processor itself.

'Intelligent' terminals take a very wide variety of forms, from relatively simple data-gathering devices which can be programmed to supervise and edit input values, to small computers which can call upon the larger processor whenever their own capacity is insufficient for the problem in hand. In this case, the satellite computer will probably have its own basic peripheral units and auxiliary storage units, as described earlier. But even the most basic communication terminal may be enhanced by the addition of a storage medium on which data can be recorded for later automatic transmission to the computer. For example, an IBM typewriter terminal is available with a simple magnetic card memory giving a capacity of 5000 characters, as a means of securing more efficient use of remote computing facilities.

Visual displays

Instead of receiving all computer output in printed or other 'hard copy' form, it is possible to have results displayed in a visual form instead (Sutherland, 1970). Analogue signals are often represented as oscilloscope traces, but to achieve a static display of digital computer output requires more elaborate equipment. Visual display units (V.D.U.'s) can be constructed in several ways, depending upon what is required of them. Equipment which can use an ordinary television set to display computer-generated images is now on the market, and in conjunction with a transmission unit which uses a telephone line brings the idea of domestic computing into the realm of practical reality. But specially designed cathode ray tube displays are the most commonly used, since they can combine brightness and clarity with rapid changes of image.

At the simplest level, alphanumeric visual displays can be seen as substitutes for printers, and show lines of characters similarly spaced to those which might appear on a printed page. Typically up to about 1000 characters can be displayed in preset matrix positions and may be arranged, in appropriate magnitudes, in variable numbers of lines on the screen. Units may show up to 30 lines or so at a time, depending upon their screen size and the available character positions, and may include a 'roll and scroll' facility. This permits the area of information displayed to be adjusted within limits 'forwards' or 'backwards' as though scanning a continuous document. Clearly, the more sophisticated the display facilities, the greater is their cost in both hardware and software.

Since character displays of this kind are essentially simpler than moving television pictures, the cathode ray tube itself can be rather simpler than a normal television tube, but continuous regeneration or 'refreshing' of the image is needed because the duration of phosphorescence after each scan is very short. With a specially designed tube a simpler random scanning can replace the serial scanning of the television tube, which removes the need to reformat the stored form of the screen image after any change (Reuben, 1969). However, the unit must still be capable of storing at least single-frame images and holding them constant with minimal flickering until the computer transmits further information. Typically, display units are not merely passive but are equipped with keyboards in the same way as teletypes, and can serve the same purposes in communications.

The minimum configuration usually offers a teletype facility in which the computer output is set up line by line on a screen instead of being typed on a roll of paper. For a constant speed of data transmission, these units can show line-by-line input and output much more rapidly than a teletype (at least by a factor of ten), but still do take a little time to build up a full frame of the screen one character at a time.

A further useful facility quite frequently found causes the 'blinking' of characters or sets of characters, which can, for example, draw attention to expected data formats in pre-arranged input routines or similar applications which call for close interaction between a user or subject and the machine. Higher priced display units may be provided with a limited additional operating capacity so that they can function on their own, if necessary, as small computers. As with other forms of 'intelligent terminal' the effect can be to shift the burden of the auxiliary processing of input and output from the main computer to the local unit, making possible a more efficient use of the large machine. When cathode ray tubes are used, it is also possible to display coloured pictures generated by a computer.

Some or all of a displayed image can be reproduced using a line-printer or page-printer in conjunction with the V.D.U. The latter is a small fast printer which on demand gives a paper copy of the lines currently on the screen. Other methods of saving the image include the use of micro-film or microfiche photographic reproduction. But selective printing of the most useful sections of output, provided the computer is suitably programmed to display results in this way, is now a viable alternative to obtaining vast quantities of line-printer output as a matter of course. For certain kinds of application, the immediacy of this type of continuous communication with a computer can be invaluable. It can mean, for example, that the formulation and testing of hypotheses about stored data can be carried out together, at a pace which can match the creative thought of an investigator by providing an immediate evaluation of ideas as they occur. This kind of equipment is also of great value in other computer assisted learning processes (Allen, 1972).

A usually cheaper technique employs a storage mesh behind the display screen's phosphorescent surface, from which the image is transferred to the screen itself. This eliminates the need for image refreshing but loses flexibility in use. Direct view storage tubes (D.V.S.T.'s) display virtually flicker-free images until they are overwritten by fresh input or erased, but the time taken to generate a full display is appreciably longer than is possible with a cathode ray tube. Considerable development of this technology would be needed before it could approach the flexibility of the cathode ray tube in interactive applications. On the other hand, greater resolution is possible in the picture displayed, which makes them attractive for the representation of graphic material.

Graphic output can often be obtained quite satisfactorily from an ordinary line-printer, and some modest examples are to be found in later chapters of this book. Reasonable graphs can be drawn, and by overprinting suitable combinations of characters illusions of shading and depth can be produced quite simply to add an apparent third dimension in plotting (Day, 1972, pages 20–34; Sterling and Pollack, 1968, pages 192–205). But if the resolution of the line-printer character plotting is not sufficient, highly accurate graphic output can be obtained from a special-purpose plotter. Here, the accuracy of plotting can be a few thousandths of an inch, and continuous lines can be drawn between specific points. Plotters are of two main kinds. Some use continuous stationery, moved by sprockets relative to a pen which moves in one dimension only, and some move a plotting head in two dimensions across a flat bed on which a piece of paper is laid. Either type operates at a much slower rate than most line-printers, although some of the latest electrostatic printers will produce both graphics and lines of characters at high speeds. An alternative method is to reproduce photographically, on microfilm, images created for visual display.

Computer graphics

Graphic input is not often used in the social sciences, although it could be useful in fitting mathematical descriptions to otherwise complex but sketchable curves for theoretical relationships, and in curve-fitting to graphical data displays. Various devices are in use for digitising graphic material by recording the digital co-ordinates of points from a diagram in a form suitable for computer input. The Benson-Lehner 'Oscar', for example, provides two movable pointers and records the co-ordinates of their point of intersection on an illuminated plane which is used to hold the diagram to be coded. The density of recording is under the control of the user.

Less laborious, but more expensive in terms of the dedicated hardware, is the use of light-sensitive 'pens' in conjunction with a visual display unit. Some V.D.U.'s can be operated in a tracking mode, which can record the co-ordinates of points on the screen at which the pen is pointed when a button is pressed, or can automatically follow, and simultaneously display, the path of the 'pen' across the face of the tube, and so store any kind of curve for future reference. Light-pens may be sensitive to the radiation from the phosphor of the screen or to the electron beam itself of the cathode ray tube.

An intermediate form of input devices uses a stylus which is tracked across a flat tablet surface to record a series of points for transmission to the computer. The RAND tablet, for example, uses the conductivity of the tablet itself to track the stylus, while a more recent acoustic technique tracks the sound of a series of small sparks between tablet and stylus along two dimensions to record co-ordinates. Either is best used for tracing designs which have already been drawn on paper, and the results must be displayed elsewhere.

Clearly, any of these devices must be buffered, to save wasting the time of a main processor as it waits for input from a human operator, and requires sophisticated circuitry to discharge its functions. The major drawback to their more general use is that the amount of storage needed to generate even quite simple graphic displays is still too large for comfort, and there remain formidable problems of achieving efficient structuring and retrieval of the data to be manipulated (Bird, 1969).

However, the effect of these sophisticated systems is again potentially to reduce the problems the eventual user has in formulating a problem for computer-aided solution. Sketching a theoretical relationship with a light-pen or stylus is much simpler than coding the same information as numbers on punched cards or tape before analysis, and reduces to a minimum the time lapse between thinking of an idea and using the computer's resources for investigating its implications. Some experiments carry the application of this equipment further. C. W. Gear, of the University of Illinois (Gear, 1969), has described an experimental means of programming a computer directly using diagrams or flow-charts of the process to be carried out. Given sufficient development, the job of programming could in this way be reduced, possibly, to the drawing of flow-charts using a graphic input device. This kind of facility could, Gear argues, dramatically change our conception of computer programming by reducing the need to think in terms of sequences of instructions and recognising something closer to the 'inherent parallelism' of most non-programmers' thinking. Similar claims are made for management information systems which also use visual displays and light-pens to manipulate and interrogate a stored data base at speeds matching the human enquirer's own formulation of a question (Machover, 1969, pages 65–67).

We have now made a very general review of the kinds of hardware commonly found in computing centres accessible to social scientists, and have introduced some frequently-encountered terms in the process. It has not been possible to deal with the relevant technology, about which a user arguably has increasingly less need for information. We have confined ourselves instead to a functional description of categories of equipment, and have emphasised the ways in which some knowledge of their various characteristics can improve the efficiency of their use. Both the very high cost of modern computers and the important considerations of numerical methods and storage organisation, when they are affected by particular hardware designs, still make it advisable to have some knowledge at least of the particular machine one is using. In the following chapter, we consider, from a similar viewpoint, aspects of computer programming and software. In most respects, our inventiveness in programming lags far behind the existing technology and imposes much more severe restrictions on the potential exploitation of computing systems than the present state of hardware development.

References

J. R. Allen (1972) 'Current Trends in Computer-Assisted Instruction', *Computers and the Humanities*, **7**, No. 1, pages 47–55.

G. A. Bekey and W. J. Karplus (1968) *Hybrid Computation*, New York, John Wiley.

S. Bird (1969) 'Computer Graphics Software Techniques' in R. D. Parslow, R. W. Prowse and R. Elliot (Editors), *Computer Graphics—Techniques and Application*, London and New York, Plenum Press.

W. J. Claffey (1967) *Principles of Data Processing*, Belmont, California, Dickenson.

A. C. Day (1972) *FORTRAN Techniques with Special Reference to Non-numerical Applications*, Cambridge University Press.

J. W. Forrester (1971) *World Dynamics*, Cambridge, Mass., Wright Allen Press.

C. W. Gear (1969) 'Computer Aided Programming Systems' in Parslow *et al.* (Editors), *Computer Graphics.*

J. N. Hambury (1969) 'Hybrid System Programs', *Computer Bulletin*, **13**, No. 3, pages 74–79.

K. A. Key (1965) *Analogue Computing for Beginners*, London, Chapman and Hall.

C. Machover (1969) 'Computer Graphics in the United States' in Parslow *et al.* (Editors), *Computer Graphics.*

J. Martin and A. R. D. Norman (1970) *The Computerized Society*, Englewood Cliffs, N.J., Prentice-Hall.

P. M. Neely (1966) 'Comparison of several algorithms for computation of means, standard deviations and correlation coefficients', *Communications of the Association for Computing Machinery*, **9**, pages 496–499.

B. Noble (1964) *Numerical Methods: 1—Iteration Programming and*

Algebraic Equations, Edinburgh and London, Oliver and Boyd, New York, Interscience.
M. A. Reuben (1969) 'Low Cost Graphics' in Parslow *et al.* (Editors), *Computer Graphics.*
W. Renwick and A. J. Cole (1971) *Digital Storage Systems*, 2nd edition, London, Chapman and Hall.
H. McGregor Ross (1972) 'Character Codes' and 'Computer Standards' in *Computer Users' Year Book*, Brighton, The Computer Users' Yearbook.
T. D. Sterling and S. V. Pollack (1968) *Introduction to Statistical Data Processing*, Englewood Cliffs, N.J., Prentice-Hall.
B. R. Schneider (1971) 'The Production of Machine-Readable Text: Some of the Variables', *Computers and the Humanities*, **6**, No. 1, pages 39–47.
J. D. Schoeffler and R. H. Temple (Editors) (1972) *Minicomputers: Hardware, Software and Applications*, New York, I.E.E.E. Press (Institute of Electrical and Electronics Engineers).
C. W. Smith, G. P. Mead, C. T. Wicks and G. A. Yewdall (1969) *Management Information*, London, Pan.
I. E. Sutherland (1970) 'Computer Displays', *Scientific American*; repr. in R. R. Fenichel and J. Weizenbaum (Editors) (1971) *Computers and Computation*, San Francisco, W. H. Freeman.
C. B. Tompkins and W. L. Wilson Jr. (1969) *Elementary Numerical Analysis*, Englewood Cliffs, N.J., Prentice-Hall.
C. A. A. Wass and K. C. Garner (1965) *Introduction to Electronic Analogue Computers*, 2nd edition, Oxford, Pergamon Press.
M. V. Wilkes (1968) *Time-Sharing Computer Systems*, London, Macdonald; New York, American Elsevier.
S. Winograd (1968) 'How fast can computers add?', *Scientific American*; repr. in Fenichel and Weizenbaum (Editors) (1971) *Computers and Computation.*

Further Reading

On computer arithmetic

D. D. McCracken (1957) *Digital Computer Programming*, New York, John Wiley

contains a still very useful introduction, and

H. Borko (1962) *Computer Application in the Behavioural Sciences*, Englewood Cliffs, N.J., Prentice-Hall, Chapters 5 and 6.

will also be found helpful.

I. Flores (1963) *The Logic of Computer Arithmetic*, Englewood Cliffs, N.J., Prentice-Hall.

provides a full and highly readable account of the topics touched on here. On other topics covered in this chapter see also:

S. H. Hollingdale and G. C. Toothill (1965) *Electronic Computers*, Harmondsworth, Penguin.

G. A. Phillips and P. J. Taylor (1969) *Computers*, London, Methuen.

The collection of readings edited by Fenichel and Weizenbaum (1971) is simple but authoritative, while A. Chandor, J. Graham and R. Williamson

A Dictionary of Computers, Harmondsworth, Penguin, Baltimore, Md., Penguin, 1970

provides an invaluable glossary of the often obscure terminology and acronyms of the computing world.

The symposium on computer graphics edited by Parslow *et al.* (1969) also has a full glossary of terms and bibliography.

3 Programs and programming

One of the best known truisms in discussion of the uses of computers is that the machine is the servant of the programmer. It may be a very efficient and startlingly obedient servant, but it can strictly speaking do nothing which it has not been instructed to do by a human master. As with all truisms, the deceptive simplicity of this idea can lead to an unwary view of its subject. If that were all there is to computing, a great deal of the work involved in the developing art of programming would be redundant. Our purpose in this chapter is to give some idea of the state of the art, but it is as well to begin with some general caveats. While it is true that computers have to be told what to do, and they cannot, in the first instance, begin to work until somebody produces a set of instructions they can digest and put to use, for most large modern computer systems, the situation is not that simple. Computers of the latest generation were partly designed using their less sophisticated predecessors, and programmed by men using earlier computers as aids in this process. It is increasingly difficult to try to understand in exact detail the steps by which a problem is solved in the machine. As computers come to understand increasingly general forms of human communication, perhaps eventually including reasonably general forms of ordinary languages such as English, the more remote we become from the actual 'thought processes' of the machinery. So while it is true that somebody must at some stage issue certain instructions, he is unlikely to do so in a form which the machine can interpret without further help in the form of translator programs, rendering the user's language into its own internal instruction code.

As a result, machines often do highly surprising and unexpected things if the human programmer's instructions are wrong, ambiguous or incomplete in some important respect. It is also possible, as will be seen later, to create sets of instructions which tell computers to modify *themselves*, in response to the conditions they generate. This kind of behaviour is then quite unpredictable in its general outcome, although the intermediate steps are all strictly the results of the programmer's efforts. However, most applications of computers to problems involving calculation require the construction and carrying out of fixed sequences of computer instructions. The key notion in understanding this kind of programming is the idea of a *process*, with which we must begin.

Processes and flow charts

A process consists of a set of defined operations performed in a definite and unambiguous sequence, and is often conveniently represented in the form of flow charts or block diagrams. These have a variety of applications in the design of data processing and computer systems, as well as in planning the structure of actual computer programs. Computer-produced flow charts can sometimes be used to summarise automatically the various steps in a program. Their use depends on their contribution to the clarification of the overall process to be described. There are, in fact, programming techniques which strictly defy this form of representation altogether, but it helps to begin in this way. A rather different approach to summarising program logic involves the use of decision-tables to specify the various contingencies in an analysis of the problem to be tackled (Cheseborough, 1971; Day, 1972; Chapter 9). Our account here is more conventional, but the references given provide an accessible introduction to another way of doing things.

A number of different symbol conventions exist but the important distinctions are simple. The main thing is to be self-consistent. Diamond-shaped blocks are usually used to indicate decisions, and rectangular blocks to denote operations of varying degrees of generality. The process shown in Fig. 3.1 is clearly more generally expressed than the program flow charts in Chapters 6 and 7. Initial and terminal points are distinguished from other operations, and when the process represents an actual computer program, input and output operations are denoted by a block of a different shape, such as a parallelogram in this book. The various blocks are linked by solid lines which occasionally have to overlap with arrows to indicate the direction of flow.

The details in Fig. 3.1 will be explained later. For the present, we need only note its general outline, which considerably simplifies the actual work involved in programming. In particular it makes no reference to the possibility of errors in the standard software, which is assumed to be available for the translation of programming languages into terms the machine can understand. It also assumes that the machine itself is free of errors or breakdown during the running of the programs, which is not always the case. Finally, the loops involved in the selection of facilities and correction of errors are theoretically endless, as shown, and should perhaps include some further decisions based on the cost of each further repetition, in terms of time or personal frustration.

Basic programming techniques

Before looking at some of the main ways of communicating processes to a computer, we can conveniently apply the general flow-charting symbols to some of the basic logical constructions of programming. The techniques illustrated form the basic building blocks of a great many problem-solving computer programs, and if properly understood can be successfully applied to a wide variety of computational problems in social science.

Computers are to be distinguished from other calculating aids, by, among other things, their capacity for being programmed to take decisions and act in different ways as a result of values generated during their own activities. Figure 3.2 illustrates the ideas behind two basic kinds of branching instruction in a program. The first, represented by a diamond-shaped box, takes one of three different routes to later operations, depending upon the decision criterion stated in the box. The separate questions which follow are arranged vertically to suggest the additional notion of an unconditional branch, missing out the next operation in the sequence, and jumping down below to form a single path again.

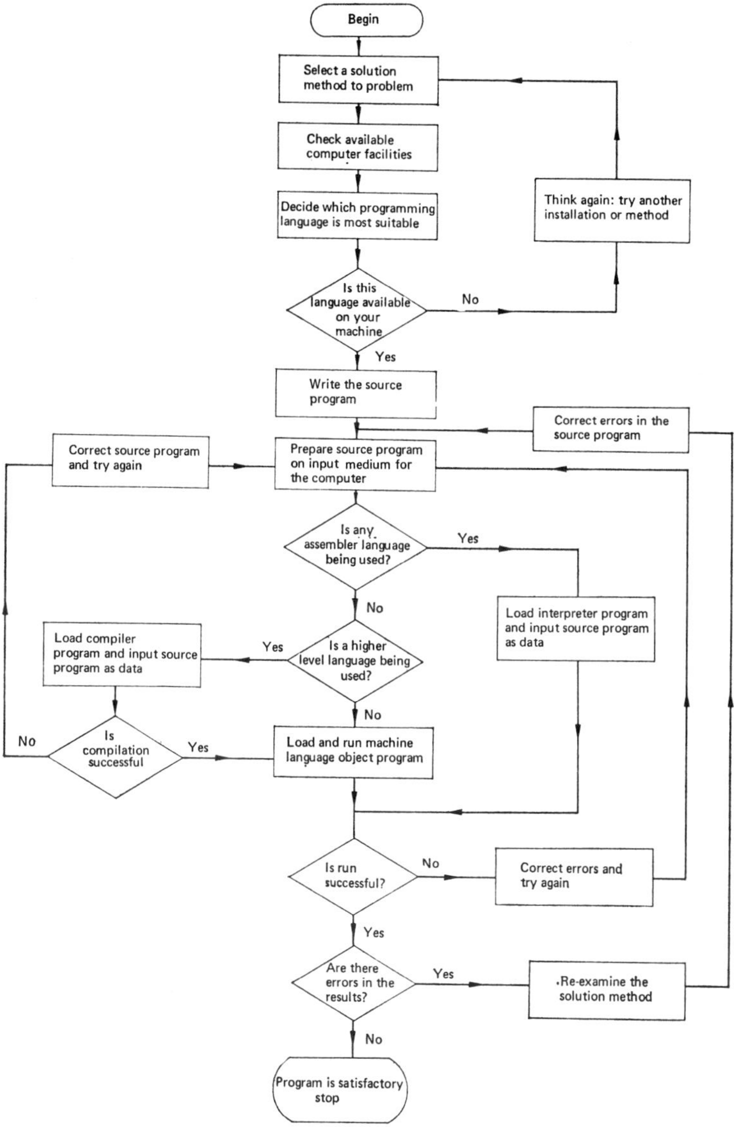

Fig. 3.1 An example of a process—programming a computer.

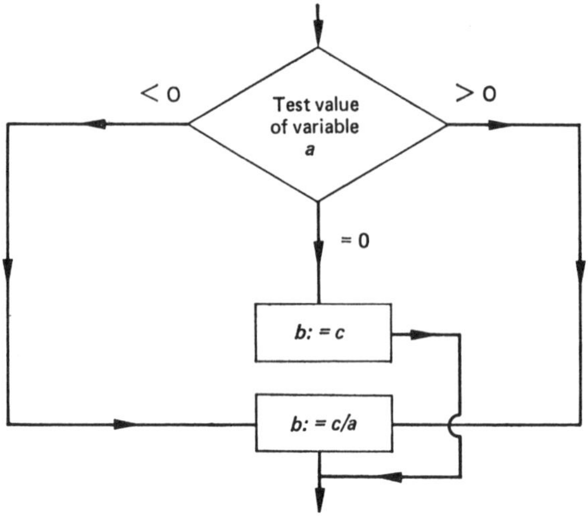

Fig. 3.2 Branching instructions.

In describing operations which correspond to actual program instructions the symbol := is used here to indicate an assignment of the value of the expression on the right to the variable on the left, and is not to be confused with the mathematical equality symbol. It derives, in fact, from the reference version of the Algol programming language, which uses it for a backward arrow (←). In these terms, variables must be considered always as names associated with the contents of particular storage registers. This kind of structure is very commonly encountered when a number of decisions are to be taken, each with different consequences.

Because digital computers can only work in a series of discrete steps, even a process as simple as adding a set of numbers must be specified in some detail. To avoid a whole series of repetitious instructions, loops are constructed and repeated as many times as are necessary by incrementing and testing the value of a counter or index variable at each cycle of repetition. Two equivalent ways of specifying this process are given in Fig. 3.3. The abbreviated form is included to show how the explicit formulation can be made implicit in a slightly shorter notation.

At the end of the loops illustrated, the variable j has a value equal to the sum of the first ten integers.

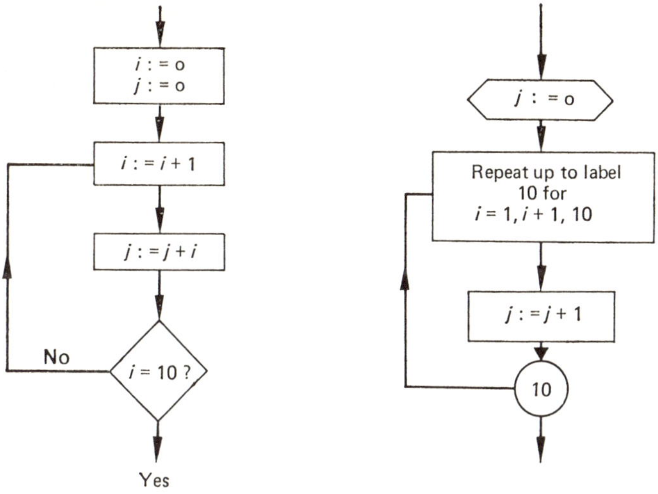

Fig. 3.3 Two ways of depicting a loop.

Figure 3.3 illustrates the use of an index variable which serves to count the number of repetitions made and bring the loop to an end after a definite number of cycles. A more general form of this process repeats a series of operations until some criterion is satisfied which is a result of the process itself. When the number of repetitions is indeterminate, until the set of instructions is carried out, the technique is termed *iteration*. This is of very general application and many numerical processes involving, for example, a convergence criterion, can be expressed in terms of iterative loops.

Figure 3.4 is a flow chart for the evaluation of the exponential function e^x, using the expanded series

$$e^x = 1 + x + \frac{x^2}{2!} + \frac{x^3}{3!} + \frac{x^4}{4!} + \ldots\ldots\ldots\ldots \text{etc.}$$

where 3! stands for the factorial of 3 and so on. Since the series is infinitely long, the evaluation process is halted after the desired accuracy has been attained. But even if a strictly convergent series is the basis for an iterative process of this kind, successive terms will not in practice be tested for strict equality, since this is unlikely to occur in digital floating-point arithmetic. A convergence test is thus made for equality only to some acceptable degree of accuracy.

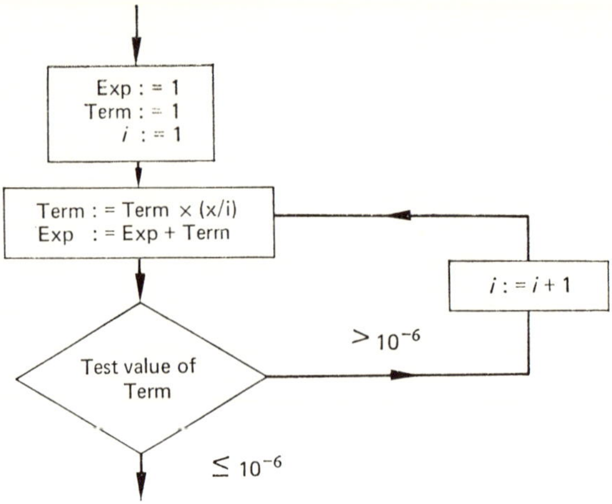

Fig. 3.4 An example of iteration.

A further application of index variables is worth notice here, since it provides a useful technique in the construction of programs, designed to perform standard operations on data under the control of a few simple instructions from the user. If the index takes only the values 0 and 1, it can be set at one stage in a program, by the user or by the input data, to be interrogated later with different effects according to its different values. The index variable behaves like a simple switch, which may be provided for, either as an ordinary variable or as a separate hardware bit, to be tested individually. The use of single bits as switches requires a special facility to be provided by a manufacturer or installation, to supplement the more general programming languages.

A programming concept which is present in some form in most computer languages, is the subprogram. This consists of a separate set of questions to perform some standard task required a number of times in a main program. A subprogram can be regarded as a self-contained module, and can usually be written and tested separately from the main process in which it is required. But it is constructed so that all the variables, in this case termed arguments, contained in its definition are regarded as dummy arguments. When a subprogram is 'called' from the main program, these dummy values are replaced by actual variables taken from the main program and returned with new values as a result of the action of the subprogram. We have earlier referred to the arrows linking the boxes of a flow chart as indicating the direction of flow of the process defined. From now on, when the diagram represents the action of an actual computer program, we will talk of the *execution* of a sequence of instructions, to be carried out by the computer. The arrows then indicate the passage of *control* in the program, from one block of statements to another. Subprograms are employed for common functions such as finding the square root of a number, which a digital computer must evaluate by some suitable iterative process to a given degree of accuracy. Operations involving the transfer and calculation of several different arguments may be cast in a different form, commonly termed a subroutine, in which the subprogram takes a more explicit form. Some illustrations of this distinction in the FORTRAN language will be found in Chapter 7 and need not detain us here.

Figure 3.5 illustrates the idea of the transfer of control to a subprogram and back again.

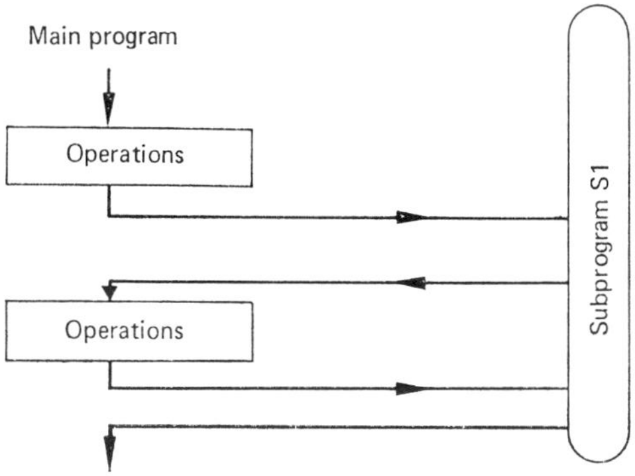

Fig. 3.5 The subprogram concept.

The subprogram S1 is used twice by the main program, although its definition, in terms of dummy arguments, need be given only once. Calling a subprogram sets up link information to indicate the point to which control must return in the main program. When the subroutine has been executed, the new argument values are available, and control passes to the next instruction after the point of departure.

Unfortunately, this takes us near the limits at which flow charts of this kind can be used very clearly to illustrate concepts in programming. We must now turn to notations more appropriate to the problem to be considered.

Most programming languages allow the use of subprograms to define functions. When they are used, it is natural to adopt a functional notation, in the mathematical sense, to represent these operations. This is, among other things, much more convenient to a user who is not a professional programmer but is used to notational convention in his own discipline. Non-mathematical social scientists may find mathematical conventions rather strange at first, since they are used to describing their problems in English. However, functional concepts will be found almost a necessity when making their ideas sufficiently unambiguous for communication to a computer.

In its simplest and most general form a function f is defined as a series of operations performed on the value x, with the result $f(x)$. In computation, x need not, as we shall see, be a number but may be an English word, or a list of words and numerical values. We can thus express the square root of a number x as the value of the expression Sqrt(x) where Sqrt stands for the function of taking the square root and x is the operand. Functions can be compounded, using this notation, so than an expression of the kind

Sqrt (Sqrt(16))

has the value 2. The 'nesting' of functions in this way can be carried on to any depth required, limited only by the need to remain reasonably intelligible to the reader.

This kind of notation is very useful in programming, but rather difficult to represent adequately in terms of a flow chart of the kind we have used so far. Beyond very simple calculation processes, the flow chart method is most likely to be useful to sketch the broad outlines of the design of a program, rather than its detailed parts. With additional symbols to represent peripheral devices, block diagrams are also very often used to illustrate the interrelations between various programs in a particular computer system or integrated set of software components.

Programming languages

Up to now we have described the various codes in which a computer can be instructed as languages without discrimination among available types of code. Further discussion of techniques of programming will arise most naturally in the context of the particular languages in which they are specially provided, or in which they were first introduced for general use by other than professional programmers.

The terminology and concepts of modern linguistic analysis have, in fact, provided a basis for the definition and sometimes the design of programming languages, and are widely adopted in the general discussion of these codes (Higman, 1967; Naur, 1960). To talk of them in these terms, then, is rather more than anthropomorphisation of communications between men and machines. In looking at different types of language, we will be concerned with those most widely used, and with the characteristics most likely to be of interest to a social science user. Since the designers of all new languages naturally enough see their efforts as offering some kind of advantage over other alternatives, we will also deal briefly with the general principles involved, to enable readers to assess further claims and developments as they encounter them.

1. Machine codes and assemblers

The most basic and tedious form of a computer language is the machine's own operating code, in which every step of every operation is defined completely in terms of shifting values from numbered storage locations, generally into specially reserved areas known as accumulators, performing manipulations of the accumulator contents, and replacing the values into store. The brief account of numerical operations in the previous chapter will have given some idea of the conditions to be considered at each stage of even these simple operations. In particular, the contents of an accumulator cell must be tested, by a specific instruction, after each numerical operation in case the condition known as overflow has occurred. From the point of the programmer, such a result would be an error, but the computer has to be instructed that this is so. The general forms of machine instructions vary according to the manufacturer and series, but the general principles are much the same. A common device in introducing texts in computer science is to represent basic programming concepts in terms of a hypothetical digital computer (e.g. McCracken, 1956). We are concerned here only with the general character of this kind of code and need only consider a simplified illustration.

Accumulators may be specially referenced storage locations in the processor, or a set of cells in the storage used for a program which are reserved for the performance of operations. Each operation within the repertoire of the machine is represented by a unique code sequence, and storage locations which contain information to be processed are referred to by unique numbers. An instruction made up of these elements is made intelligible to the machine by its fixed format, which is determined by the logical design of the computer. A set of three machine instructions, in binary form, might look something like Fig. 3.6.

Operation code	Accumulator	Storage address
0001010	01	000000000000010
0001100	01	000000000000011
0000011	01	000000000000001

Fig. 3.6 An example to illustrate a hypothetical machine code.

For the sake of this illustration, we assume that each machine instruction addresses a single accumulator, shown here as a two-bit binary code, and one storage location, whose absolute address in the main storage is expressed as a 15-digit binary number. In the computer, these elements could thus occupy one 24-bit word, or four 6-bit bytes, according to the mode of storage. We leave it to the reader to check that there are no more than four accumulators, 128 separate instruction codes, and possibly 32768 storage addresses. Any real machine of course would allow considerably more flexibility than this.

Programming in this kind of code is not only very tedious, but also likely to involve many errors. Whether instructions of this kind are expressed in binary, base eight, otherwise called octal, or in more familiar decimal form, they remain essentially strings of digits whose meaning is obscure to the uninitiated and are difficult to manipulate even for the professional. Two improvements make programming at this level much more straightforward. These are the introduction of mnemonic codes to represent operations, and the assignment to storage locations of addresses numbered relatively within programs, and not absolutely, within the whole machine store. It is then a fairly natural extension to regard storage locations as having names, to be assigned by the programmer, and not numbers. Figure 3.7 treats the example of Fig. 3.6 in this way. This kind of code is usually termed a *mnemonic assembler language*, since it is one step 'higher' than the basic machine code.

Operation	Accumulator	Storage location
LDX	01	B
ADX	01	C
STO	01	A

Fig. 3.7 An example of a hypothetical Assembler Code.

This should clarify the meaning we have assigned to operations 10, 12 and 3 in the earlier example. LDX places the contents of a stored variable B into accumulator 1. ADX adds another value to the accumulator. STO stores the result as a variable A. Clearly, we assume that the variable names have been assigned by other instructions to specific storage locations, and assigned values earlier in the program. It should be apparent that even this kind of language is not the same as the machine code, and must be translated into a form the machine can understand, before a program can be executed. This involves the creation, once and for all for any design of machine, of a translator program, which treats instructions on this format as data, and causes the assembly of the corresponding sequence of machine instructions. Most assembly language operations maintain the strict one to one correspondence between their statements and machine instructions, which is apparent in our illustration. Their translation is a relatively simple process of substitution according to specified equivalences, and is often achieved in one pass of the program through the computer, translating and executing in one go. The translator program is usually called an *interpreter*, to distinguish this process from the *compilation* of programs from *higher level* languages, which is why the distinction was made in Fig. 3.1 earlier in this chapter.

Assembler languages give convenient and complete control over operations within the computer, and are used professionally when special effects or efficiency of execution are important. They are unlikely to be of interest directly to a social scientist, unless some unusual facility is thought to be desirable. Since assembler instructions are treated as data values to the interpreter, instructions can be inserted which actually change other instructions according to conditions generated during a program run. However, except in the simulation of 'intelligent' behaviour, this is unlikely to be found strictly necessary.

Before leaving the topic, it is also interesting to note that apart from some initial machine code to start the process of translation, graphically described as *boot-strapping*, translators and eventually compilers can be written in the language which they exist to translate, which amounts to a considerable simplification of the job of language creation.

2. General purpose languages at a higher level

Higher level languages can be classified in various ways, but have some common features, which we will illustrate by reference to those most likely to be encountered in general use. Most generally they condense many machine operations into a single statement, so that their translation involves a complicated instruction explosion. The essential rationale is to make available a notation for the definition of problems which is as close as possible to the terms in which a human user thinks of his problem. The considerable developments of the past decade in the design of software to support man-machine communications are an attempt, often rather conservatively, to exploit the enormous information processing power of computers in ways which are increasingly simple for the non-professional user. One of the earliest developments, for example, was to permit the use of common mathematical notation in calculations involving simple arithmetic. The result is that

A:=B+C
or even ADD B, C GIVING A

can be written to represent the simple operations of our earlier example in Figs. 3.6 and 3.7. Because of this matching of notation to particular applications, higher level languages are often loosely described as problem-solving languages, although, as in the case of certain special purpose languages, they often serve as much to define problems in some areas, where the correct specification of a problem achieves the desired result. (Sammet, 1969; Chapter 1). They are also distinguished by the manner in which they are commonly translated. A program written in a higher level language is termed a source program (see Fig. 3.1) and is translated by a special program, called a *compiler*, into a machine-code *object program*. This program is then capable of being stored and run as many times as is necessary without recourse to the source. Since compilation involves an instruction explosion it inevitably takes much longer than interpretation of assembler languages, but this is often compensated by the possibility for independent compilation and testing of program modules, which can be combined later in their machine code form to make a single large program.

Intermediate between assemblers and the higher level languages, both in conception and period of development, are the so-called autocodes, also usually interpreted. These represented the initial automatic programming languages of the 1950's and contained facilities for the definition of subprograms and elaborate branching facilities (Higman, 1967; pages 65–74).

Pursuing linguistic terminology a little further, some of the best known languages have variant dialects, either because a manufacturer's version is modified from the version of the original designers, or because variants have grown up during the protracted MIT international gestation process of a language such as Algol 60. Some examples are MADTRAN (MIT's version of FORTRAN), Balgol or Burrough's Algol, and JOVIAL (in some accounts 'Jules' own version of Algol', a more powerful general purpose language developed for the United States Air Force). In the rest of this chapter, we shall confine ourselves to the main general purpose languages in common use, and special purpose languages which offer facilities of special interest to social scientists.

The most widely used language of all, FORTRAN, began in the mid-1950's as IBM's attempt to provide a general purpose language using mathematical notation, hence its name (from FORmula TRANslation). We hope that the short account in Chapter 7 bears out the contention that the language is easy to learn, although it is still heavily dependent on a fixed statement structure derived from the earlier experiments with machine auto-codes. The statement format and set of possible characters is also derived from IBM's own ubiquitous punched card, and card punch machines, which offer a limited range of symbols compared with the full mathematical usage. Despite these limitations, FORTRAN, in its later and standardised version FORTRAN IV, has survived to become the only really widespread language in scientific use, for which compilers are available from all major computer manufacturers. Because of its rather clumsy format, it is little used for *communicating* programming techniques, in the form of algorithms for particular problems, but is very common in the social sciences for all kinds of computation. Its universality and ease of learning outweigh for most current users any of its inherent disadvantages, deriving from its period of development in the rapid growth of computer science. Above all, programs in FORTRAN are quite easily converted to run on a wide variety of machines, which considerably reduces the problem of dissemination of techniques. Newer extensions by various manufacturers easily overcame its basic weakness in handling alphabetic characters, for example in processing textual information, but these solutions are still unfortunately tied to the particular machine for which they are devised. On the other hand, its modular structure, into units called segments, including its subprogramming or subroutine facilities, have made possible a number of extensions, using programs in FORTRAN to translate newly defined terms. Many special purpose languages have begun life in this way, with the backing of readily available FORTRAN compilers, and originally consisted of sets of FORTRAN subroutines called into action by the terms of a new language read and decoded by a suitable FORTRAN program. Many users have become so attached to the language that they seek ways of achieving, by subterfuge based on the system architecture of a particular computer, what the source language cannot achieve at all (Barron, 1968; pages 37–39). There are still two basic drawbacks to this approach, which point to the eventual obsolescence of FORTRAN IV. Because of its period of development, and a rather conservative approach even then by its IBM designers, it cannot properly achieve some facilities now regarded as important by programmers. In particular, the recursive methods introduced later in this chapter are not possible at all in the standard language, and in general only the kind of sequences which can be represented by continuous flow charts are permissible. It is essentially a sequential procedural language, in which each step in a calculation is executed in turn after the one before. The speed of the latest processors requires some means of multiprocessing even statements inside individual programs, which was hardly envisaged when FORTRAN was written. It is also impossible to avoid inefficient storage use, sometimes with considerable overheads in computing costs, since each program reserves and retains a fixed amount of storage while it is in the computer, and cannot adjust its allocation to suit its needs at any point in time. Nevertheless, FORTRAN remains a very useful general purpose high level language, with few serious rivals for the attention of a busy researcher.

Input and output is specified as for ICL 1900 series computers.
The purpose of the program is explained by the initial **comment**.

```
begin  comment A program to perform a swap sort of ten integers into
                 ascending order;
       integer array A [1:10];
       integer i, p, hold;
       select input (3);
       for i:=1 step 1 until 10 do
             A [i]:=read;
loop:  p:=0;
       for i:=1 step 1 until 9 do
       if A [i+1]<A [i] then
       begin hold:=A [i];
             A [i]:=A [i+1];
             A [i+1]:=hold;
                   p:=p+1; end;
       if p>0 then go to loop;
       free input; select output (0); paper throw;
       write text ('Ascending ␣ order ␣ is'); newline (2);
       for i:=1 step 1 until 10 do
             print (A[i], 10, 0);
       free output;
end
```

The sorting method of this example should be compared with Example 7.3 and the Appendix in Chapter 7, and with the sorting example in Chapter 5. Pairs of elements in the list of ten numbers are 'swapped' as necessary in a series of passes through the list, until no further changes are found to be necessary. The number of interchanges made depends on the initial order of the numbers to be sorted, so that the method is relatively efficient in its use of the computer.

Fig. 3.8 An example of an Algol program.

Algol, developed by an international committee of computer

scientists and mathematicians between 1958 and 1960, represented in many ways an advance over FORTRAN, which is recognised implicitly by its use in a publication form from the inception of the Association for Computing Machinery's collection of problem-solving algorithms for the purposes of communicating solutions among programmers (A.C.M., 1966 ff). This was despite the fact that until very recently, Algol compilers were actually tested in FORTRAN. Algol features have been influential in a number of newer languages, and it remains an excellent language for the description of computational problems. For the social scientist interested in manipulating textual data, the availability of Algol depends heavily upon extensions and special features provided by particular installations, since input and output arrangements were deliberately left undefined by the authors of the language. It cannot, then, be regarded as transferable between different machines or installations in the same way as FORTRAN, or COBOL, which we consider shortly. Our main reason for mentioning Algol is to take note of its innovatory facilities, which actually create problems of inefficient implementation in an almost opposite sense to FORTRAN. Algol's difficulties arise from ambitious attempts to conceive a language close to ordinary mathematical notation, with the addition of a few English words to make the result more intelligible. An attempt was made to design a language in which, as in mathematics, more than one way of saying the same thing was possible and any apparently sensible construction should have a meaning. The effect is to bring the syntax much closer to the 'natural' form of expression of at least one large class of potential users. Mistakes are still easily made with punctuation of statements, but otherwise the format is quite free, no spaces being of any significance in the syntax of the language. The main features of Algol to note are its generalisation of the FORTRAN idea of the subroutine into the *procedure*, and its easy acceptance of functional notation and *recursive definition.*

The advantages of recursion are by no means confined to numerical work, but we can best illustrate what is meant by the term by considering two ways of defining a function to calculate the factorial of an integer number. The function is fact $(n)=1\times2\times3\times\ldots\times(n-1)\times n$. By convention fact $(0)=1$. One obvious way is the iterative approach shown in Fig. 3.9.

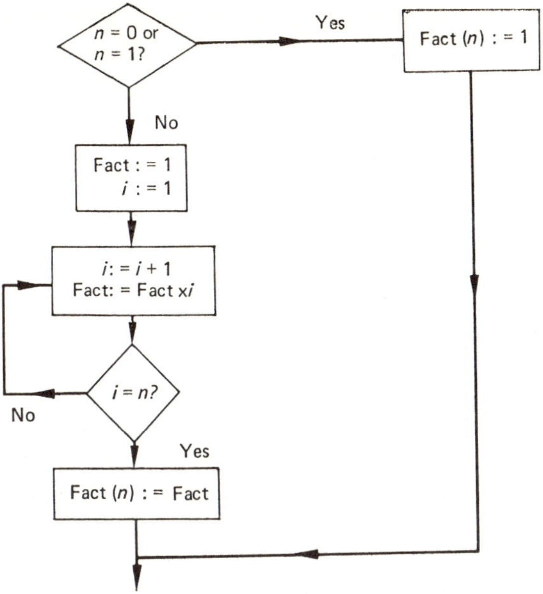

Fig. 3.9 Iterative calculation of a factorial.

A recursive definition expresses the function in terms of itself, and the 'depth' of recursion is only apparent at run-time. In Algol, the following expression

$$\text{fact } (n) := \textbf{if } n = 0 \textbf{ then } 1$$
$$\textbf{else } n \times \text{fact } (n-1);$$

has the same effect, and can be used anywhere in the program where the declaration is effective.

This kind of indefinite construction clearly cannot be displayed on a flow chart. However, there must be at least one non-recursive statement in such a definition, in this case fact (0):=1, to prevent the recursive equivalent of an infinite loop. To accept this kind of construction, Algol compilers had to introduce a new concept into computer software, now commonly available. This is the stack or pushdown storage cell, with which we deal later as an idea in list-processing. Associated with the use of this technique in compiling Algol source programs is their ability to increase their storage requirements during the course of execution to meet their exact needs. The relative inefficiency of the stack principle on most machines is offset by the avoidance of unused areas of reserved storage, which almost inevitably occur in running FORTRAN programs.

Recursive definition also plays an important part in the general theory of computability. While all recursive relations can be shown to be capable of reduction to iterative equivalents, recursion can be most conveniently used to define any function which a digital computer can compute (Barron, 1968; Chapter 4). In languages whose executable statements are all cast in the form of functions, recursion becomes essential, since iteration is not possible.

The third of the widely used higher level languages, COBOL (Common Business Oriented Language) was developed following an initiative in 1959 by the United States Department of Defense, to secure a flexible subset of English suitable for data processing. As with other languages of its period, it has a number of drawbacks for current use, and might be considered only by social scientists who need to exchange programs with the business or commercial world, or with solely data processing requirements. The distinctive structure of COBOL, in particular the so-called Environment Division of the program, is of interest as an attempt to deal with the requirements of machine-independent programming (Sammet, pages 330–377) but the claim to have achieved general readability through use of English forms needs to be treated sceptically. In order to allow constructions such as

```
IF A EXCEEDS B OR EQUALS B AND X EQUALS Y THEN
IF GREATER THAN B MOVE C TO D OTHERWISE ADD
B TO D
```

an example of the kind of eliptical but highly flexible conditional structures possible in COBOL, a large number of alternative forms are permitted with a consequent loss of efficiency in compilation. But while one is making the effort to express a computational routine in a suitably precise form, it is hard to see the benefits of using English words simply to replace the logical and arithmetic operators found in other languages.

The chief advantages of COBOL lie in its facilities for file description, which while precise, and definitely not English, give a better means than any other of specifying the names of data items and their structure. The Data Division of COBOL, which defines structures for input and output, is based on the idea of a *file*, described in terms of the *records* it contains. The following forms can all describe a field in a given file which is to be interpreted as a three-digit real number, with one decimal place;

```
PICTURE IS 99▽9
PICTURE IS 99·9
USAGE IS COMPUTATIONAL     POINT 1 LEFT
```

but each produces a different kind of storage use in the object program. COBOL can also handle alphanumeric data in a more straightforward manner than most languages using verbs such as MOVE . . . TO, which shifts character-strings without regard to their content, and SORT, which automatically gives a re-ordering of items in a file. Some of the more useful COBOL features have been included in the newer general purpose language PL/1. Similar flexible file descriptions and conditional construction are to be found in various interrogation languages available as part of systems for information retrieval.

This example produces a tabulated listing of input data cards.

```
IDENTIFICATION DIVISION.
   PROGRAM-ID. ESTAO1.
   ESTATE AGENT CARD TO PRINT.
   AUTHOR UNIVERSITY OF SOUTHAMPTON D.P.U.
ENVIRONMENT DIVISION.
CONFIGURATION SECTION.
SOURCE-COMPUTER.
   ICL–1901
OBJECT-COMPUTER.
   ICL–1901.
   MEMORY 13500 WORDS.
INPUT–OUTPUT SECTION.
FILE-CONTROL.
   SELECT CARD-FILE ASSIGN CARD-READER 1 RESERVE 1.
   SELECT PRINT-FILE ASSIGN PRINTER 1 RESERVE 1.
DATA DIVISION.
FILE SECTION.
FD  CARD-FILE.
       LABEL RECORDS OMITTED.
       DATA RECORD IS CARD-REC.
```

```
01    CARD-REC.
      02 A–C  PIC X(15).
      02 B–C  PIC X(23).
      02 C–C  PIC X(23).
      02 D–C  PIC X(19).
FD    PRINT-FILE
      LABEL RECORDS OMITTED.
      DATA RECORD IS PRINT-AREA.
01    PRINT-AREA.
      02 A–P  PIC BXXBXXBXXBXXXBBBXXXBBBXBBBBBXX.
      02 B–P  PIC XXXXBXBXXXBXXXBXXXBXXXBXXXBXXX.
      02 C–P  PIC XXXBXXXBXXXBXXXBXXXBXXXBXXXBXX.
      02 D–P  PIC XBXXXBXXXXXXXXXXXXXXXBBBBBBBB.
WORKING-STORAGE SECTION.
    77    LNCT PIC 9(6)     COMP SYNC RIGHT VALUE 0.
PROCEDURE DIVISION.
PAR-1.
      OPEN INPUT CARD-FILE
        OUTPUT PRINT-FILE.
P2.   READ CARD-FILE AT END GO TO P8.
      MOVE SPACES TO PRINT-AREA.
      MOVE A–C TO A–P.
      MOVE B–C TO B–P.
      MOVE C–C TO C–P.
      MOVE D–C TO D–P.
      IF LNCT=40 MOVE ZERO TO LNCT GO TO P5.
      WRITE PRINT-AREA AFTER 2.
      ADD 2 TO LNCT.
      GO TO P2.
P5.   WRITE PRINT-AREA AFTER CHANNEL-1.
      ADD 2 TO LNCT.
      GO TO P2.
P8.   CLOSE CARD-FILE PRINT-FILE.
      STOP RUN.
```

Fig. 3.10 An example of a COBOL program.

Special purpose languages

1. List processing

One of the most valuable means yet devised for handling general information is *list processing*. The initial impetus came from researchers interested in automatic language translation, and in the imitation of human thought processes in general problem solving. List processing techniques become virtually essential whenever large data structures are involved in a problem, whether the data consist of numbers, individual data files containing some alphanumeric information, or texts in natural languages. In many applications, it is difficult to arrange data sequentially for all operations, since the structure of the data itself may be highly relevant, and subject to changes during the running of a program. It is sometimes possible to overcome the inherent inefficiencies of repeated sequential processing of, say, a dictionary of English words, with the resources of the languages discussed so far. This can be done to some extent by constructing a table containing the addresses of the starting points of various subdivisions of the data structure to be searched, and beginning the search at a more appropriate place in the list instead of starting at the beginning for each consultation of its items. This is the computer equivalent of remembering the order of the letters of the alphabet, and beginning to consult a dictionary or index at the correct section, instead of leafing through the whole volume. This is quite adequate, so long as the list to be consulted is of fixed length, and remains the same throughout the process. If, however, we are trying to construct a dictionary, there must either be a large number of empty cells reserved in each alphabetic section ready to receive new items as necessary, or we must have some equivalent of a file-card box in the computer, into which new words can be slotted whenever the need arises.

Because rearranging a large number of items in store is wasteful of valuable computer time, list structures are represented by stationary items, which consist of two elements. The first element of a pair contains the data item itself, and the second is a link which contains the storage address of the next item on the list. As we need some general terms, we will call the individual list items *atoms*, and arrange atoms to form lists, by setting the link values appropriately. The last item of a list is most conventionally a *null item*, with no pointer link. The structure is then manipulated not by moving items around but by resetting links in an appropriate way.

Figure 3.11 illustrates two ways of thinking about list structures. While they may be stored in a series of consecutive locations, list elements can be thought of as having any ordering required by a particular problem. Items in a list, treated as list elements, may consist of other sublists as well as of individual pieces of data. In this way, tree-like structures are easily accommodated, in which

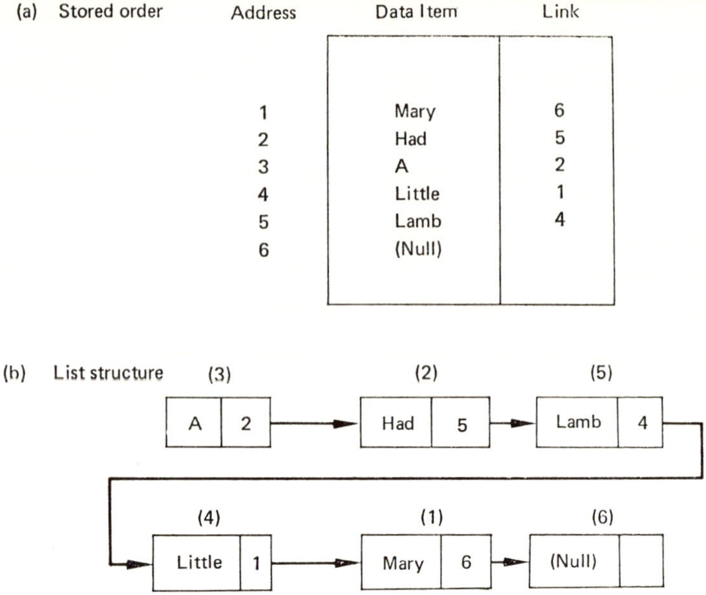

Fig. 3.11 List structure for alphabetic ordering. To insert the word BLACK into this list, these characters are placed in another storage location. Its address becomes the link of the preceding list item, and the new item takes the forward link of that item. Deletion simply reverses this process.

atoms are combined into lists, which are themselves combined to form higher level lists, and so on. An obvious application is in storing complicated classification structures, which embody a hierarchy of characteristics. As a simple illustration consider a list composed of names and addresses with elements of varying levels of generality in the information they contain. We can represent lists as a set of items in order, separated by commas, and enclosed in square brackets to denote the limits of the list. If the structure is as follows:

List element=[name, [house number, street, town, county]]

it is a simple matter to search a list of names and addresses for occurrences of any required items and remove them for processing. It is also easy to amend the list at any time.

A secondary advantage of this technique lies in its inherent economies of storage use. Space not currently needed is returned to a separate list of unused cells, serving the program as a whole. In its implementation, along with other concepts discussed here, in a language called LISP (Sammet; pages 405–416), this was termed graphically 'garbage collection'. New list items can then be assigned to one of the addresses on this free list.

One of the first realisations of the idea of list structure, in a language called IPL (Information Processing Language) manipulated the basic structure and links in a form akin to a machine code for a hypothetical computer. LISP adopted a set of basic functions to permit these list manipulations, and other languages have since followed suit. To give a general idea of how this works out in practice, we will consider two functions which provide a means of accessing list items, and then give an example of their use. In languages of this type, lists are given names, which make the whole list available for operations. The function *hd* or *head* is used to pick out the first item in a list, and *tl* or *tail* refers to the items remaining.

So that, if a list x consists of $[a,b,c,d]$
then $hd(x)$ has the value a,
and $tl(x)$ has the value $[b,c,d]$

These functions can be compounded, so that $hd\ (tl(x))$ refers to the element b, and $hd(hd(tl(x)))$ refers to the next element in the list, and so on.

As an example of list processing, we can use these functions to construct another, this time one which takes the value *true* when an element is found to be included in a given list, and *false* otherwise. Bearing in mind that all operations are defined on lists or list elements, we can define a function *member* in the following way. We assume that the constant *null* is available as a test of an empty list, so that the end of a list can be identified without knowing in advance how many elements it contains.

```
loop: if list=null then member b:=false
      else if hd(list)=x then member b:=true
      else list b:=tl(list); goto loop
```

This formulation is intended to be more or less self explanatory, but is in no particular extant programming language. 'loop' is a *label* which serves simply to locate the point at which each repetition of the search routine must begin. The expression member (x, list), using this function, takes the value *true* if the element x is found in the named list, and false otherwise.

In our imaginary language, we could also write

$$hd\,(\text{list})b := x$$

to add an item to the beginning of a list, or

$$hd(tl(\text{list})) := x$$

to put it as a new second item.

An important allied concept in programming such languages for the machine itself is the stack or pushdown storage. It should be apparent by now that lists are treated as being of indeterminate length, subject to the physical limitations of an individual computer. Pushdown storage is designed to behave in a similar way to the spring-loaded plate stacks often found in self-service cafeterias. A number of plates is contained in the stack, but only the top one is visible at any time. Remove a plate and the whole stack 'pops up', add a plate and the stack is 'pushed down' so that the latest addition only appears at its head. Storage which behaves in this way is very useful, since the job of locating the latest value of a series is considerably simplified. Apart from the Burroughs B5700 and larger computers, which embody the stack principle as part of the hardware circuitry itself, this effect must be achieved by programming. A stack *pointer* is established, which at any time contains the address of the item on the 'top' of the stack. The stack itself is a series of consecutive locations, so that the following operations are sufficient to achieve the desired effect. To add an item to the stack, $p := p+1$

$$c[p] := x$$

and to take off the top item $x := c[p]$

$$p := p-1,$$

where $c[p]$ refers to the *contents* of storage register p, and p is the pointer value.

Since the stack must consist of a suitably large number of reserved locations, it is easy to see how such a practice can be inefficient in storage terms. This is overcome in the newer languages PL/1 and CPL by facilities providing for the separate specification of areas of the program which require the use of a stack.

List processing facilities have been increasingly recognised as essential to general purpose languages, and should form part of the repertoire of techniques available in any future language with a claim to generality. Other earlier languages were also devised specifically to operate on values consisting of strings of characters, rather than on arithmetic values. The best known string processor languages are probably COMIT and SNOBOL, in which expressions resembling ordinary arithmetic statements are used to rearrange, amend and delete characters in string form. Figure 5.3 contains an example of SNAP, a more recent string-processing language which is based on a restricted form of natural English (Barnett; 1969). COMIT was originally developed at MIT in 1960 for application to problems of machine translation of natural languages. (Sammet; pages 416–448). At one level, this kind of concept shades over into the increasing application of computers to the job of type-setting ready for normal printing operations. Here the main concern is to select appropriate type-faces and produce any desired effect by manipulation of the text in the computer instead of in the conventional forms of type.

2. *Simulation*

Computer simulation of dynamic systems (see Chapter 6) can be undertaken using any general purpose programming language. Indeed, many special simulation languages are in effect 'conversion kits' to extend the facilities already available in an existing general language (Higman; page 140).

For reasons of space we will discuss only the simulation of systems which can be described in terms of discrete events, rather than quantities which are continuously variable over time. Continuous systems are encountered, for example in Economics, but most are conceived in discrete terms or can be treated as a series of events separated by very small intervals of time.

Two different languages are considered here by way of illustration of the facilities which can be made available. The General Purpose Systems Simulator (GPSS) developed for IBM (Sammet; pages 653–655), uses an extended set of flow chart symbols to describe a system. Conversion from this form into a sequence of instructions is then very straightforward. A process is defined as a series of blocks, each representing some kind of operation on an object passing through the system. Each block contains at least a simple indicator of the simulated time needed before the object advances to the next stage of the process. This consists of a mean time plus a modifier giving the range above and below the mean within which variation can be randomly constructed during a run of the simulation program. This approach is best suited to the representation of systems involving queuing problems or the optimisation of processes in manufacturing or distribution services. This method however is of general interest for its simplicity of conception and complete independence of individual machine characteristics. GPSS charts can be understood by those familiar with the systems under study, without the need for special programming knowledge.

SIMSCRIPT, developed by the RAND Corporation also in the early 1960's (Sammet; pages 655–656), on the other hand, uses a statement structure based on FORTRAN, and provides some additional commands to simplify the problem of describing a system. Its basic elements are conceived as sets of separate entities, representing the changing quantities in a system. Entities may be described at any point in time in terms of their set of parameters, or variables which monitor the condition of a basic part of the system. Thus, the state of the simulated model at any point is completely described in terms of its entities and their parameters. Events, which may be endogenous or exogenous according to the origin of their generation, inside or outside the operation of the model itself, are simply changes from one state to another. In common with several other simulation languages, SIMSCRIPT was originally written as a set of extensions to FORTRAN, by the provision of new subprograms to perform common tasks in simulation more easily. Programs could then be compiled using an ordinary FORTRAN translator program, with the support of a new library of facilities.

All simulation languages include a range of methods of generating values for variables which are treated as subject to random fluctuations, and commonly include means of specifying the range and probability generating function of their hypothetical distribution. Their other basic facility generates and tabulates the results of a simulated run on the computer. The ability to summarise the behaviour of a system is as important as the ability to describe it in conveniently simple terms. A number of statistical and tabulation options are very useful as a means of understanding the output from a simulation experiment, since without them the computer's capacity for generating results soon overwhelms the researcher. There is nothing unusual about these provisions, and they have much in common with the specialised report and sorting program generators now supplied by most computer manufacturers for data processing purposes. The idea is that a few simple commands, in terms based on the user's own terminology, can be used to replace the elaborate sequences of instructions necessary to perform the same tasks in a language such as FORTRAN.

Conversational languages

Conversational, or interactive, use of computers, from a remote terminal operating in real time, requires some very sophisticated software support. Since this kind of use began with the development of special purpose language systems for man-machine communications, some discussion follows naturally at this point. The languages mentioned are really of a general purpose sequential kind, devised specifically for on-line operation.

The requirements of conversational use are different from those of more conventional batch-processing of jobs through basic peripheral devices. Any work requires the construction of a program, which can be executed by the machine, but holding 'conversations' with a program in a computer through an on-line device such as a console typewriter relaxes many of the strict requirements of a conventional language. It is still possible, given a suitable supervisory system at an installation, to deal with facilities for time-sharing, to communicate, compile and run whole programs in a batch-processing language and have the results returned to a remote peripheral device. But given a suitable language construction, it becomes possible to abandon the idea of a complete program altogether. At the lowest level, a computer can be used as a calculating machine of enormous power, possibly with the aid of programs already stored at an installation ready for cueing-in with a single command. At a higher level, programs can be developed a few statements at a time, and corrected with the help of messages from the machine itself, which can be programmed to point out errors and omissions, and generally guide a user to a satisfactory solution of his problem. The chief advantage of conversational systems lies in the user's relative freedom from the mechanical processes of preparation of programs, and his ability to concentrate on problem-solving in direct and personal communication with the computer.

One very influential model for this kind of communication is a language called JOSS (for Johnniac Open Shop System) developed in 1964 using the ageing Johnniac computer at the RAND Corporation (Shaw, 1965). Unlike more conventional languages, this requires the provision of line numbers to indicate the programmer's intended sequence of instructions. A numbering system leaving suitable intervals makes it very easy to insert or delete lines in a program, with statements being executed in indexed rather than input order. By giving steps a part number as well as a line number: 1.1, 1.2, . . . 2.1, 2.2, . . . etc., execution can be partial, to test the effect of a few lines or even a single line considered separately. A loop can be executed by typing a command such as

DO PART 1 FOR X=1 (1) 10

where the 1 in brackets is the unit of incrementation and the other figures represent the range of the index variable X. Format in its simplest form is given by a statement such as FORM 1, followed on successive lines by a schematic picture of the desired layout.

JOSS, and its many derivatives, contain a wide range of replies to cover errors. In JOSS, for example, the reply EH? would follow an unexpected input message not understood, and helpful remarks would sometimes reach the stage of 'IT'S A MESS. LET'S START OVER'. This type of language thus has a useful built-in teaching function, although its approach is more informal than a conventional batch-processing language.

These systems have the advantage of simplifying the process of extracting useful information from a computer. On-line systems are also frequently designed to help a casual user find his way around the facilities available to him at an installation, as a more graphic alternative to printed material. They also carry considerable overheads of cost and computer use which can only be justified by providing services for a large number of users, or for very important purposes needing immediate answers.

An on-line system requires a supervisory program resident in the main computer, as well as the additional hardware to cope with incoming and outgoing messages in a number of different channels. This program ensures that any necessary language translators are provided at the correct time to different users, and generally makes possible the experience of each that he is in sole personal contact with the computer. Conversational compilers must also be able to check statements as they are entered, and stop the user whenever he makes a mistake. To accommodate these facilities, a language system which attempts to offer much guidance to a user inevitably takes up a lot of valuable storage space which might otherwise be employed by working programs. Such systems become really viable only when a relatively sizeable computer is available, in conjunction with an efficient network for handling communications from a large number of users.

In a suitable environment, a suitable language design does help considerably in obtaining a 'feel' for programming (Sharpe, 1967). Another such successful language is BASIC (Beginner's All-purpose Symbolic Instruction Code), which is deliberately simplified to make assumptions about the programmer's intentions in default of the specification of operations more complicated to learn. Two attractions of BASIC for the programmer are its facility in handling strings of characters, which it does with much greater ease than, for example, FORTRAN, and its matrix operations which combine considerable power with great simplicity. It is possible, if A, B and C have been earlier defined as matrices and given maximum dimensions, to carry out matrix arithmetic directly by statements such as

```
MAT A=B+C
MAT C=A * B
```

Another command often found might read

```
MAT C=INV(A)
```

and carries out the matrix operation

$$\mathbf{C}=\mathbf{A}^{-1}$$

leaving the inverse of **A** in **C**. These operations would require special definition by a user of other languages such as FORTRAN or ALGOL.

Other methods of on-line communication involve the use of very terse commands using elaborate codes which the machine is already programmed to recognise. Examples are to be found in the enquiry languages of systems designed for remote interrogation of large data files in commercial and industrial situations. These make more effective use of on-line devices by minimising the amount of data to be transmitted by the enquirer, and may send back results to a cathode ray tube display unit rather than as hard copy.

In common with list processing facilities, the possibility of being used interactively is likely to form part of the specification of new languages in the future. In 1963 IBM devised the QUIKTRAN system, making available virtually a full version of FORTRAN for use on-line, with the corresponding advantage that programs could also be used for conventional processing using FORTRAN compilers. The system requires provision of a full program to be meaningful, with execution caused by a separate command, and facilities for editing a program to remove errors before a re-run. Dual modes of operation can considerably enhance the use of general purpose languages, and this kind of FORTRAN application is now possible using a number of manufacturers' systems. The chief advantage is that modification and the removal of errors can take place at the same time as a program is being constructed. Instead of a series of runs under batch processing, correcting errors if they appear, the process can be completed in a single, if extended, session of communication with the computer.

Computer graphics

Interactive applications which use the various graphical input and display equipment described in the preceding chapter have also generated software systems of differing levels of generality. Direct graphic input may use, for example, a cathode ray tube display in conjunction with a light-pen and control keyboard. This requires supporting programs at different levels, corresponding roughly to the levels of programming language discussed earlier, and ranging from basic sub-routines for the operation of the hardware itself to processors for special purpose graphic languages (Wagner and LaHood, 1967). Whether the mode of operation is interactive or not, graphic data may be handled by special purpose commands, or by the extension of the systems which accept some general purpose language.

Some systems for graphic communication operate directly in graphic terms using a tracking device such as a light-pen or a 'joy-stick' to accept input and require only a few keys with specially assigned functions to initiate the available analysis routines. 'Perspective' displays are quite possible, and special graphics software can be used to construct, modify, and rotate 'three-dimensional' drawings as required. These systems are, of course, limited in scope, and the approach is probably better suited to special applications such as computed-aided design. Social scientists may well prefer the combination of a general purpose computing language with some relatively simple graphic facilities to a specialised system which would be more efficient in computing terms (Bird, 1969).

Newer developments

The new social science user faces a choice between two main alternatives in deciding which language he should learn to solve his problem. Assuming nobody else can be found who has already written or is prepared to write a suitable computer program, he may attempt to become sufficiently proficient in a general purpose problem orientated language, or seek the more limited facilities of a language specially designed to serve his immediate needs. Since learning any new means of communication requires some effort, a flexible general purpose language, which can easily be adapted to a range of computer environments, is likely to be preferred to some kinds of code which offer superficially simpler solutions to a limited range of problems. Languages such as DATA-TEXT, developed for sociologists at Harvard (and not to be confused with IBM's text editor called DATATEXT), or the control code for the Michigan Statistical Package for the Social Sciences (Sammet; pages 646–647; Armor and Couch, 1972; Nie *et al.*, 1970), are inevitably more limited in application outside the statistical and text-handling functions which their designers have been able to provide. Both of these examples, in common with some other special application languages, are, in effect, elaborate extensions of an existing higher level language. They were implemented using FORTRAN compilers for the bulk of their needs, but exclude the use of general FORTRAN language facilities in their present form. They permit a user to define his needs in words similar to those current among sociologists concerned with data processing and statistical analysis, but this is a comparatively small gain compared with the loss of inherent generality. DATA-TEXT is available only for quite large IBM and CDC computers, and allows a range of commands to be used for statistical analysis of variables defined by statements such as:

```
*VAR(1)=X(1)=SEX OF SUBJECT (MALE/FEMALE)
*VAR(5)=ORDER X(2)=VERBAL IQ (1–4=LOW/*
*      5–7=AVERAGE/OVER 7=HIGH)
*VAR(6)=1 IF X(10)=5
*OR    =2 IF X(19)=10 AND IF X(11) LESS THAN 3
```

The X—variables in this illustration refer to temporary storage areas used when data are to be recoded prior to analysis. The instructions shown would be preceded by commands to read in the raw data.

Although conceived as a kind of 'natural' language for social scientists engaged in statistical analysis of data (Armor and Couch, 1972), the main strength of the DATA-TEXT system lies in its convenient provision, as illustrated, for the description, recoding and transformation of data values. This, for example, automatically associates the researcher's own labels with possible values of variables which are categorised, or non-continuous, and these labels conveniently appear in the results of statistical analyses subsequently requested of data defined in this way. The other main commands of the language simply specify which of a range of statistical tabulations and tests are to be applied.

Raw data may be coded in alphabetic characters, or groups of characters, as well as numerically, although this obviously limits subsequent statistical analysis to cross tabulations and frequency counts of variable values in this form. An original intention to provide commands for various kinds of content analyses of text material in DATA-TEXT (Couch, 1967) has unfortunately not been realised in the current release of the system.

Facilities of this kind are particularly useful when a social scientist requires to perform extensive re-coding of his raw data, particularly by creating new composite variables or scales from the results of a basic set of observations or the application of a questionnaire. A considerable amount of effort can be devoted simply to rendering the raw data into a form suitable for otherwise routine statistical analysis. Packages such as DATA-TEXT and SPSS, and others which provide for an interactive mode of operation (for example the IMPRESS system, David and Sternick, 1971), can help to overcome this problem. For a researcher whose needs are adequately met by the range of standard statistical procedures which they offer, they may be a sufficient and highly useful research tool. On the other hand they can be considered as providing computer users' languages in only a very limited sense, while still demanding a considerable effort of learning to achieve a reasonable fluency in their available commands. Programming ability in a general purpose language is still needed to extend the range of options offered, and the researcher with this kind of knowledge will clearly be able to devise his own routines for transforming data values and formats with little difficulty. A decision to invest time or money in such a system must depend upon the kind of skills and resources available, and the relative costs of convenience in the short term over the use of general purpose computing facilities.

In addition, the large size of these systems of programs in their current mode of implementation and stage in development suggests that, for many research purposes, use of a good set of single purpose packaged programs, of the kind discussed in the following chapter, is likely to be more efficient in computing terms. Also, statistical routines are commonly available as subprograms in the libraries of computing centres, and can be called more efficiently in this form into users' programs written in a general higher level language.

The facilities we have discussed in this chapter are all to be found in some way in newer languages, except for special simulation requirements which can be provided by the definition of new procedures as subprograms. A language called PL/1 (Programming Language One) available on IBM computers at present, offers a very high degree of generality with a format reminiscent of FORTRAN, plus some COBOL features for file-handling. This is not particularly well suited to list processing, but represents a considerable improvement over FORTRAN in methods of handling files and character strings.

It is possible to produce programs using only very simple subsets of the language, which it is claimed will help the beginner, but a very wide range of possibilities exist for the specialist. This great flexibility initially led to criticisms of the language based on the relatively poor performance and the size of its compiler, but as with other developments in programming, ways are being found to improve its implementation and make it more generally acceptable. We have earlier noted that PL/1 may use the stack principle selectively, which helps to improve efficiency on most current computers, but this language is innovatory in other important respects. It is the only widespread language to recognise the inefficiency of sequential structure, and allow the programmer to execute different parts of calculations simultaneously, to produce a faster run. And although it has the drawback of not being suited to direct conversational use, it does have one other feature which is prophetic of likely future trends. This lies in an inherent ability to extend the language at will, using not subprograms but new definitions of commands. It can be adapted in this way to suit any special purposes, without any sacrifice of generality in its overall construction (Bates and Douglas, 1970). Another language developed about the same time in Britain, and called CPL (Higman, pages 102–124), uses a similar approach, while following the Algol tradition, with the addition of list processing methods.

It is possible in several current languages to redefine notation or sections of the grammar of the main language itself, to suit the user. A natural extension of this idea is the provision of aids to the development of new languages specially tailored to particular uses, and deliberately chosen to use the terms of a highly specific field. We have already noted several attempts to achieve general problem-oriented languages, while retaining an algorithmic character suitable for a wide range of applications. In these languages, it is a common practice to write user-oriented 'packaged' programs to suit individual applications. An example is the provision of sets of generalised subprograms for common statistical processes, which are activated by very simple commands given together with a set of data.

As an illustration of how the process may be extended while making minimal extra demands on professional programmers, Burroughs' recent Problem Oriented Language Generator (POLGEN) (Burroughs Corporation, 1971) can be used to create new languages in a simplified way. A suitable grammar must first be negotiated to contain the terms and operations needed for the required field of application. The POLGEN system develops a language processor capable of translating these terms, which is subsequently available whenever the new language is needed.

Grammar definitions are expressed in terms similar to those of COBOL, and the system itself uses COBOL compilers in the course of producing the final translator. Any new computational procedures necessary to match the terms of the new user-oriented language are also written in COBOL and merged by POLGEN into the final software product. While restricted in this case to one manufacturer's machines and to a rather cumbersome basic language, the idea is clearly capable of extension. The development of systems of this kind will then considerably reduce the programming effort needed to convert a new grammar into a usable means of communicating with a computer.

Finally we should note the availability at present of another powerful general purpose language which is capable of being used either on-line or in batch-processing, and contains most of the facilities found useful up to the present. This is POP2 (Burstall, *et al.*, 1971), designed in the Department of Machine Intelligence at the University of Edinburgh to provide conversational facilities in a language with a notation giving full mathematical generality, akin to algebra. The result is a powerful but, in storage terms, surprisingly compact language system which is very convenient for non-numerical work as well as numerical calculation, and has a syntax which is capable of extension by the programmer. As an aid to its dissemination as a language, a machine-independent POP2 compiler written in POP2 itself is available. An example which conveys the flavour of the language will be found in Fig. 5.5. Considerable advantages of efficiency and brevity seem to make the POP2 approach preferable to, for example, the FORTRAN-extension DYSTAL (Sakoda, 1968) which attempts to provide some similar facilities in a form which will be familiar to users of FORTRAN.

Basic computer software

Little use can be made of a computer without the provision from some source of some basic software to control the computer's activities and to translate incoming messages not already in machine code form. We conclude this chapter with a brief discussion of the way these affect the user.

1. Compilers A well-designed compiler is a considerable asset to a programmer in any higher-level language. For some reason it did not, apparently, occur to the mathematicians responsible for the original development of programmed computers that a programmer was likely to prove fallible. Experience soon showed that a great deal of the time needed to develop working programs was taken up in the correction of mistakes made by their authors or those who prepared them for input into the computer. Higher-level languages reduce the likelihood of errors in punctuation or format, but simple slips can still prove fatal on execution. The correction of errors is commonly termed 'debugging'.

Errors in source programs can be detected by introducing syntax checks into compilers, and causing error messages to be output in the event of unsuccessful computation. However, syntactic correctness is not sufficient condition for a program to make semantic sense, and still less a guarantee that the programmer's intentions are correctly realised. This is the reason for the introduction of the final decision box in the flow chart in Fig. 3.1. It is always necessary to check that a program is actually giving the kind of results expected, and if it is not, the fault probably lies with the programmer. It is also possible that semantic errors will appear during the course of execution of a program. For example, a divisor may become zero for unforeseen reasons. To assist in finding the source of this type of mistake, compilers in general insert extra code into an object program to generate and temporarily store a trace of the working values resulting from successive statements. In the event of an execution error, a portion of this trace information can be output, to show at what point things went wrong.

Like other programs, compilers themselves should not be considered completely error free, although prolonged use will usually reveal most of their shortcomings. A programmer can help to demonstrate the more obscure sources of error, including hardware malfunctions, by arranging for monitoring statements to be output at various stages of his program, especially if the compiler's assistance is insufficient to clarify a fault.

Compilers can also be designed to try to create the most efficient possible machine code from source statements. For example, if they discover statements written by the programmer inside a repeated loop which do not seem to depend upon changes in the loop counter, they may cause these statements to be compiled outside the loop, to save wasted repetitions. Optimising compilers of this kind are not really a substitute for good programming, and sometimes produce unexpected results if their rules for finding short cuts conflict with the problem-solving method employed by the user. But subject to careful comparisons with the results of normal compilation, they can help to save some work in creating efficient programs.

2. Operating systems The increase in operating speeds with successive generations of computers has led to the development of other important basic software, to try to keep pace with the machine's appetite for work. Initially, computers were operated by manual instructions from a control console typewriter, with the assistance of a control or executive program permanently resident in the machine. But reliance on human operators became increasingly uneconomic when the waiting time between job runs so clearly exceeded the time taken for the performance of calculations. Even with careful manual batching of jobs using similar facilities, for example of all programs needing the same compiler system, the need for an automatic multi-processing method was obvious, if expensive equipment was not to be wasted.

This was the motivation for the development of so-called operating systems, as substitutes for many of the routine tasks of job control formerly performed by human operators. Operators are always required to load and supervise the various peripheral units for input and output of information. The job of loading, compiling and running separate programs, however, was much better handled automatically. Characteristically, operating systems of this kind call in appropriate compilers and other software needed by a user's job, allocate storage and peripherals to a program, and schedule simultaneous processing of several jobs in the input 'stream' to ensure the maximum possible use of the computer at all times. When provided with sufficient input material, the process is continuous for as long as the system is active in the computer, and human intervention is required only to load and start the operator program, or in the event of breakdown. Operating systems are usually controlled by messages in codes designed to describe each job and the facilities it requires. Users are therefore required to master the techniques of communicating with the operating system as well as the facilities of the program they wish to run. But since the control language of an operating system has been written to suit users rather than the machine's own vocabulary, successful submission of jobs for batch processing is considerably simplified. The operating system can also offer comments on the progress of a job, as a guide to error-tracing, and output general statistics concerning its use of available facilities.

The development of conversational languages was also accompanied by supervisory systems to cope with the problem of storage allocation and control of a number of jobs simultaneously transmitted by various users. Similar, still more complex, supporting systems are needed to operate cathode ray tube display devices, when used directly for input and output of data.

Finally, operating systems characteristically include some means of combining sections of a program written in different source languages, so that the resultant object program can be run as one.

The latest stage in the development of such systems is a fusion of these various elements into a single software package, containing all the facilities needed for communication and control in large computer systems, with the maximum economy. The ways in which an operating system affects the user are discussed in the chapter which follows.

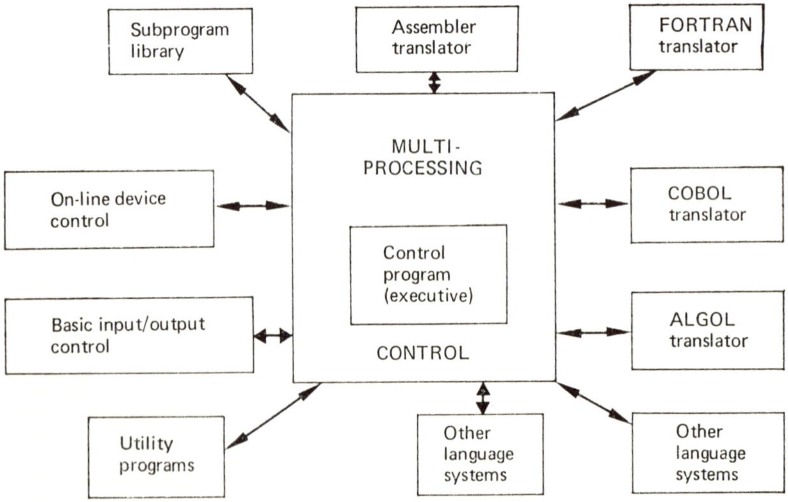

Fig. 3.12 Operating system facilities.

References

D. J. Armor and A. S. Couch (1972) *The DATA-TEXT Primer*, New York, The Free Press.

Association for Computing Machinery (1966) *Collected Algorithms from the Communications of the A.C.M., New York.*

M. P. Barnett (1969) *Computer Programming in English*, New York, Harcourt Brace and World.

D. W. Barron (1968) *Recursive Techniques in Programming*, London, Macdonald.

F. Bates and M. L. Douglas (1970) *Programming Language/One* (2nd Edition), Englewood Cliffs, N.J., Prentice-Hall.

S. Bird (1969) 'Computer Graphics Software Techniques' in R. D. Parslow, R. W. Prowse, R. Elliot Green (Editors), *Computer Graphics —Techniques and Applications*, London and New York, Plenum Press.

Burroughs Corporation (1971) *B2500 and B3500 Systems Problem Oriented Language Generator (POLGEN) Reference Manual*, Detroit, Michigan.

R. M. Burstall, J. S. Collins and R. J. Popplestone (1971) *Programming in POP2*, Edinburgh University Press.

W. C. Cheseborough (1971) 'Decision Tables as a System Technique' in D. D. Benice (Editor), *Computer Seelctions*, New York, McGraw-Hill.

A. C. Day (1972) *FORTRAN Techniques with Special Reference to Non-numerical Applications*, Cambridge University Press.

J. A. David and J. H. Sternick (1971) *The IMPRESS Primer*, Dartmouth College, N.J.

B. Higman (1967) *A Comparative Study of Programming Languages*, London, Macdonald.

P. Naur (Editor) (1962) Revised Report on the Algorithmic Language Algol 60. I.F.I.P. (Also in *Computer Journal*, **5** (1963), pages 349–367, and *Comm. A.C.M.*, **6** (1963), pages 1–17.)

N. H. Nie, D. H. Bent and C. H. Hull (1970) *Statistical Package for the Social Sciences*, New York, McGraw-Hill.

J. M. Sakoda (1968) 'A General Computer Language for the Social Sciences' in J. M. Beshers (Editor), *Computer Methods in the Analysis of Large-Scale Social Systems*, (2nd Edition), Cambridge, Mass., and London, MIT Press.

J. E. Sammet (1969) *Programming Languages: History and Fundamentals.* Englewood Cliffs, N.J., Prentice-Hall.

W. F. Sharpe (1967) *BASIC: An introduction to Computer Programming using the BASIC language*, Glencoe, Ill., Free Press.

J. C. Shaw (1965) 'JOSS: Experience with an Experimental Computing Service for Users at Remote Consoles', RAND Report P-3149 in W. D. Orr (Editor) (1968) *Conversational Computers*, New York, John Wiley.

F. V. Wagner and J. LaHood (1967) 'Computer graphics—software design' in F. Gruenberger (Editor), *Computer Graphics*, London, Academic Press; Washington, Thompson.

References to the list processing language LISP apply also to LISP2, which is effectively an extended Algol, with many other useful features besides those noted (Sammet, pages 589–598).

Further reading

D. W. Barron (1971) *Computer Operating Systems*, London, Chapman and Hall.

N. Chapin (1971) *Flowcharts*, Princeton, Philadelphia, New York, London, Auerbach.

J. M. Foster (1967) *List Processing*, London, Macdonald.

P. J. Kinat, 'Simulation Languages', Appendix C in T. H. Naylor (Editor) (1971) *Computer Simulation Experiments with Models of Economic Systems*, New York, John Wiley.

M. Levison and W. A. Sentance (1968) *Introduction to Computer Science*, London, Oldbourne.

D. D. McCracken (1957) *Digital Computer Programming*, New York, John Wiley.

D. D. McCracken and U. Garbassi (1970) *A Guide to COBOL Programming* (2nd Edition), New York, John Wiley.

C. M. Reeves and M. Wells (1964) *A Course on Programming in ALGOL 60*, London, Chapman and Hall.

References on FORTRAN are to be found at the end of Chapter 7.

For practical purposes, the user's manuals describing any particular implementation are necessary to supplement texts concerned with individual programming languages.

4 Data processing—survey and statistical analysis

The area of computer application which the social scientist is most likely to meet is the analysis of large, or complex, batches of quantitative data. In the past, business investigations and social research had to be strictly limited in scope to enable statistical processing to conform to the restrictions of the relatively few mechanical devices available. Alternatively, calculations effectively delayed the completion of research so that the maximum value of the results was often lost. For example, the advent of the computer cut years off the time previously taken for full population census results to be calculated, a reduction of inestimable value for social and economic planning. The coming of fast and accurate computing has not only made much existing research easier to analyse but has led to the expansion and development of many types of application. Two of the most useful ways in which the computer is available as a research tool to the social scientist are in the processing of social surveys and in the general statistical analysis of a wide range of quantitative data. Although at a basic level many operations may be common to both, somewhat different computing problems are presented. In the first area, we will be mainly concerned with discrete variables and counting operations, while the second involves mainly continuous variables and problems of numerical methods. Therefore, for the purposes of this chapter, these two areas of application are treated separately. We further take the opportunity, in this chapter, of introducing some general problems in the use of 'packaged' programs not written by the user for himself.

The structure of a social survey computer program

The social survey, accepted as one of the main means of information-gathering in the social sciences, can be analysed with substantial gains on the computer, provided certain limitations are borne in mind. It is worth considering the structural features of this type of program as they give a good indication of the problems to be overcome in machine terms. A basic requirement is that it should be able rapidly to produce contingency tables, of at least a bivariate nature, and frequency counts for any, or all, combinations of the variables input. The basic counting operation to produce tables such as Figs. 4.1 and 4.4 is computationally trivial. However, storage requirements and reworking of contingency tables may present substantial problems in the organisation of data and the construction of programs. To justify the use of computers it must be said that in any but the smallest survey, the formation of complex contingency tables would immediately put the analysis of a survey beyond the reasonable capacity of any other mechanical aid. This can be illustrated by considering a data set of say 60 variables, each punched in a separate column of a data card, such as was illustrated in Fig. 2.2. If a standard 64 character set is used, the maximum number of different column punches which could represent discrete variable values is 65, if a blank column is treated as a separate value. Cards which are also to be sorted using an electro-mechanical device will usually be coded only in single punched characters, that is, as reference to Fig. 2.2 will show, the numerical codes 0 to 9, and the two additional 'zone' punches, in this case called '&' and '—'. Including the blank column, this gives a maximum of 13 separate value codes for each variable which is to be processed (Claffey, 1967).

The number of simple contingency tables which could be calculated for all combinations of variables is:

$$\frac{60 \times 59}{2} = 1770 \text{ tables}$$

The problem for the program comes not only from the large number of tables, but also the fact that each table may be a 13×13 matrix,

EXAMPLE RUN FOR REVOLUTIONARY INCIDENTS DATA 09/02/73 PAGE 5

FILE CALVERT (CREATION DATE = 09/02/73) PETER CALVERT'S DATA FILE

VARIABLE VAR005 PERSONNEL

VALUE LABEL	VALUE	ABSOLUTE FREQUENCY	RELATIVE FREQUENCY (PERCENT)	ADJUSTED FREQUENCY (PERCENT)	CUMULATIVE ADJ FREQ (PERCENT)
MILITARY	1.00	123	33.9	33.9	33.9
CIVILIAN	2.00	170	46.8	46.8	80.7
MILITARY-CIVILIAN	3.00	70	19.3	19.3	100.0
	11.00	0	0.0	MISSING	100.0
	12.00	0	0.0	MISSING	100.0
	13.00	0	0.0	MISSING	100.0
	TOTAL	363	100.0	100.0	100.0

VALID OBSERVATIONS - 363
MISSING OBSERVATIONS - 0

Fig. 4.1 Survey analysis—an example of a frequency count. The data shown are also to be found in P. A. R. Calvert's study of 'revolutionary incidents' between 1901 and 1960 (Calvert, 1970, page 209; cf. pages 86–92). The print-out was produced using the SPSS system (Nie *et al.*, 1971).

representing 169 separate cells to be calculated and output in one medium or another. In addition, it is obvious that each separate variable must be available at all times for the program to call up and work upon. The key elements in this situation must therefore be program flexibility, and the easy storage of data until it is accessed for analysis. These are usually provided by the use of magnetic tape or discs as backing store, and the use of a series of interrelated, but distinct, routines which allow the process to be broken down into machine manageable components. Most programs are divided into at least two sections. One of these reads the data, usually on punched cards, and transforms it, as card images, to data blocks on a magnetic tape, whilst at the same time providing as printout, from a line-printer, a straightforward count of column punches. A second set of routines, using the backing store file constructed from the first routine, forms contingency tables, and prints them out to a user's specification. Because of practical limitations of storage space, there may well be more than two separate routines in a survey analysis package, running as a chain.

In practice, a survey analysis series of programs is considerably more complicated than this outline. For instance, although the variables may be used just as they are punched on data cards, in the event of errors, other more complex operations may be required. Thus some form of suppression, alteration or elimination of data is usually incorporated into one or more of the programs. Additionally facilities may be added to provide mathematical or statistical aids to analysis (such as weighting and transformation of values) and such operations as filtering through a series of control or background variables in the formation of tables for subgroups of the original data.

The reading and storage of data, the adding and percentaging of numbers, the formation and printing of contingency tables, the formation of statistics on the basis of these tables, and the possible use of more complex statistical operations, all require separate computing solutions. The most obvious way of meeting these is to present one complete lengthy program in which linking sections transfer relevant information to each other without the complications of peripheral storage. However the requirement that a single program accomplish all the operations in a *single pass of the data* (for example, one complete run-through of a deck of cards or a tape file) is, in effect, insuperable, unless a remarkably inefficient system is sanctioned. It may be easier to start each separate operation in a social survey analysis on the basic data which are input rather than perform a hierarchy of increasingly complex statistical processes. For example, Veldman (1967, pages 326–338) notes how difficult it is to integrate a chi-squared program completely with a contingency-table-forming program. This is because the technique of chi-square formation may involve the amalgamation of separate cells in a contingency table, which for other purposes must be kept separate. Although a separate program may be written which achieves a satisfactory reworking of a contingency table, it inevitably will mean a second pass of the data. Therefore, the almost invariable solution is to use a work-file which is created by a separate program, and then read as a preliminary to each sequence of computed operations.

On computers with a strictly limited amount of immediate access storage, or where very large surveys are being run, in effect the only way of working with a survey analysis program is to overlay temporarily sections either of the program or data to some form of backing store. The flexibility of a series of programs which can do this may not be only immediately useful in so far as it allows the program to run at all, but if a package is written in discrete segments, may allow the modular modification or development of the program for different or unexpected requirements. This latter point would hold, even with the development of different storage arrangements on some of the newer ranges of computers, where immediate access to stored programs or data is virtually limitless.

Different possible specifications of such programs can be illustrated by a number of American examples analysed by Janda (1969). In these, the number of variables allowed ranges from 40 to a (theoretically) unlimited number, table size varies from 4×4 to 34×99 (compared to our earlier maximum of 13×13), the number of cases permitted (respondents) varies from 1500 to an unlimited number, and there may be restrictions based on the number of separate tables calculated on a single pass of the data. There appears on this basis to be no such thing as a perfectly written survey analysis package suitable for everyone. For many programs are still constructed for specific research purposes, or involve a loss in one dimension of the available facilities for a gain in another.

The use of a social survey computer program

Efficient computer analysis of survey material essentially involves pursuing a logical and coherent experimental design from the inception of a project. The possibilities of analysis are greatly reduced by failure to appreciate the capabilities of a particular available program. Even more disastrous is the completion and coding of a social survey, without reference to computing facilities until the moment of hypothesis testing, or contingency table formation. The stages through which it is advisable for the experimenter to pass in progressing from the conception of a project, to a completed survey analysis on the computer, can be shown by a flow chart which details the most important features of the process.

It is necessary not only to identify the problem and ask pertinent questions in relation to a given hypothesis, but also to make sure that the analysis of the data obtained is as exhaustive and efficient as possible.

One of the most crucial operations to be considered is the extent to which the design of the social survey must be manipulated in order to provide a suitable data base for a computer program. Inevitably as all answers must be coded to be used on any input medium, the emphasis will usually be on structured, rather than unstructured, questions in a questionnaire. To some extent this is a defect, but echoes controversies (still raging) over the rigidity and restrictions imposed on difficult and elusive concepts by structured survey questions (Moser and Kalton, 1971; Galtung, 1967). The *process of computing* itself does not impose any more drastic constraints on data than other mechanical, or manual, methods of producing quantitative data. However in a situation of limited computing knowledge and the absence of recognised alternatives, a potential user may in fact unduly restrict the kind of data he collects, and subsequently analyses.

The general point here is that given suitable programs a researcher need not feel constrained by a 'punched-card' mentality in his data-gathering. Developments in programming techniques, some of which will be discussed in later chapters, make it possible to consider submitting much less restricted codes to the computer for subsequent analysis. It is now quite feasible to use optical character recognition techniques to input transcripts of interviews, after which a computer

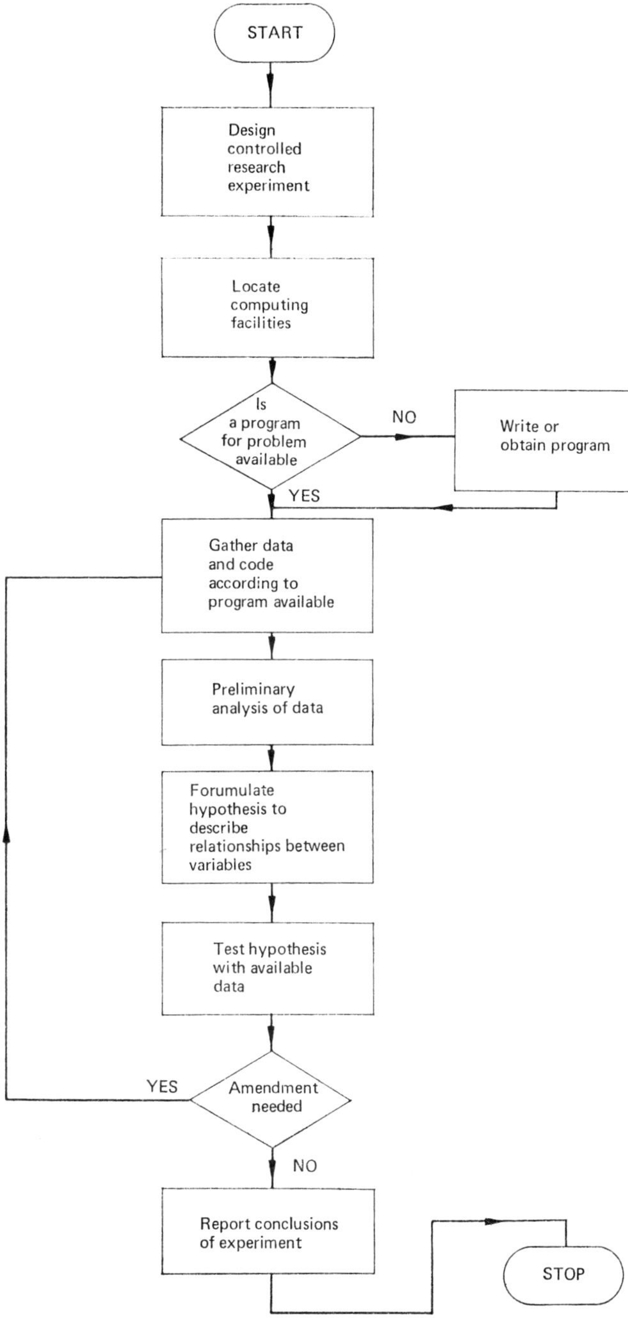

Fig. 4.2 The use of computing facilities in research.

analysis of the content can be performed. Other combinations of free-response answers and pre-coded data can be directly input in the same way, if the equipment is available. Coding routines will, of course, still have to be used as part of any quantitative treatment, but they can be based on all the data obtained and not on an *a-priori* categorisation.

```
50/ 63
M
.....................................MATRIX.....................................
        50  POLITIES                                               50  POLITIES
            WHERE FREEDOM OF THE PRESS IS           .                  WHERE FREEDOM OF THE PRESS IS
            COMPLETE  (43)                          .                  INTERMITTENT, INTERNALLY ABSENT, OR
                                                    .                  INTERNALLY AND EXTERNALLY ABSENT  (56)
                                                    .
                                                    .
                                       63  POLITIES
                                           WHERE THE RELIGION IS
                                           PREDOMINANTLY
                                           SOME KIND OF CHRISTIAN  (46)
                                                    .
AUSTRALIA   AUSTRIA     BELGIUM     CANADA      CHILE       .ARGENTINA  BRAZIL      BULGARIA    CUBA        CZECHOS'KIA
COLOMBIA    COSTA RICA  DENMARK     DOMIN REP   FINLAND     .FRANCE     GERMANY, E  HUNGARY     PARAGUAY    POLAND
GERMAN FR   ICELAND     IRELAND     ITALY       JAMAICA     .PORTUGAL   RUMANIA     SPAIN       VENEZUELA   YUGOSLAVIA
LUXEMBOURG  MEXICO      NETHERLANDS NEW ZEALAND NORWAY      .
PANAMA      PHILIPPINES SWEDEN      SWITZERLAND UK          .
US          URUGUAY                                         .
                                                         27 .  15
. . . . . . . . . . . . . . . . . . . . . . . . . . . . . . . . . . . . . . . . . . . . . . . . . . . . . . .
                                                         16 .  40
                                                    .
                                       63  POLITIES
                                           WHERE THE RELIGION IS
                                           PREDOMINANTLY OR PARTLY
                                           OTHER THAN CHRISTIAN  (68)
                                                    .
CAMEROUN    CHAD        CYPRUS      ECUADOR     INDIA       .AFGHANISTAN ALBANIA    ALGERIA     BOLIVIA     BURMA
JAPAN       MALAGASY R  MALAYA      MALI        MAURITANIA  .CAMBODIA   CHINA, PR   CONGO(LEO)  ETHIOPIA    GHANA
NIGER       SIERRE LEO  SOMALIA     TANGANYIKA  TRINIDAD    .GUINEA     HAITI       INDONESIA   IRAN        IRAQ
UGANDA                                                      .ISRAEL     JORDAN      KOREA, N    KOREA REP   LAOS
                                                            .LEBANON    LIBERIA     LIBYA       MONGOLIA    MOROCCO
                                                            .NEPAL      NIGERIA     PAKISTAN    PERU        SA'U ARABIA
                                                            .SO AFRICA  SUDAN       SYRIA       THAILAND    TUNISIA
                                                            .TURKEY     UAR         VIETNAM, N  VIETNAM REP YEMEN
                                                            .
```

Source: Banks and Textor (1963)

Fig. 4.3 A contingency table with named elements.

The contingency table of Fig. 4.3, taken from Banks and Textor's *Cross Polity Survey* (1963) is an excellent example of the imaginative use of explanatory text combined with a quite straightforward contingency table program. In this analysis, 57 different variables were gathered for 115 countries as a basis for analysing relationships between certain political and social dimensions of classifications of nations. These variables were all dichotomised and used to produce a series of two-by-two matrices, for which statistics could be calculated to measure the degree of association between variables. The example shown is their cross-tabulation of countries based on the degree of competitiveness of the electoral system and freedom of the press. The study from which this is taken has formed the basis for many later analyses of the basic associations between features of this kind.

At a more modest level, two or more columns of a card could be used for codes, as could data without imposed intervals, for instance exact ages instead of a series of age ranges. This may not only make the survey analysis more accurate, but leads to the possibility of interchange of data between researchers on a less constricted basis. This latter point is of particular importance where survey analyses assume more than local importance to an individual or group of users. The increasing prominence and use of data banks for survey data implies at the very least a willingness to consider the needs and structure of other researchers' survey projects. The aim ultimately is to have a sequence of wide ranging surveys done both at the same time and over a long time period. Those may prove more useful in any particular area of study than individual surveys researched on the basis of limited resources.

Bearing in mind the problems described above, a busy researcher is very unlikely to want to write himself the kind of survey analysis program described in the preceding section of this chapter. Nor, given a reasonably well-developed computing centre, will he normally have to do so, for many of the kinds of programs he needs are likely to be available in one form or another. However, these programs may prove to have incompatible format requirements when compared with each other, or with the format of the data which has been assembled and coded. This is a problem particularly when information is obtained from another researcher, and local format conventions differ.

In order to overcome these problems there are two main possibilities. If the program to be used is available in source form, rather than ready compiled, it should be a relatively simple matter to alter the input formatting statements to suit the data which are to be analysed by the program. If the source program is written in one of the higher level languages, this can be done with the help of any proficient programmer. However, it may be that some programmers, anxious to safeguard their own ideas, will withhold the original source program, in which case it is necessary to change the format of the data to suit the program rather than the other way round. For this a knowledge of a general purpose programming language, such as FORTRAN (described in Chapter 7), is useful. The program that needs to be written is a trivial one, which simply reads one format and outputs another, but the process can also conveniently include some editing or transformation of data values. If the data are not already stored on such a medium, it is probably a good idea at this stage to transfer values to a magnetic tape or disc store, from which afterwards they can be obtained for input to the computer much more quickly than from cards or paper tape. Finally, a problem may arise with data that are received from another researcher on a magnetic tape coded in a form which is not standard for the computer to be used. In this case a transcription program is essential if the data are to be used at all, but with a little ingenuity should not be too difficult to devise. In fact this kind of programming skill may be the most useful of all for the researcher to acquire, and can open the way for much more effective exploration of the efforts of statisticians and programmers.

Assuming the availability of a suitable program to perform all the analyses required, the first step then, is to see that the data are coded in a suitable format. We earlier described some alternatives which may be possible in survey analysis applications. A basic distinction to note is that between fixed formats and free formats. In a fixed format coding, all values are expressed in the same self-consistent way in 'fields' of equal length. For example, one of the possibilities we noted earlier was to use each column of a punched card to convey a separated variable value. In free formats, variable values are expressed in fields of varying lengths, separated by spaces or commas. The computer program, in this case, must be able to read a series of characters in sequence until it recognises a blank or comma, and record the information read up to that point. Either method may be provided for by a suitably written program, but of course this has to be ascertained in advance. Highly developed general purpose program 'packages' such as the SPSS (Nie *et al.*, 1971) from which two of our text illustrations are derived, allow the user to specify which system he will use, and in the case of fixed formats to indicate the format of his data as part of his instructions to the program. Since the format specification uses FORTRAN conventions, it also helps to know something of this computer language in using SPSS. Once format conventions have been adopted and the data are in machine-readable form, say on punched cards, the next stage is to prepare a set of instructions for the program. These will specify the dimensions of the data, the number of columns, and cards for each respondent, the number of respondents and an identification for the survey. In addition, there may be parameter cards specifying such things as data editing or recording facilities, if used with the initial run of the program. A standard facility is the counting and printing out of character frequencies in the relevant columns as in Fig. 4.1. This is a useful exercise in two ways, because first it may be a necessary first stage in the testing of hypothesis or a search for relevant variables, and secondly it is the main means of identifying whether there are any errors or mispunches. This phase of the operation also usually includes the creation and naming of a backing store file, which the remaining sections in the particular survey package will use as a work-file. Once this data file has been created, the editing and recording which may be required can be undertaken. This may involve a further run, or series of runs, to identify and alter the relevant data records.

With editing complete, the main contingency table formation phase can be accomplished. Although the type of table available varies in detail between various programs, the main outlines are as follows. Two-way tables are produced as raw frequency counts in a matrix, and percentaged by row, column and grand total. In addition there may be filtering options available, or means of selecting sub-groups by certain values of the variables, and a variety of statistics on the tables. On some of the more sophisticated survey packages, 3, 4 or 5-way contingency tables are available.

Figure 4.4 represents, from the SPSS system, a highly developed solution to the problems of table construction for the line-printer. The titles, variable and variable value names were all supplied on the initial run of the program as additional data, and reappear in any subsequent print-out of an analysis of these particular variables. The obvious advantage of using a well-developed system of this kind is that tabulations from it are immediately intelligible, and even ready to publish without further modification. Although the construction of such tables is not difficult to conceive, there are few programs which achieve the standard of clarity seen here. In addition, Fig. 4.4 shows the full range of contingency statistics which can be requested on the SPSS system.

Two important stages of a survey analysis are apparent for the user. First, it must be emphasised again that the initial questionnaire must be designed bearing in mind available facilities for computation. Secondly, the structuring of a table-forming run of the program must be done in such a way as to provide an efficient test of the hypothesis previously considered in relation to the survey.

Some indications of the possibilities and hazards of indiscriminate table forming have already been suggested. Given a survey of 60 variables printing even all simple cross-tabulations yields 1770 tables. With even a fast line-printer this is wasteful of machine time as well as of paper. Whilst this operation is an entirely feasible one on many computers, for reasons of expense and the time needed for later analysis, it is not advisable. Even with the aid of individual statistics, such as chi-squared for each of these tables, the time required to analyse the print-out of all these results and their significance is obviously large. For reasons of efficiency as well as methodological rigour, the process must be more structured. The real problem associated with survey analysis on the computer is, then, to restrict the potentially large number of operations between variables, through judicious use of preliminary print-out of variable frequency counts and prior assessment of hypothesis. Otherwise, although there are likely to be interesting and rewarding results thrown up serendipitously, there are serious problems of deciding whether relationships are valid, or merely spurious ones (Moser and Kalton, 1971).

Even in a well-planned survey, it is sometimes the unexpected associations of variables which are most fruitful for the later revision of hypotheses. When a computer is used in the process of a search, it is again quite feasible to substitute a preliminary statistical scan for the generation of large numbers of contingency tables. One possibility, which is admittedly rather wasteful of computer time, is to request supporting data for a series of intuitive hunches, using an interactive system and a visual display unit, as described in Chapter 2. A more efficient alternative is to generate matrices of coefficients of association, or of chi-squared values, instead of the full cross-tabulations. Again, the sheer volume of data may very easily defeat this design too. There remains a suggestion that all variables, however coded in the raw data, should be dichotomised, possibly automatically by the computer at or near the median of any more or less ordered measures. Phi coefficients (the equivalent of the correlation coefficient for dichotomised data given the dummy values 0 and 1) can then be calculated, and the matrix of these values can be used as a basis for some of the multivariate factor or cluster analyses described later in the chapter (McKennell, 1970). Despite theoretical objections to the use of ordinary correlation coefficients for ordinal or non-metric data, this procedure seems to work reasonably well in practice as a means of pin-pointing areas for detailed examination. It might, however, be more desirable if substantial non-linear relationships in the data are suspected, to *trichotomise* variables and use some other measure for the significance of an association (Galtung, 1967, page 259). Various short-cut methods of this kind can be devised, with the help of a suitable computer program, to assist in the fuller analysis of survey data.

Statistical data processing

Whereas the use of computer programs in relation to social survey analysis is more or less obligatory in all but very small surveys because of the sheer volume of work involved, the decision to use a computer for statistical analyses is less straightforward. In some cases, where an intimate 'feel' for the nature of the data is essential, it may even be preferable to use an alternative calculating aid, such as a programmable desk calculator or micro-computer. Apart from the volume of data to be processed four considerations may guide the user in choosing between these possibilities. First, the complexity of the statistical operation to be applied; second, the number of times that the same batch of data is to be used in a series of operation; third, the number of times the same operation is to be repeated; fourth, and in practice the most important, is the availability and ease of operation of relevant programs. This may be especially significant when using small machines, and where there are few social science users of an installation.

We can conveniently discuss these considerations in order of the complexity of the statistical operation involved. The following sections will deal with data organisation and univariate analysis, bivariate analysis and multivariate analysis.

Data reorganisation and univariate analysis

Some of the statistical operations required in the social sciences are of a relatively unsophisticated nature, but may be rather repetitive. Data reorganisation may take many forms dependent on the subject matter of the research and the aims of the investigator. Probably the most irritating difficulty, mentioned already in the context of social surveys, arises when a number of different programs are to be used on the same set of coded data. The problem of matching format requirements where necessary may seem a trivial one, but some skills of the kind indicated earlier can help a researcher through a number of possible sources of frustration.

A fortunate user will have available at his own computing centre one of the widely used general packaged programs for routine analyses of social data. The best known of these take two different forms. The widely available Biomedical Computer Programs (BMD) developed and distributed by the Medical Centre of the University of California, Los Angeles, consist of a set of separate routines which together cover most of the commonly required tasks in data processing and statistical analysis. Data and instruction cards for the various analyses must be prepared as specified in the available manuals (Dixon, 1969 and Dixon, 1971). Some programs in the later X-series BMD group contain open subroutine sections, into which a user can insert his own FORTRAN statements among his instruction cards. This facility covers the possibility that a non-standard data transformation may be needed for particular application, and helps to make the programs more flexible than a closed package would be. In the program for general non-linear curve fitting by least squares, it is possible to provide FORTRAN definition of the functions to be fitted, together with its derivative, as additional code to be executed when the program is run. For the user who knows some FORTRAN and is reasonably familiar with his local computer installation, these programs are often a more efficient way of performing many of the analyses which are also available in program packages which are operated by means of a fuller instruction language. Two of these, SPSS and DATA-TEXT, have been discussed in the previous chapter, and their details will not be repeated here. A major advantage of these systems is their comprehensive facility for data manipulation and transformation,

```
EXAMPLE RUN FOR REVOLUTIONARY INCIDENTS DATA                                          09/02/73        PAGE    2

FILE    CALVERT   (CREATION DATE = 09/02/73)    PETER CALVERT'S DATA FILE

* * * * * * * * * * * * * * * * * *    C R O S S T A B U L A T I O N   O F   * * * * * * * * * * * * * * * * * *
    VAR004     DURATION                                      BY  VAR005     PERSONNEL
* * * * * * * * * * * * * * * * * * * * * * * * * * * * * * * * * * * * * * * * * * * * * * * * *   PAGE  1 OF  1

                     VAR005
             COUNT   I
           ROW PCT   IMILITARY CIVILIAN MILITARY    ROW
           COL PCT   I                  -CIVILIA   TOTAL
           TOT PCT   I     1.00I    2.00I    3.00I
VAR004     --------I--------I--------I--------I
              1.00   I    62  I    59  I    12  I    133
  UNDER 1 DAY        I  46.6  I  44.4  I   9.0  I   37.5
                     I  51.2  I  35.8  I  17.4  I
                     I  17.5  I  16.6  I   3.4  I
                    -I--------I--------I--------I
              2.00   I    51  I    50  I    32  I    133
  1 TO 30 DAYS       I  38.3  I  37.6  I  24.1  I   37.5
                     I  42.1  I  30.3  I  46.4  I
                     I  14.4  I  14.1  I   9.0  I
                    -I--------I--------I--------I
              3.00   I     8  I    40  I    17  I     65
  1 TO 12 MONTHS     I  12.3  I  61.5  I  26.2  I   18.3
                     I   6.6  I  24.2  I  24.6  I
                     I   2.3  I  11.3  I   4.8  I
                    -I--------I--------I--------I
              4.00   I     0  I    16  I     8  I     24
  OVER 1 YEAR        I   0.0  I  66.7  I  33.3  I    6.8
                     I   0.0  I   9.7  I  11.6  I
                     I   0.0  I   4.5  I   2.3  I
                    -I--------I--------I--------I
            COLUMN        121      165       69      355
             TOTAL       34.1     46.5     19.4    100.0

CHI SQUARE =     44.50162 WITH    6 DEGREES OF FREEDOM
CRAMER'S V =     0.25036
CONTINGENCY COEFFICIENT =     0.33376
KENDALL'S TAU B =      0.27086
KENDALL'S TAU C =      0.26616
GAMMA =     0.40595
SOMER'S D =      0.28164

NUMBER OF MISSING OBSERVATIONS =        8
```

Fig. 4.4 A contingency table with statistics. The data shown are also to be found in P. A. R. Calvert's study of revolutions (Calvert, 1970, page 209; cf. pages 86–92). The print-out was obtained using the SPSS system.

for example recoding values or producing scales from raw data. This is done in instructions to the program which are very close to the sociologists' mode of expressing these questions verbally. The comprehensive labelling of variable values, apparent in Figs. 4.1 and 4.4, is also retained throughout in the construction of new operations. In both systems it is a simple matter to locate and re-structure large data files. Large general packages, however, usually involve some loss of computing efficiency in the particular case, for a gain in convenience.

Once a data file is established it is easy to compute such measures as means and standard deviations. Univariate descriptive statistics are useful to pin-point general characteristics of the distributions of variables and can be generated with simple computer programs such as those found in Chapter 7. However the choice of whether to write programs or not will again depend on the number of operations required, the availability of other mechanical aids and the question of whether a data set has to be specially prepared for this single job. A single calculation of a mean or a standard deviation is just as well performed using a good calculating machine, preferably one which is programmable. However, when some further measures of variation are considered, like the 3rd or 4th moments of the distribution, the work of calculation becomes such that writing a small computer program may be less time-consuming than the tedious process of hand calculation. A further useful descriptive aid is the computer-produced histogram or bar chart, which readily draws attention to the shape of raw data distributions. Here again, our earlier remarks about exhaustive table generation must be borne in mind.

Obtaining measures of distribution is a necessary descriptive step in the processing of many data sets, but is generally a preliminary operation to bivariate and multivariate analyses.

Bivariate analysis

By far the most common statistical procedures in the social sciences are those that trace association between two or more variables. At a minimum level this involves the formation of contingency tables for discrete variables or grouped data, but invariably for detailed hypothesis testing it is desirable to express relationships as single statistics. A single measure of the association of discrete distributions might be chi-squared, while for a continuous variable a correlation coefficient can be calculated. Much data obtained in categories from social surveys is open to only limited analysis, particularly if values cannot be scaled convincingly by one of the recognised scaling techniques (Coombs, 1964). Nonparametric, or ranking, statistics, however, such as the Spearman and Kendall rank order correlation coefficients, may be used where the data can be ordered. Some examples of ranking methods are given in Chapter 7, to illustrate how the calculations can be programmed. Ranking is also related to the processes of sorting and searching which are discussed in the next chapter.

On data that are arguably cardinal in nature, computationally more convenient measures can be applied. The most important of these from the point of view of further analysis is the Pearson product-moment correlation. Indeed, both of the types of coefficient mentioned above can be used as the basis for the formation of a correlation matrix. This is generally the starting point for multivariate procedures such as partial correlation, multiple regression, casual modelling and factor analysis. Correlation coefficients can therefore be calculated as bivariate measures of association which on their own can produce interesting relationships, but are normally the necessary preliminary computation for other statistics.

As a basic tool, a simple program to calculate and print a correlation matrix is extremely useful for a preliminary examination of bivariate relationships in a set of variables. If measures of statistical significance are also integrated into the printed matrix (as probability levels or simply asterisks shown against values with a given degree of significance) a visual identification of salient relationships may conveniently be obtained. With a modern digital computer, very large matrices of coefficients can be calculated as rapidly as any researcher is likely to require them. Using the kind of single-pass method which was mentioned in Chapter 2 for accumulating sums of squares and cross-products, the number of observations which can be handled is virtually without a practical upper limit. Contrary to the normal 'desk-calculator' formulae, used again in Chapter 7 for simplicity, this one-pass algorithm permits the direct accumulation of a matrix of sums of squared deviations and corrected cross-products. That is, a matrix is formed (in a triangular form because it is symmetric, so saving storage capacity) in which the diagonal elements are for each variable x_i

$$\sum(x_i - x)^2$$

and the remaining cells contain

$$\sum_i (x_i - \bar{x})(y_i - \bar{y})$$

for each pair of variables x_i and y_i. Dividing this matrix by the

```
VARIABLE   3 ( SENIORTY )  ON VARIABLE   2 ( AGE       )

N =   406

VARIABLE    3  SENIORTY
MEAN = 227,998
SKEW IS POSITIVE
STANDARD DEVIATION =  148.598      BETA1 (SKEWNESS) = 0.558427    BETA2 (KURTOSIS) = 3,26557
RANGE. 1,00000       TO 601,000

VARIABLE    2  AGE
MEAN = 440,818
SKEW IS POSITIVE
STANDARD DEVIATION =  143.917      BETA1 (SKEWNESS) = 0.421906    BETA2 (KURTOSIS) = 3,03624
RANGE '202,000       TO 786,000

R = 0.972742      F =  7109.14      (D.F,  1,N-2)


REGRESSION OF VARIABLE   3 ( SENIORTY ) ON VARIABLE   2 ( AGE       ) )

 REGRESSION EQUATION        <SENIORTY>  = -214.752      +  1.00438     <AGE     >
```

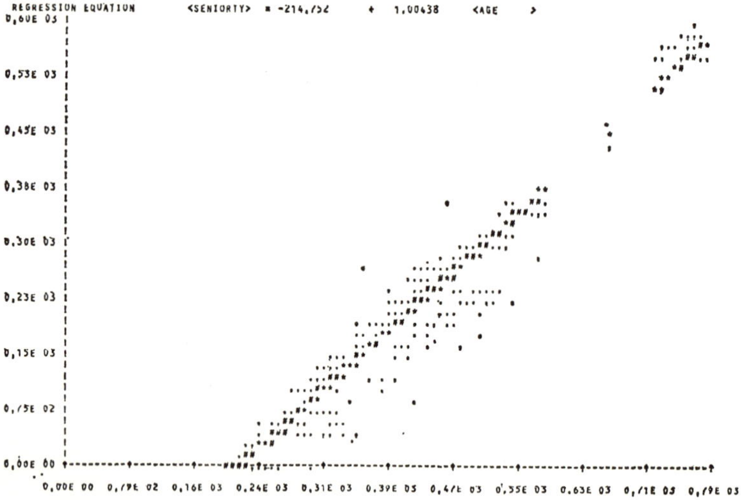

Fig. 4.5 Correlation, distributions and a scattergram. The data are taken from a sample of employees of British Rail, kindly supplied by Dr. P. Hollowell. The character ♯ indicates the regression line.

number of observations (minus one for a population estimate from a sample) and taking the square root, we obtain the correlation matrix.

If there are a large number of elements in this matrix, our earlier cautions regarding generation of too much output again apply. A very large correlation matrix may still be difficult to understand, so that some further summary of its contents is needed to render its structure more intelligible.

To avoid possible errors of interpretation due to non-linearity of relationships summarised in this way, it can be useful to generate bivariate graphic plots on a selective basis. An advantage of graphic presentation is that it expresses more information more intelligibly to a human reader than a page of figures. Again, a small program to generate displays of data is a very useful asset.

Fig. 4.5 shows a computer generated scattergram of two variables, seniority and age, with the regression line printed out in addition to the individual points. The program also provides a series of statistics to summarise important variations not immediately evident from the scattergram.

Multivariate analysis

The most dramatic impact of computers on statistical procedures has been in the area of multivariate techniques. Indeed the ease of access to programs to perform these analyses is sometimes seen as dangerous in view of possible nondiscriminating use of sophisticated methods. However, although there are some dangers inherent for a novice, it is arguable that the use of multiple regression and factor analysis has provided new dimensions to research and theory in many of the social sciences. Without the computerisation of these techniques it is improbable that econometrics or quantitative psychology would have taken the path they have taken, and ambitious quantitative work in other disciplines would have been impossible. The more-or-less routine application of many theoretical multivariate models in data analysis would have been virtually inconceivable without the help of a computer. The operation of matrix inversion, which is fundamental to most continuous-variable models, is extremely time-consuming for even a matrix of ten-by-ten variables using a desk calculator. A general FORTRAN method for inverting matrices of any reasonable size will be found at the end of Chapter 7 (Van de Geer, 1971).

Part of the process has been the development of what are often regarded as automatic search techniques, in which the computer, given certain criteria, searches for relationships amongst a series of variables. In two situations this has been of immense advantage. First, in research where the investigator has a large number of hypotheses covering a wide range of variables, the testing of which would be inconceivable given time contraints unless a computer were available. Second, it may be that an investigator has an open mind concerning the possible associations in a data set, and by positing certain search criteria can be given an assessment of the 'fit' of the data to a number of possible models of multivariate interrelationships.

This in some respects has led to reorientation of information-gathering and hypothesis testing in the scientific world, a revolution that, apart from economics and psychology, has only just begun to affect the social sciences. Instead of studying what may now appear in retrospect to be a rather simplistic bivariate view of the world, much more emphasis has now been placed on constellations or clusters of variables which are likely to be related. This in turn has led to a greater complexity and sophistication in explanations in the social sciences. Of course at the same time it must not be implied either that all types of data in the social sciences are amenable to this type of multivariate analysis, or alternatively that all applications of these techniques are invariably productive empirically or theoretically.

Three types of multivariate analysis will be examined to illustrate the kind of advantages and difficulties encountered. These are, first, multiple regression, second, some of the factor analytic methods, and third, less constrained search algorithms for pattern discovery. The object in each case is to obtain a simplified and statistically efficient summary of the total variability in a set of observed data values, in terms of a model which can be given a convincing theoretical interpretation. The amount of computation required increases considerably with the relaxation both of assumptions about the nature of the data and the constraints imposed on the search for correspondence between the model and the observations.

Multiple regression applications

There are a number of variations of multiple regression techniques readily available as algorithms which can be expressed as computer programs. Here we will confine ourselves to the widely-used linear least-squares method in which the coefficients of a linear equation of the form

$$y = c + b_1x_1 + b_2x_2 + \ldots b_nx_n$$

are determined so as to minimize the squared-deviations of the observed values from the values predicted by the equations (Sterling and Pollack, 1968, Chapter 8). This is simply the extension to n independent variables of the simple bivariate regression model of Fig. 4.5.

In its simplest form, the independent and dependent variables for the multiple regression are selected by the investigator and are given as input parameters to a suitable computer program. This is most helpful in cases where hypotheses about the behaviour of variables are structured, and a series of co-ordinated computer runs can produce the required results. Figure 4.6 shows some typical print-out for this case. In other programs 'automatic' search techniques are incorporated. A number of rules may be used to bring in independent variables to the regression equation in a 'step-wise' fashion. One of these, the 'backward' solution, starts with the largest possible predictive set of variables, and eliminates the least predictive ones in successive stages. The criteria used for deletion may include consideration of the relative statistical significance of the regression coefficient of the independent variables, or the effect which the removal of a variable has on the percentage of the total variation explained by the regression equation. Another, the 'forward' solution adds variables according to their predictive capacity until a point at which the prediction given by the equation is not appreciably improved. To save computing time, a minimum percentage increase in predicted variation may be specified as a criterion for ending the search for new variables to add to the equation. Each of these methods requires the storage of a covariance matrix in the computer, that is, the mean squares and cross products matrix described earlier. This, of course, increases rapidly in size as the number of variables in the original data set rises. Indeed, with only a relatively small number of variables, the main storage capacity of some smaller computers might well be exceeded. It may be wise therefore to attempt more limited analyses initially, until the characteristics of the data are better known.

If on the other hand there are strong theoretical guidelines available to assist in this process, investigation can be confined to the testing of predetermined hypothetical linear models. It is then possible to specify a limited number of variables to be included in the regression equation, and to make a routine application of a simple computer program.

Using the predicted values from one application of linear multiple regression and storing them as new 'observed' values, a multi-stage iterative procedure can be used quite simply to introduce non-linear effects into the model to be fitted to the data set. For example, if theoretical considerations suggest a relationship such as

$$y=a+bx_1+abx_2+e$$

(where e is an error term) a series of estimates of a and b can be obtained by regressing y on a constant and x_1 to give the coefficients of $y=a_1+b_1x_1$. Further regression of $(y-a_1b_1x_2)$ on a constant and x_2 will produce new estimates a_2 and b_2. Repeating the process produces a series of estimates of the hypothetical parameters required. The iteration can easily be performed by a suitable program, which will terminate when the difference between successive values for a and b reaches an acceptable tolerance level.

Factor analysis

A variety of variance-reduction techniques fall under the general heading of factor analysis. These, when mathematically formalised, are models for reducing a number of variables to a smaller number of factors which can be held to represent the 'underlying' dimensions of the variables. For large matrices of variables, these are virtually impossible to solve unless programmed on a computer, for the complexity is such that it requires many hours, if not days, of calculation by other means. The easiest of these in computing terms is what is normally called principal component analysis, which needs no preliminary assumptions about the underlying structure of

```
42/73    LIBERAL VOTE EXAMPLE RUN,LIMITED VARIAPLE SET

    62 OBSERVATIONS ON     49 INPUT VARIABLES     49 VARIABLES IN TRANSFORMED FILE

TRANSFORMATION PARAMETER =      2

MI 1 (BY OBSERVATION)

VARIABLE  NAME          MEAN           S.D.         ACCURACY, COEFF OF VARIATION
   0   CONSTANT                                     0.10E-05
   1   VAR1          17.9258        5.21225         0.10E-05  -  0.290768
   2   VAR2          37.2048        5.15273         0.10E-05     0.138496
   3   VAR3          18.0145        5.04972         0.10E-05     0.280314
   4   VAR4          17.5097        6.59967         0.10E-05     0.376916
   5   %AGRICUL      6.70323        7.92651         0.10E-05      1.18249
   6   VAR6          45.8742        10.2828         0.10E-05     0.224152
   7   VAR7          49.7048        29.1757         0.10E-05     0.586979
   8   VAR8          15.5113        9.98131         0.10E-05     0.604514
   9   VAR9          9.59516        6.83847         0.10E-05     0.712700
  10   VAR10         28.8581        7.42328         0.10E-05     0.257234
  44   VAR44         25.1806        25.2548         0.10E-05      1.00295
  45   VAR45         8.06452        9.93773         0.10E-05      1.23228
  46   VAR46         49.8710        52.5237         0.10E-05      1.05319
  47   VAR47         8.00161        10.2766         0.10E-05      1.28431
  48   VAR48         50.9258        14.5039         0.10E-05     0.284805
  49   LIB.VOTE      15.3516        6.94247         0.10E-05     0.424574

  REGRESSION OF VARIABLE    49  (LIB.VOTE) ON     0  (CONSTANT)
                                                  5  (%AGRICUL)
                                                 11  (%FEMALE )
                                                 33  (MAJORITY)
                                                 40  (DISTANCE)

   NO.  NAME          COEFFICIENT    STD DEVIATION     T RATIO     RSQ IF VAR DELETED

   0 CONSTANT        -52.719626       20.235712       -2.605276
   5 %AGRICUL          0.419457        0.095943        4.371937        0.400876
  11 %FEMALE           1.265557        0.391032        3.236452        0.468879
  33 MAJORITY          0.011127        0.061887        0.179789        0.551075
  40 DISTANCE          1.506326        0.524440        2.872257        0.486391

  RSQ=0.551329      SE OF RESID=       4.810671

   NO.       OBS            PRED           RES       %OBS/PRED %RES2/RSS  CONTRIBUTIONS
    1      10.9000        15.7309       -4.83093      69.3      1.77      0.5872        65.56      0.1458
                                                                           2.162
    2      26.7000        28.0116       -1.31165      95.3     0.130      10.44         66.32      0.2036
                                                                           3.768
    3      17.6000        12.2395        5.36053      144.      2.18      1.930       . 63.40      0.1624
                                                                          -0.5373
    4      12.2000        14.4034       -2.20338      84.7     0.368      3.523         63.53      0.9903E-01

   56      10.9000        10.7727        0.127268     101.    0.123E-02    0.4195        64.92      0.1446E-01
                                                                          -1.865
   57      7.80000        8.27617       -0.476174     94.2    0.172E-01    0.4195E-01    65.18      0.1558E-01
                                                                          -4.238
   58      25.6000        23.8955        1.70450      107.     0.220       7.299         66.69      0.0000E 00
                                                                           2.622
   59      19.1000        19.4376       -0.337621     98.3    0.864E-02    2.894         68.09      0.2092
                                                                           0.9668
   60      6.90000        12.4136       -5.51364      55.6      2.30       0.8389E-01    68.47      0.5118E-01
                                                                          -3.468
   61      16.9000        12.1314        4.76856      139.      1.72       0.7970        65.18      0.2581


                                                                          -1.380
   62      17.8000        24.4092       -6.60919      72.9      3.31       1.091         75.81      0.4239
                                                                          -0.1926

  D-WSTAT =   1.8636          ERROR MEASURE =    0.000000
```

Fig. 4.6 An example of simple multiple regression. The data are taken from work in progress by A. P. Hill. The Liberal share of the 1966 General Election vote in each constituency is the dependent variable, and the independent predictors are (1) per cent employed in agriculture in the constituency (2) per cent of women in the population (3) 1964 majority for the winning party and (4) distance from London. Output is taken from ERP (Econometric Regression Package) developed in the Department of Economics, University of Southampton.

the variables, and works by finding which of a linear additive combination of variables accounts for the most variance in the data set. The other most commonly used method of factor analysis is the common factor solution, the so-called classical method, which does assume that there is some recognisable structure amongst the group of variables to be analysed.

The basic model assumes that the variation of the observed n variables $x_1, x_2 \ldots x_n$ is to be explained by a smaller number of common 'factors' and a variation specific to the variable itself. That is to say,

$$x_i = \sum_r l_{ir} f_r + e_i \quad (i=1,2, \ldots n)$$

where f_r is the r-th common factor and r is appreciably less than n. The terms l_{ir} are generally called the 'loadings' of the variable x_i on the r-th common factor and e_i is the variation specific to the variable (Lawley and Maxwell, 1963). The model represents a hypothesis about the data which can be tested using a number of different estimation procedures. Factor analysis using this model can only be carried out by iterative methods producing a series of estimates of the factor loadings, and at each iteration at least one matrix inversion is required.

Factor solutions consist of sets of estimates of the loadings of each variable with the common factors extracted. These can be regarded as the correlations of the initial variables with the hypothetical variables underlying the observed values. An example is shown in Fig. 4.7, which is taken from Alker and Russett's work on the underlying dimensions of conflict indicated in the correlations of roll-call votes by the various nations in the U.N. General Assembly.

This is a fairly typical example of the results obtained from factor analysis of multivariate data. In the original, nine factors were extracted and Fig. 4.7 includes only a selection of the General Assembly resolutions included in the study. Groups of resolutions with relatively high loadings for a particular factor provide a basis for interpretation of the new dimensions. The first two factors shown in the extract seem to represent independent but rather generalised attitudes concerned with anti-colonialism and U.N. budgetary matters. The third and fourth factors shown are more specific in character. The investigation broadly confirms in a statistical sense that votes on superficially different issues tend to be determined by a

ROLL CALL		FACTOR I	FACTOR II	FACTOR III	FACTOR IV
8004	CENSURE SOUTH AFRICA	.77	.02	.00	.17
8022	SANCTION SOUTH AFRICA	.88	–.10	.19	.13
8023	SECURITY COUNCIL & S. AFRICA	.91	–.06	.25	.16
8024	NO ARMS TO SOUTH AFRICA	.82	–.12	.28	.08
8025	NO PETROLEUM TO SOUTH AFRICA	.84	–.14	.24	.11
8027	OMAN SELF DETERMINATION	.67	–.19	.15	.51
8029	CHINA QUESTION IMPORTANT	–.22	.20	–.83	–.30
8030	CHINA DECLARATION	.34	.13	.86	.12
8031	SEAT PEOPLE'S REP. OF CHINA	.33	.16	.84	.08
8032	REPRESENTATION OF CHINA	.33	–.17	.87	.12
8008	STOP 50 MEGATON BOMB	–.22	.79	–.21	–.16
1010	GENERAL AND COMPLETE DISARMAMENT	.69	–.16	.42	.33
8009	REGRET TESTS: NEED TREATY	.24	.76	–.04	–.02
8065	FRIENDLY RELATIONS WITH CUBA	.67	–.15	.54	.29
2002	TRADE CONFERENCE	.83	–.06	.31	.19
8039	CAPITAL & TECHNICAL ASSIST.	.06	.78	–.07	–.10
8011	ALGERIAN PRISONERS	.69	.01	.35	.09
8017	1962 END OF COLONIALISM	.72	–.30	.45	.19
8019	W. IRAN SELF DETERMINATION	–.32	.16	–.35	–.65
8020	COMMISSION ON W. IRIAN	–.36	.16	–.38	–.63
8021	INDIAN RES. ON W. IRIAN	.37	–.09	.35	.63
8073	1 MAN 1 VOTE' S. RHODESIA	.86	–.07	.23	.20
8075	REGRET UK ON S. RHODESIA	.82	.05	.02	.23
8056	CONDEMN PORTUGAL	.76	–.21	.40	.25
4001	BURUNDI PRIME MINISTER	–.85	.06	–.22	–.30
8051	CONGO COST	–.28	.83	–.01	–.00
8052	U.N.E.F. EXPENSES	–.36	.76	.02	–.11
8053	BUDGET FOR YEAR 1962	–.12	.76	–.03	–.29

Source: Edited from Alker and Russett [1965]

Fig. 4.7 Factor analysis in research: dimensions of conflict at the Sixteenth U.N. General Assembly.

similar underlying set of divisions among the voting nations (Alker and Russett, 1965). However, the verbal interpretation given to this particular transformation of the original observations is clearly a matter for some ingenuity on the part of the researcher. By facilitating the extraction of a large number of factors the use of a computer in this task can actually make it more difficult to attach sensible meanings to the results.

The analysis can be taken further if the original individual observations are re-expressed as sets of scores on the new factor structure. The voting position of each nation could be summarised efficiently by its score values for the extracted factors, instead of by its recorded votes in the much larger number of separate roll-calls. If, in turn, the intercorrelations of those first-order factor scores are computed, they can be submitted to a further analysis to produce second-order factors of greater generality, and so on into higher orders if they are of theoretical interest.

The problem of interpretation of higher-order results becomes more acute, and it is questionable whether the assumptions of the general factor model can reasonably be met by much of the data to which factor analysis may be applied. The model assumes that relationships between observed variables are wholly explained by the underlying factors, but many observable social variables are not generally thought to be mutually independent. Nevertheless, for heuristic purposes, the method may still be of interest. For example, R. J. Rummel's study of 'the dimensionality of nations' obtained an economical set of first-order factors broadly interpreted as the level of economic development, the power base or size of a country, and so on. These expressed the intercorrelations observed in such statistics as the number of unemployed, the rural/urban ratio and the size and composition of the population. 236 variables in all were available for 83 countries. To some theorists, it may be of more interest that a few dimensions can effectively summarise the world's diversity than to study the individual correlations of, say, poverty and mortality rates. Rummel took his analysis to the stage of second-order factors, based upon the first-order factor scores. To three of these he gave such names as 'international rank disequilibrium' to denote discrepancies between economic development and international power, 'political stability', and 'subsistence'. Some second-order factors had no intuitive explanation. Experts in the subject must judge whether these insights into the structure of national characteristics constitute a theoretical advance. Rummel has made the striking assertion that many, if not most, theories of international relations and national development could be tested in half an hour's computing time (Rummel, 1968).

An acknowledged difficulty in the interpretation of such results is the lack of a unique solution to the analysis. The matrix of loadings can be considered as the co-ordinates of a set of points, each representing an initial variable, in a hypothetical space of the same number of dimensions as there are factors extracted. The number of factors used in a solution depends upon the definition of some criterion for the 'completeness' of the explanation it offers of the observed variations. Different numbers of factors produce different patterns of initial loading estimates using some methods of factor analysis, but there are recommended statistical criteria which can be incorporated into a computer program to determine a 'best' solution.

The relative positions of variables in the solution space are often given a graphical representation in terms of point co-ordinates measured from pairs of factors. Alternatively, triplets of factors can yield the results by the projection of a spherical map as a two-dimensional plot. Thinking of the loadings as defining geometrical points in this fashion gives a simple way of understanding the idea of the rotation of the factor axes, so that they pass through the main clusters of points. The co-ordinates of the points are themselves, consequently, redefinable in terms of any arbitrarily chosen set of axes. The factor axes themselves may be kept at right angles to each other, in an *orthogonal* solution, or allowed to rotate closer to each other, in an *oblique* or *correlated* solution. Again, there are various proposed criteria for this process of oblique rotation, but it would be fair to conclude that no generally accepted method exists to determine which of an infinity of possible positions for the reference axes should be preferred in interpreting the results (Horst, 1965; Cooley and Lohnes, 1971).

Factor analysis is often used to search for possible summarising variables, to explain observed variables by a smaller number of underlying factors. In this application, the possibility of using a computer for the work of generating estimates and plotting various rotated factor patterns has undoubtedly influenced the spread of the method. Critics of this proliferation argue that the lack of a unique solution means that data could be fitted fairly easily to any predetermined interpretations, and their position is strengthened by the kind of controversies that have arisen in the field of personality measurement. The same evidence has sometimes been used to support quite different theoretical interpretations according to whether the initial factors were rotated or not (Diesing, 1971, pages 267–268).

Differences in the parsimony with which British and American psychologists for a long time constructed their theories of primary mental abilities can adequately be traced to the relatively greater availability of computers to the latter in contemplating multifactor rotated interpretations of their test results. These differences in thinking have, to a large extent, diminished with the routine application of computers to the problem in Britain (Wrigley, 1962, pages 165–170).

The method is more properly applied when it is required to investigate the degree to which observed data fit a particular theoretical factor pattern, and not to an almost unguided search for patterns to which some meaning can afterwards be attached. However, when applied cautiously, and as part of a process of considering different hypothetical factor structures, factor analysis can be a valuable statistical technique.

Further multivariate techniques

Some social researchers have regarded the mathematical assumptions of factor analysis and multiple regression as too restrictive for their purposes. Despite the kind of cautions we have already entered, there is a tendency to give the results of multivariate analyses causal interpretations rather too readily. Even though as variance ordering techniques they are clearly based on linear additive models, their heuristic possibilities tend to be confused with their validity in testing hypotheses. Other more general assumptions about the structure of observed data may be more appropriate to initial explanations which are more or less unguided by theory.

The main problem is raised if interaction between observed variables is strong enough to invalidate the assumption that they are mutually independent. If there is no theory to guide an investigation, one approach is to search for empirical interactions in as unconstrained a way as possible. For discrete or categorical variables such as are common in social survey data, some computer routines developed at the University of Michigan can assist in the development of a kind of regression analysis. The procedure called A.I.D. (Automatic Interaction Detection) is a computer program to conduct an automatic search for a series of predictor variables which, given the units of analysis under consideration, provide the maximum improvement in capacity to predict the values of a dependent variable (Sonquist and Morgan, 1969). The search may consider predictors in a completely free manner, or may be constrained to treat pseudo-continuous categorical variables monotonically. It proceeds by seeking a series of binary splits of the population of observations into subgroups. The program can consider all possible dichotomisations of all available predictor variables each time it looks for the best split, which is the kind of simple repetitious process at which a computer excels. The results can be summarised in the form of a tree diagram, as shown in Figs. 4.8 and 4.9, and an analysis of variance is performed on the final group solution.

The process is terminated when one of a number of conditions occurs. First, the group may be too small in terms of number of observations to split it again. Second, what is called an *explained group* materialises in which the variation within the group is too small to attempt a split, or, third, an *unexplainable group* is reached in which no variable within the data set is useful to reduce the variation within the group. In the extract given in Fig. 4.8, two of the splits result in variables being added to the final predictor set, and others result in either a group too small for further analysis, or groups which the program later splits again. Interpretation is still largely a matter of intuition, but the method improves on multiple regression by revealing interaction effects as asymmetries in the variables used as the bases for splits at various nodes in the tree. If different variables are used for splits at the same level of the tree they are involved in some asymmetric effect which deserves investigation. Also, unlike adaptations of the multiple regression model to categorised data, predictors may be used more than once in the dichotomisation process and do not constrain the later search when they have been used for a split.

A.I.D. has a companion program, M.C.A. (Multiple Classification

```
                              * * * S U M M A R Y * * *

    DEPENDENT VARIABLE  21  ( WAGE RATE H )

    WEIGHTED  BY  VARIABLE   26

 ** TOTAL  GROUP

       N  =       2546          MEAN =  .23069163E 03          SUM Y =  .26937631E 08        TSS =  .24445921E 10
 TOTAL WT SUM=  116769      STD. DEV. =  .14469030E 03     SUM Y SQ. =  .86588781E 10

 *  GROUP  NO.   2  SPLIT  FROM  GROUP   1  ON  VARIABLE    3 (EDUCATION   )
    VALUES  OF  PREDICTOR  INCLUDED  ARE    0    1    2    3    4    5
       N  =         2262            MEAN =  .21559815E 03      GROUP DEVIATION = -.15093479E 02      SUM Y =  .22243908E 08
  WEIGHT SUM =    103173        STD. DEV. =  .13220740E 03                TSS(I) =  .18033398E 10   SUM Y SQ. =  .65990852E 10
 PCT OF TOTAL =     88.4       WTD. MEAN SQ. =  .47957454E 10      (TSS(I)/TSS(T)) =  .73768536E 00

 *  GROUP  NO.   3  SPLIT  FROM  GROUP   1  ON  VARIABLE    3 (EDUCATION   )
    VALUES  OF  PREDICTOR  INCLUDED  ARE    6    7
       N  =          284            MEAN =  .34522822E 03      GROUP DEVIATION =  .11453660E 03      SUM Y =  .46937230E 07
  WEIGHT SUM =     13596        STD. DEV. =  .17977870E 03                TSS(I) =  .43942789E 09   SUM Y SQ. =  .20538335E 10
 PCT OF TOTAL =     11.6       WTD. MEAN SQ. =  .16204056E 10      (TSS(I)/TSS(T)) =  .17975509E 00

 *  GROUP  NO.   4  SPLIT  FROM  GROUP   2  ON  VARIABLE   25 (BACKGROUND  )
    VALUES  OF  PREDICTOR  INCLUDED  ARE    4    5    6
       N  =         1244            MEAN =  .24302012E 03      GROUP DEVIATION =  .12328487E 02      SUM Y =  .14640504E 08
  WEIGHT SUM =     60244        STD. DEV. =  .12983906E 03                TSS(I) =  .10156043E 10   SUM Y SQ. =  .45735412E 10
 PCT OF TOTAL =     51.6       WTD. MEAN SQ. =  .35579370E 10      (TSS(I)/TSS(T)) =  .41544937E 00

 *  GROUP  NO.   5  SPLIT  FROM  GROUP   2  ON  VARIABLE   25 (BACKGROUND  )
    VALUES  OF  PREDICTOR  INCLUDED  ARE    1    2    3
       N  =         1018            MEAN =  .17711579E 03      GROUP DEVIATION = -.53575834E 02      SUM Y =  .76034039E 07
  WEIGHT SUM =     42929        STD. DEV. =  .12575165E 03                TSS(I) =  .67885677E 09   SUM Y SQ. =  .20255397E 10
 PCT OF TOTAL =     36.8       WTD. MEAN SQ. =  .13466829E 10      (TSS(I)/TSS(T)) =  .27769735E 00

 *  GROUP  NO.   6  SPLIT  FROM  GROUP   4  ON  VARIABLE   22 (SEX         )
    VALUES  OF  PREDICTOR  INCLUDED  ARE    1
       N  =         1037            MEAN =  .25978099E 03      GROUP DEVIATION =  .29089361E 02      SUM Y =  .13111926E 08
  WEIGHT SUM =     50473        STD. DEV. =  .13164685E 03                TSS(I) =  .87474220E 09   SUM Y SQ. =  .42809713E 10
 PCT OF TOTAL =     43.2       WTD. MEAN SQ. =  .34062291E 10      (TSS(I)/TSS(T)) =  .35782747E 00

 *  GROUP  NO.   7  SPLIT  FROM  GROUP   4  ON  VARIABLE   22 (SEX         )
    VALUES  OF  PREDICTOR  INCLUDED  ARE    2
 *** THIS  GROUP  IS  RETAINED  AS  ONE  OF  FINALS.
       N  =          207            MEAN =  .15644028E 03      GROUP DEVIATION = -.74251348E 02      SUM Y =  .15285780E 07
  WEIGHT SUM =      9771        STD. DEV. =  .73953599E 02                TSS(I) =  .53438918E 08   SUM Y SQ. =  .29257008E 09
 PCT OF TOTAL =      8.4       WTD. MEAN SQ. =  .23913117E 09      (TSS(I)/TSS(T)) =  .21860055E-01

 *  GROUP  NO.   8  SPLIT  FROM  GROUP   6  ON  VARIABLE   12 (AGE         )
    VALUES  OF  PREDICTOR  INCLUDED  ARE    1
 *** THIS  GROUP  IS  RETAINED  AS  ONE  OF  FINALS.
       N  =           95            MEAN =  .18442677E 03      GROUP DEVIATION = -.46264641E 02      SUM Y =  .83231900E 06
  WEIGHT SUM =      4513        STD. DEV. =  .82819856E 02                TSS(I) =  .30955248E 08   SUM Y SQ. =  .18445733E 09
 PCT OF TOTAL =      3.9       WTD. MEAN SQ. =  .15350208E 09      (TSS(I)/TSS(T)) =  .12662745E-01

 *  GROUP  NO.   9  SPLIT  FROM  GROUP   6  ON  VARIABLE   12 (AGE         )
    VALUES  OF  PREDICTOR  INCLUDED  ARE    2    3    4    5    6    7
       N  =          942            MEAN =  .26718030E 03      GROUP DEVIATION =  .36488676E 02      SUM Y =  .12279607E 08


                    * * *   ANALYSIS  OF  VARIANCE  TABLE   * * *

          SOURCE OF          SUM  OF          DEGREES OF        MEAN
          VARIATION          SQUARES           FREEDOM          SQUARE              F

          T O T A L      .24445921E 10         116723

          BETWEEN        .59073587E 09             12       .49227989E 08     .30991909E 04

          WITHIN         .18538562E 10         116711       .15884142E 05


            RESIDUALS  ARE  OBTAINED.

     TIME IS NOW 12. 12. 32. 14.

              RESULTS  ARE  ON  TAPE.


                              * * *   E  N  D   * * *

     TIME IS NOW 12. 12. 32. 20.
```

Fig. 4.8 Part of the print-out from an A.I.D. analysis.

Analysis), which provides a multiple regression equivalent for categorical variables and is intended to form the next stage of multivariate model building (Andrews, Morgan and Sonquist, 1969).

Other dimensional analyses which can really be contemplated only when using a computer include a variety of non-metric scaling and classification techniques. Their existence as computer programs has popularised the use of methods which, like A.I.D., involve large amounts of simple-minded searching but may be relatively simple in

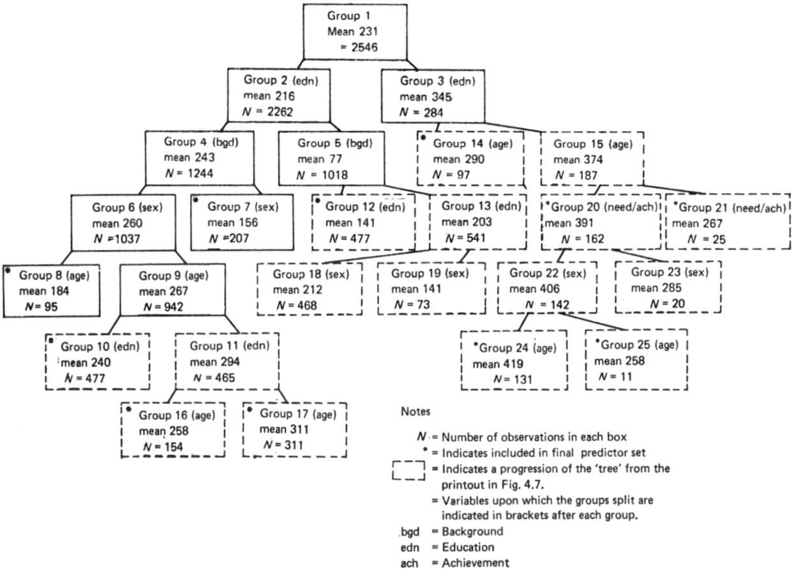

Fig. 4.9 An A.I.D. tree diagram.

their mathematical form, compared with factor models. The essence of what are called non-metric methods is that the distances of observations along the dimensions produced in the analysis are recovered only in ordinal terms, and with a minimum of assumptions about the distributions of the variables (Coombs, 1964; Tryon and Bailey, 1970; Green and Carmone, 1970).

Some methods exist in the manner of A.I.D. only as computer programs, with manuals giving them some mathematical specification. Carroll and Chang's non-metric INDSCAL, for example, provides for the calculation of a series of dimensions to cover the 'group space' of a set of multivariate observations, in a similar fashion to the dimensions extracted in a factor solution. The program also constructs a set of weightings of these dimensions for each individual observation to attempt to represent the salience of each dimension in its classification. Intuitively, this method can cover the possibility that the classification of attitudes held in common by a group of people may mask considerable differences in the weight each person gives to any particular component attitude. Indeed, the group attitude space may not correspond to any individual's own personal construction of reality. The INDSCAL model tries to comprehend this possibility in its estimates of salience weightings (Coxon, 1972).

The confusing variety of computerised 'pattern discovery' techniques may well induce bewilderment in researchers attempting to build multivariate models in their field of interest. Inevitably, both their availability and relative familiarity have tended to produce champions of one or other as a recommended general method. Here again, computer facilities can be seen guiding the course of enquiry. But paradoxically, the discovery of the full implications of a particular data set may well depend upon more and not less use of computer analysis. A comparison of the results of various procedures based upon different assumptions is probably the best possible research design in the absence of theoretical guidance.

The use of packaged programs

The use of a packaged program for any kind of computer analysis involves a few basic principles, which are conveniently mentioned here. First, the program has certain storage requirements which must be discovered and may use named tape or disc files as backing storage. Some estimates of its running time may be obtainable, to help in deciding how long it will take to produce the desired results. If, as is usual, the job is to be run under an operating system, as described in the previous chapter, all of these details must be communicated to this system as a set of requests for allocation of resources to the job. The program source will usually be located on another backing store file, which may also have an identification. This must be given to the system at the same time, with a request to load the program and cause it to start working on the data file provided.

We mention all this because many beginners tend to assume that the computer can discern their intentions without specific instructions how to run their program and how much time and storage they need. The operating system manual for a particular installation is the necessary source of this information.

Programs themselves, of course, have particular requirements for data formats, and so on, as we have already noted in passing. Obviously, they will not run unless the user has correctly prepared all necessary instructions and input his data correctly. Two further methods may be encountered of giving commands to a program. The first is to enter the program at a different *entry point* in the code according to certain conditions of operation. Different entry points may be used, for example, according to whether the data are input on cards or paper tape. The other is to make use of hardware sense switches, if they are provided on a particular machine, as an economical method of conveying commands. These are separately accessible binary registers, which can accordingly be set on or off on request by the operating system before a program is executed.

Some probable sources of error

In addition to errors due to mistakes in programming, there are other problems of which the researcher must be wary. Packaged programs, which have been developed by others, place the user in a vulnerable position. Complete understanding of the numerical or logical methods employed in these programs is a counsel of perfection which few have the time to observe, although it is necessary in a strict sense to determine whether techniques are really appropriate to the problem in hand. The source form of a package is unlikely in any event to be readily available, especially if it is part of a 'library' of programs, and, even if it were, it is not particularly easy to follow if the procedure is at all complicated.

Apart from deciding whether the model used by a programmed procedure is appropriate to one's own data, the major difficulty facing an inexperienced computer user is the interaction between program logic and data which can produce erroneous results in some cases. Some reasons for this were illustrated in Chapter 2. No program can be considered free of errors until it has been widely used on all kinds of data, and any user should try to avoid undue reliance on a packaged program to the extent that he treats it as a wizard in a black box. The acronym GIGO has been coined in computer circles to cover the possible consequences of too great a detachment from the actual processes involved. It stands for 'Garbage In, Garbage Out'.

The worst possibility is that plausible-looking but quite erroneous results may be produced by a computer program which has been used as an act of faith rather than reason. To some extent, this can be avoided by a deliberate policy of testing an available package on data which as closely as possible resemble those to be used in a real analysis, but which can be checked by hand calculations as well. A few short trial runs to check that all is working as expected are much preferable to launching into a large scale analysis only to find it becomes an expensive failure due to a program fault. An understanding of the numerical methods employed, together with some kind of error analysis, is also important, but it may not prove feasible in the end to check their realisation in the program logic, except by some test runs.

Our last word on this subject is a quotation from a recent note by David Muxworthy of Edinburgh University (Muxworthy, 1972). While we fervently hope it refers to a rare example of the problem, nobody can afford to be too sanguine.

'I wonder how many users of the canonical correlation program [in Cooley and Lohnes' 1962 edition of *Multivariate Procedures for the Behavioral Sciences*] have discovered that the canonical coefficients are calculated wrongly. This has been corrected in their new work but as IBM used Cooley and Lohnes as their text for the Scientific Subroutines, the erroneous algorithm is still available for use at 75% of the Western World's computer installations. Since the error must have been known to the authors for at least two years and they must have been aware that IBM followed their method, it would be interesting to know why it has not yet been corrected in the IBM library. It is to be hoped that anyone finding a mistake in the 1971 edition will make it known and not allow errors to go unnoticed for 10 years presumably on the assumption that if Wiley published it, it must be correct.'

References

H. R. Alker and B. M. Russett (1965) *World Politics in the General Assembly*, New Haven, Yale University Press.

F. M. Andrews, J. N. Morgan and J. A. Sonquist (1967) *Multiple Classification Analysis: A report on a computer program for multiple regression using categorical predictors*, Ann Arbor, University of Michigan, Survey Research Center.

A. S. Banks and R. B. Textor (1963) *A Cross Polity Survey*, Cambridge, Mass., MIT Press.

P. A. R. Calvert (1970) *A Study of Revolution*, Oxford, Clarendon Press.
W. J. Claffey (1967) *Principles of Data Processing*, Belmont, California, Dickinson.
W. W. Cooley and P. R. Lohnes (1971) *Multivariate Data Analysis*, New York, John Wiley.
C. H. Coombs (1964) *A Theory of Data*, New York, John Wiley.
A. P. M. Coxon (1972) *Differential cognition and Evaluation: an Introduction to Carroll and Chang's Multidimensional Scaling Models*, Project on Occupational Cognition, Research Memoranda 1, Edinburgh University Department of Sociology.
P. Diesing (1971) *Patterns of Discovery in the Social Sciences*, Chicago and New York, Aldine Atherton.
W. J. Dixon (Editor) (1969) *BMD: Biomedical Computer Programs X-series Supplement*—University of California Publications in Automatic Computation 3; Berkeley and Los Angeles, University of California Press.
W. J. Dixon (Editor) (1971) *BMD: Biomedical Computer Programs*—University of California Publications in Automatic Computation 2, 2nd Edition (revised), Berkeley and Los Angeles, University of California Press.
J. Galtung (1967) *Theory and Methods of Social Research*, London, George Allen and Unwin.
P. E. Green and F. J. Carmone (1970) *Multidimensional Scaling and Related Techniques in Marketing Analysis*, Boston, Mass., Allyn and Bacon.
P. Horst (1965) *Factor Analysis of Data Matrices*, New York, Holt, Rhinehart and Winston.
K. Janda (1969) *Data Processing: Applications to Political Science*, Evanston, North Western University Press.
D. N. Lawley and A. E. Maxwell (1963) *Factor Analysis as a Statistical Method*, London, Butterworth.
A. McKennell (1970) 'Attitude Measurement: Use of Coefficient Alpha with Cluster or Factor Analysis', *Sociology*, **14**, pages 227–245.
C. A. Moser and G. Kalton (1971) *Survey Methods in Social Investigation*, London, Heinemann.
D. Muxworthy (1972) in *Newsletter 7*, British Sociological Association Mathematics and Computing Applications Group, page 11.
N. H. Nie, D. H. Bent and C. H. Hull (1970) *Statistical Package for the Social Sciences*, New York, McGraw-Hill.
R. Rummel (1968) 'International Pattern and National Profile Delineation' in D. B. Bobrow and J. L. Schwartz (Editors), *Computers and the Policy-Making Community*, Englewood Cliffs, N.J., Prentice-Hall, pages 154–195.
J. A. Sonquist and J. N. Morgan (1969) *The Detection of Interaction Effects —A report on a computer program for the selection of optional combinations of explanatory variables*, 5th Edition, Ann Arbor, University of Michigan, Survey Research Center.

T. D. Sterling and S. V. Pollack (1968) *Introduction to Statistical Data Processing*, Englewood Cliffs, N.J., Prentice-Hall.
R. C. Tryon and D. E. Bailey (1970) *Cluster Analysis*, New York, McGraw-Hill.
J. P. Van de Greer (1971) *Introduction to Multivariate Analysis for the Social Sciences*, San Francisco, W. H. Freeman.
D. J. Veldman (1967) *Fortran Programming for the Behavioral Sciences*, New York, Holt, Rhinehart and Winston.
C. Wrigley (1962) 'The University Computing Center' in H. Borko (Editor), *Computer Applications in the Behavioral Sciences*, Englewood Cliffs, N.J., Prentice-Hall, pages 140–171.

Further reading

In ascending order of difficulty, the following books provide general introductions to the subject matter of this chapter, with a computer orientation.
Sterling and Pollack (1968); Veldman (1967) and Cooley and Lohnes (1971).

The manuals for the SPSS and DATA-TEXT systems mentioned in the references to Chapter 2 are both good, brief and practical introductions to applications, in terms of their respective packages.

On multivariate analysis and multidimensional scaling methods Van de Greer (1971) and Green and Carmone (1970) provide fairly accessible but comprehensive surveys of available possibilities. The latter is particularly recommended for its bibliography.

5 Text processing and information retrieval

Although the major use of computers in social science research so far has been in arithmetic processing of numerical data, there are other areas in which a computer can be of immense benefit. The most obvious of these is the manipulation of alphabetic character strings—words in a non-computer sense. As the digital computer normally works from individual characters of input, it should be as easy to work in strings of alphabetic characters as it is to work in strings of numeric characters.

Information storage and retrieval

The use of computers for information storage and retrieval has been one of the major growth areas in data processing. The increase in numbers of individual records in commercial transactions, inventories of stock in industry the problems of stock-taking in libraries and the data collection activities of governments led to the search for systems whereby such information could be easily stored and accessed mechanically when the need arose. It was obvious in the early 1950's that the quantity of manual processing, and hence personnel, employed by organisations was such that it was absorbing an unacceptable amount of time and resources. Indeed it was mainly through the demands of these commercial exigencies that the complex computational systems of today have been developed.

The information storage and retrieval systems in current use vary widely in their approach to the problem. In a sense the basic processes can be seen in an examination of any number of everyday experiences. Thus, the use of the library, accounting systems, or correspondence files, can be described as information storage and retrieval systems, as can the use of a dictionary. If the process of, say, looking up a word in a dictionary is described in mechanical terms, its correspondence to computer-based storage and retrieval systems is clear. The dictionary may be conceived of as a group of ordered records of which certain allowable questions may be asked, within the range of words in the dictionary. There is a reasonable probability that the records will correspond to these questions; relevant information is then extracted from the records.

The key process in information retrieval is comparison, either between records, or between features already singled out for examination and the relevant records. However, as will be noted with respect to the analogy of retrieving information from the dictionary, the process broken down into its component elements may be complex to mechanise. It presupposes that a collection of records has been created and organised *before* questions are asked, so that such a set of records has to be created anticipating these questions. At the same time, one of the criteria of effectiveness of the system must be its flexibility in meeting new and different demands. In general, therefore, no information storage and retrieval system can hope to be completely suitable for every demand made upon it, but if computer-based systems can be specified accurately they can at the very least save a great deal of time and energy. In addition replacement and amendment of the stored records may be accomplished more speedily.

There are two general strategies that may be employed in the computer information storage and retrieval systems. First, a collection of records may be partially processed before retrieval. Second, the records may be fully analysed, and organised, usually by means of an index. These approaches are of use in varying circumstances. Generally, the first is employed where the indexing process is difficult or costly, where rapid retrieval is not essential, and where the searching of all the records for each query is not prohibitively expensive. More often, however, at least some indexing is necessary because of the time-consuming nature of a complete search of the data. Normally, in computation, some processing of records, by indexing or abstracting information, is needed. In fact it would be true to say that if no indexing or abstracting were needed then a threshold would probably have been reached below which computation would be too costly. For example, a small collection of long records (a small personal library of books) or a larger collection of short records (names and addresses in an address book) may need only minimal organisation; any further processing and computational analysis would be redundant. Most of the programs and processes outlined here have encompassed some prior processing of the collection of records. In practice, the two processing strategies are combined, in order to make the retrieval process quicker, and to ensure that the range of data stored and available is as wide as possible.

The process can be illustrated in the following stages:

Stage 1—A COLLECTION OF RECORDS
(a number of books)

Stage 2—ANALYSIS OF RECORDS ON RELEVANT CRITERIA
(division into politics, sociology, psychology, economics books—compilation of author and subject index)

Stage 3—STORAGE OF RECORDS
(storage under relevant categories in library)

Stage 4—REQUEST
(all books dealing with economics)

Stage 5—SEARCH
(a) (look at subject and/or author index)
(b) [look at shelves for the books (if not present on shelves, look at records of loans)]

Stage 6—RETRIEVAL
[collect relevant books (if books on loan, request books for return)]

Stage 7—PRINT-OUT
(used in computation only)

These stages represent the breakdown of the relevant operations involved and are applicable generally to the process of information storage and retrieval. Computational methods have not as yet been applied to the mechanical retrieval of books themselves in libraries, due largely to the complex questions borrowers might ask and the difficulty of handling books. However, they have been applied to keeping track of borrowed books, and keeping catalogues up to date. Many libraries, by the use of punched cards in books and a machine-readable borrowers' card are able to store details of borrowings. Requests for the return of books then start at Stage 4 in the illustration above and continue until details of the books are printed-out at Stage 7. However, there are a number of difficulties which have so far defeated attempts to create completely automated and foolproof library systems. Not least of these is the coding of books so that speed of access and indexing is equivalent or better than that in manual processing. For example, it is not uncommon to find library records categorised in many ways in manual systems. Barraclough *et al.* (1971, page 80) suggests it would be improbable in the present state of computer science that all the following would be recognised as identical, without creating a totally unwieldy system.

SHAW, George Bernard
SHAW, Bernard
SHAW, G. B.
SHAW, (George) Bernard
G.B.S.

The computer can only treat things as equivalent if they are identical, or if the computer has a series of discriminating rules to apply. In the event there initially proved to be a very fine economic balance between setting up a complete computer system in a library and maintaining the standard manual system of processing borrower and book records. The fact that many university, and an increasing number of public, libraries have now installed computerised systems serves to indicate that the economic equation may prove less significant than first thought.

This procedure can be effective in its application to uses in industry and commerce or administration. However, problems do arise in the definition, storage and retrieval of information much more than in a library situation. In library terms the possibilities and needs for defining information are more limited. That is, a borrower number and book number are theoretically all that is needed, although book names, authors' and borrowers' names may be added to save complex referencing. In administrative terms a process which may deal with complicated financial transactions, or with details of personnel, requires a larger number of indexing categories (Blackney and Scatcherd, 1970). This in itself does not render the computation impossible but means that all information processed has to be carefully prepared so that the most effective use is made of input media, and the interrogation and retrieval phases. There are several crucial stages in this type of programming. First, the 'population' (in the statistical sense) to be covered must be known, for adding records with radically different characteristics may involve excessive and wasteful, redesigning of the system (Rees and Schultz, 1967). Second, the analysis of these records must be carefully planned so that the space on the input media, and hence storage, is treated with economy. At the same time all the relevant records should be covered in an adequate way, so any foreseeable request for information can be met (Vickery, 1968). Third, the records, stored on a medium such as magnetic tape, should be in as compact and accessible form as possible, so that search times are low. It is generally more economical to process a number of interrogations of the file at one time rather than require each query to complete a full pass of the data each time. Indeed, if this latter approach were adopted, it could be that the cost would be prohibitive, and moreover the whole retrieval operation would be slower than if done manually (Tauber, 1967).

A system which encompasses most of the features of programs in current operation is that shown in Fig. 5.1 (ICL, *Find 2*, 1969). The

```
♯Dictionary
    Staff-No,C,W1,2W        Join-date,W,W3,1W           ♯Birth-date,W,W4,1W
    Grade,C,W5C1.1C         Degree-class,C,W81C,C1       Name,V,O/  ,  W10

♯Enquiry
?Question                   [To identify individuals with required
                            characteristics]

(Any 2 from birth-date LEQ 01/01/47 or join-date
LEQ 01/01/68 or degree-class EQL 1 or grade GEQ D)

♯Option LP120 Print
♯Form
 Name, Staff-No
```

These instructions define the layout of individual records in an input file, and request a line-printer listing of any in which specified conditions are satisfied. This (simplified) example locates by name any company employees with at least two of four desired characteristics, and illustrates the kind of abbreviated code characteristics of this kind of application.

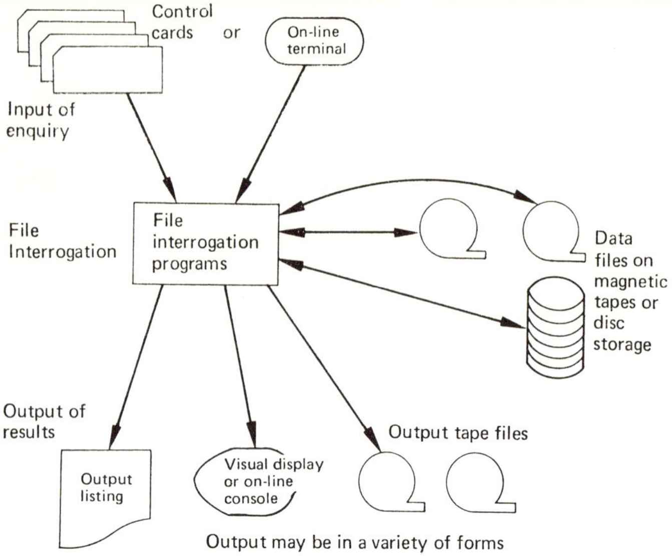

Fig. 5.1 Diagram to show information retrieval by file interrogation, and an example of a special-purpose enquiry language, for use with ICL's *Find* 2 enquiry system (1969).

diagram illustrates the components of the operation, and also contains a sample interrogation. The program uses magnetic discs or magnetic tapes as the main means of storing data. Data are stored using either fixed formatted or free formatted fields, and are accessed by means of standard enquiries as illustrated. A 'dictionary' of record formats has to be specified in detail indicating the (computer) words, characters or bits which are used. Key words and ordering categories are stored, and referred to in the enquiry procedure (Stone *et al.*, 1968A).

A basic development of information storage and retrieval programs has been the indexing system. This has entered the field of what is normally regarded as a more complex operation than some 'book-keeping' operations (although library programs have begun to meet with similar complexities). It is obvious that it is generally inefficient to store all of a particular record on a computer such as a complete book or a substantial personal history, and some means of *data reduction* must be employed. An extract from the record can be made machine readable, and also retain a sensible connection to the original. As instanced above, the extract in a library situation may be self-evident, but in other cases the best choice is not obvious. Facing conceptual and linguistic problems several attempts have been made to provide a coherent and meaningful approach to indexing. In general the difficulty has been to ensure that the indexing makes logical and semantic sense, without overtaxing the storage capacity of the computer, or making the process too long and costly. The first indexing programs were generally statistically based, in so far as they relied on the frequency of words in a text—usually a title of an article or book. There was the assumption that unusual words frequently used presented suitable index terms. However, by and large, many of the terms obtained in this manner were meaningless for index purposes, even if words such as prepositions were excluded. This led to a later development of studying the words in context, and particularly what has been called 'permutation' indexing. This process consists of cycling the title of book or article so that each significant or 'key' word is placed in a fixed index position surrounded by a fixed length context

The cycling method of KWIC demonstrated

Step 1		COMPUTERS	and the Social Sciences
Step 2	Computers and the	SOCIAL	Sciences
Step 3	Computers and the social	SCIENCES	

A 'forbidden word' dictionary is built up whereby irrelevant words are *excluded* from the analysis. In this case it varies from many 'computer type dictionaries' which represent the words, or instructions, to be *included.* An example of this type of indexing is shown in Fig. 5.2. In this illustration the KWIC (Key Word In Context) (Luhn, 1959) index has the key word in the centre of the page, and the context, being of fixed length, is often incomplete. However, the information is usually sufficient to discern the sense of a title, and is often aided by references to an author's name and the relevant journal or book. As variants on the KWIC indexing theme, the KWOC (Key Word Out Of Context) and KWAC (Key Word Augmented In Context) approaches have been developed. The former uses the same method of operation as KWIC but prints out the key word separately from the context, the latter uses also a cycling method but it is based on the addition of key words to a given piece of text by a subject specialist. There have been further developments of the indexing programs in an attempt to produce more meaningful indexing, and in the same process to provide an index which anticipates as many demands as possible. Two approaches have been particularly important, citation indexing and association indexing (Kent, 1971). The former is based on the idea that a more central relationship between books and articles occurs between works which the author cites, than between the titles themselves. Hence one looks for relationships between works cited, instead of those between titles. The latter approach assumes that the human mind associates ideas, rather than topics alphabetically, and so links what seems to be the main ideas rather than alphabetic lists of key words in titles.

Although indexing has primarily been discussed in relation to library use, it is evident that much wider applications are possible. For instance, once an indexing program is available individuals or firms can search a great deal of material from catalogues of personal libraries to indexes of commercial documents. The problems largely centre around the cost and time of the indexing operation and the meaningfulness of the completed index. Costs increase rapidly as indexes' meaning and usefulness improves and beyond a certain point the development of a system becomes considerably more time consuming than manual indexing. With all systems there is the initial labour of placing the relevant information on an input medium (probably punched cards at first) and storing this material. This a long, slow process, but once it has been achieved the data can be analysed repeatedly. Certainly the approaches based on citation, or associative, indexing require considerable work. In their final form they become highly specialised, and of specific rather than general reference. These two approaches in many aspects resemble the content analysis programs which will now be discussed.

Content analysis

As with information storage and retrieval there has been a great increase in the use of computers in content analysis. Indeed it is really only for reasons of clarity that the two types of computer use are treated separately, for many of the problems and techniques applicable to one field are also applicable to the other. In the context of politics, Kaplan (1943, page 230) has described content analysis as 'The statistical semantics of political discourse', whilst

ROOSEVELT'S LATIN-AMERICAN	POLICY.=	MATHEW	JM35	1304
BLIC OPINION IN FORMULATING FOREIGN	POLICY.= THE ROLE OF CONGRESS AND PU	COLEGR	K 44	1741
IENTISTS IN RECENT AMERICAN FOREIGN	POLICY-- SCHOLARSHIP OR INDOCTRINATION.= T	HOUGHT	ND58	2405
THE MAINSPRINGS OF AMERICAN FOREIGN	POLICY-- THE NATIONAL INTEREST VS. MORAL A	MORGEN	HJ50	2039
FOREIGN	POLICY-- THE REALISM OF IDEALISM.=	COOK	TI52	2112
N DIPLOMACY (DEMOCRATIZING FOREIGN	POLICY-MAKING).= CITIZE	MARSHA	J 49	1959
-- THE CASE OF PUBLIC INFORMATION.=	POLICY-MAKING AND SECRETARIAT INFLUENCE IN	GORDEN	L 60	2472
MILITARY LEADERS AND FOREIGN	POLICY-MAKING.=	EDINGE	LJ63	2608
SCIENTISTS, FOREIGN	POLICY, AND POLITICS.=	SCHILL	WR62	2558
S AFFECTING SOVIET RUSSIA'S FOREIGN	POLICY, I AND II.= LEGAL AND ECONOMIC FACT	PRINCE	C 44	1728
GEOGRAPHIC OBJECTIVES IN FOREIGN	POLICY, I AND II.=	SPYKMA	NJ39	1493
GEOGRAPHY AND FOREIGN	POLICY, I AND II.=	SPYKMA	NJ38	1427
CY AND THE ORIGINS OF PARLIAMENTARY	POLICY, I AND II.= THE BRITISH BUREAUCRA	AIKIN	C 39	1470
MAN PUBLICATIONS AND GERMAN FOREIGN	POLICY, 1933-1945.= RECENT GER	CARROL	EM52	2125
URY.= ANDREAS FRICIUS MODREVIUS-- A	POLISH POLITICAL THEORIST OF THE SIXTEENTH	ULAM	A 46	1826
Y WITH GERMANY LEGALLY POSSIBLE AND	POLITICALLY DESIRABLE.= IS A PEACE TREAT	KELSEN	H 47	1907
INTERVIEWING SOUTHERN	POLITICIANS.=	HEARD	A 50	2042
PAROCHIALISM IN TRANSITION (ETHNIC	POLITICS).= NEW MEXICO-- A PROBLEM OF	RUSSEL	JT36	1332
TIONAL CONFERENCE ON THE SCIENCE OF	POLITICS - INTRODUCTION.= REPORTS OF THE N	HALL	AR24	695
PRESENT TENDENCIES IN AMERICAN	POLITICS (APSA PRESIDENTIAL ADDRESS).=	FORD	HJ20	541
TVA AND POWER	POLITICS (CONSERVATION OF RESOURCES).=	WILDAV	A 61	2531
TIDES AND PATTERNS IN AMERICAN	POLITICS (ELECTION ANALYSIS).=	BEAN	LH42	1629
PHYSICS AND	POLITICS (IN AN ATOMIC AGE).=	MERRIA	CE46	1824
ENT).= THE PRIMACY OF	POLITICS (POLITICAL SCIENTISTS IN GOVERNM	POLLOC	JK51	2052
PATHOLOGICAL PROBLEMS IN	POLITICS (POLITICAL SCIENCE).=	SPENCE	HR49	1954
CALHOUN'S NEW SCIENCE OF	POLITICS (POLITICAL THEORY).=	LERNER	R 63	2630
THE PRAGMATIC APPROACH TO	POLITICS (POLITICAL SCIENCE).=	SABINE	GH30	1024
ELATIONS).= PERSONAL ATTENTION IN	POLITICS (REPRESENTATIVE - CONSTITUENCY R	SALTER	JT40	1511
THEORY AND THE STUDY OF	POLITICS (RESEARCH).=	APTER	DE57	2362
THE PHYSIOLOGY OF	POLITICS (THE SCIENTIFIC APPROACH).=	LOWELL	AL10	061
N BUNDESRAT (PARLIAMENT).=	POLITICS AND BUREAUCRACY IN THE WEST GERMA	NEUNRE	K 59	2450
ALLOWELL.=	POLITICS AND ETHICS-- A REPLY TO JOHN H. H	WHYTE	WF46	1822
AM F. WHYTE.=	POLITICS AND ETHICS-- A REJOINDER TO WILLI	HALLOW	JH46	1823
	POLITICS AND ETHICS.=	HALLOW	JH44	1726
INTERNATIONAL	POLITICS AND HISTORY.=	SPENCE	HR23	671
THE PATTERNS OF INTERNATIONAL	POLITICS AND OF INTERNATIONAL LAW.=	KAPLAN	MA59	2449
T).= ASPECTS OF PUBLIC OPINION (	POLITICS AND PSYCHOLOGY-- CONFERENCE REPOR	THURST	LL26	791
C IMPERATIVE.=	POLITICS AND RELIGION-- LUTHER'S SIMPLISTI	WOLIN	SS56	2291
TICAL THEORY).=	POLITICS AND THE CONTEMPLATIVE LIFE (POLI	DEGRAZ	S 60	2479
THE CANADIAN SENATE--	POLITICS AND THE CONSTITUTION.=	ALBINS	HS63	2607
ONE - PARTY	POLITICS AND THE VOTER.=	MILLER	WE56	2312
'MOVEMENT - REGIMES' (COMPARATIVE	POLITICS AND TOTALITARIANISM).= COMMENT O	WILES	P 61	2515
IONAL).= POWER	POLITICS AND WORLD ORGANIZATION (INTERNAT	HERZ	JH42	1648
JUDICIAL REVIEW AND	POLITICS IN AUSTRALIA.=	VILE	MJ57	2345
LEGISLATIVE	POLITICS IN CONNECTICUT.=	LOCKAR	WD54	2207
Y.= GOVERNMENT, ADMINISTRATION, AND	POLITICS IN EAST GERMANY-- A SELECTED BIBL	MASON	JB59	2413
RITICAL BIBLIOGRAPHY.= THE STUDY OF	POLITICS IN FRANCE SINCE THE LIBERATION--	MACRID	RC57	2367
ALCOHOL AND	POLITICS IN FRANCE.=	BROWN	BE57	2371
UNDERGROUND	POLITICS IN POST-WAR JAPAN.=	WILDES	HE48	1950
AL APPROACH TO THE SUBJECT OF WORLD	POLITICS IN TEACHING AND RESEARCH (CONFER	WRIGHT	Q 27	005
IOGRAPHICAL SURVEY FOR THE STUDY OF	POLITICS IN THE FORMER BELGIAN CONGO.= SEL	LEMARC	R 60	2490
MENT).= PARTY	POLITICS IN THE NEW JAPANESE DIET (PARLIA	WILLIA	J 48	1951
THE ISSUE OF A SCIENCE OF	POLITICS IN UTILITARIAN THOUGHT.=	KORT	F 52	2150
Y.= GOVERNMENT, ADMINISTRATION, AND	POLITICS IN WEST GERMANY-- A SELECTED BIBL	MASON	JB58	2400
ED LITERATURE ON THE GOVERNMENT AND	POLITICS OF BRITISH WEST AFRICA.= A SURVEY	COLEMA	JS55	2288
.=	POLITICS OF BRITISH CONSERVATISM (PARTY)	EPSTEI	LD54	2201
STWAR RECORD IN STEEL.= THE	POLITICS OF COLLECTIVE BARGAINING-- THE PO	HARBIS	FH54	2225
NT SUKARNO AND THE COMMUNISTS-- THE	POLITICS OF DOMESTICATION (INDONESIA).=	HINDLE	D 62	2586
GANIZATION OF THE EXECUTIVE).= THE	POLITICS OF MANAGEMENT IMPROVEMENT IN THE	ROSWOR	KA53	2156
IANISM).= TOWARDS A COMPARATIVE	POLITICS OF MOVEMENT - REGIMES (TOTALITAR	TUCKER	RC61	2514
THE PRAGMATIC	POLITICS OF MR. H.J. LASKI.=	ELLIOT	WY24	696
COMPARATIVE	POLITICS OF NON-WESTERN COUNTRIES.=	KAHIN	GM55	2292
THE TEXAS - MEXICAN AND THE	POLITICS OF SOUTH TEXAS.=	WEEKS	OD30	1012
THE INSULATION OF LOCAL	POLITICS UNDER THE NONPARTISAN BALLOT.=	WILLIA	OP59	2459
POLITICAL THOUGHT AND THE STUDY OF	POLITICS.= AMERICAN	MCCLOS	RG57	2336
D AN UNDERSTANDING OF PUBLIC SCHOOL	POLITICS.= TOWAR	ELIOT	TH59	2458
LOGY AND LEADERSHIP IN PUERTO RICAN	POLITICS.= IDEO	WELLS	H 55	2246
TOWARD A THEORY OF INTERNATIONAL	POLITICS.=	THOMPS	KW55	2274
HE PLACE OF PARTIES IN THE STUDY OF	POLITICS.= T	LEISER	A 57	2369
OF INTRANATIONAL AND INTERNATIONAL	POLITICS.= COMPARISON	ALGER	CF63	2609
SCIENTISTS, FOREIGN POLICY, AND	POLITICS.=	SCHILL	WR62	2558
THE TWO - PARTY SYSTEM IN BRITISH	POLITICS.=	LIPSON	L 53	2164
ROLE OF THE MILITARY IN MIDDLE EAST	POLITICS.= THE	KHADDU	M 53	2173
SCIENCE AND	POLITICS.=	KELSEN	H 51	2076
A REVISED THEORY OF AMERICAN PARTY	POLITICS.=	HUNTIN	SP50	2036
SM AND RELATIVISM IN PHILOSOPHY AND	POLITICS.= ABSOLUTI	KELSEN	H 48	1941
NATIONAL PARTIES AND LOCAL	POLITICS.=	ELLIS	ED35	1270
ANCE OF PSYCHOLOGY FOR THE STUDY OF	POLITICS.= THE SIGNIFIC	MERRIA	CE24	712
FFECT OF THE DEPRESSION ON CANADIAN	POLITICS.= THE E	REID	E 33	1181
THE SCIENTIFIC SPIRIT IN	POLITICS.=	MACY	J 17	409
STION AND ITS RELATIONS TO EUROPEAN	POLITICS.= NORTH AFRICAN QUE	ANDREW	GF03	039
THE PRESENT STATE OF THE STUDY OF	POLITICS.=	MERRIA	CE21	584
THE DRIFT IN FRENCH	POLITICS.=	SCHAPI	JS13	253
HEMATICAL REASONING TO THE STUDY OF	POLITICS.= SOME CONTRIBUTIONS OF MAT	FAGEN	RR61	2545
IN WESTERN EUROPEAN GOVERNMENT AND	POLITICS.= A SUGGESTED RESEARCH STRATEGY	ALMOND	GA55	2283
TIONAL CONFERENCE ON THE SCIENCE OF	POLITICS.= INTRODUCTION-- REPORTS OF THE S	HALL	AB25	772
TIONAL CONFERENCE ON THE SCIENCE OF	POLITICS.= INTRODUCTION-- REPORT OF THE TH	HALL	AB26	790
NS IN COMPARATIVE AND INTERNATIONAL	POLITICS.= TOWARDS AN INVENTORY OF BASIC T	DEUTSC	KW60	2465
COMPARATIVE	POLITICS-- A COMPREHENSIVE APPROACH.=	SPIRO	HJ62	2572
AL SCIENCE.= BUSINESS AND	POLITICS-- A CRITICAL APPRAISAL OF POLITIC	DAHL	RA59	2430

Fig. 5.2 A Key-Word-In-Context Listing. This illustration is taken from Janda (1964) and is part of an index to the *American Political Science Review*, volumes 1–57. Titles of articles are arranged around key words and referenced by the author's name, date of publication, and a code number.

Holsti (1969, pages 2–5) in a more general sense sees it as dealing 'with any problem in which the content of communication serves as a basis of inference'. The requirements of an analysis of communication are generally considered as *objectivity* in the sense that the categories and analysis are replicable by other researchers, *systematic* in that consistent rules are applied to any given research project and *generality* so individual findings have some theoretical reference point. These concepts are also applicable to much information retrieval and storage work, but have become more sophisticated in general content analysis as communication problems have had to be overcome.

The computer has been used at various points in this process, for although it must be obvious that initially great intellectual effort is required to meet the requirements above, the actual technique of content analysis, once the guidelines have been laid out, is often a boring and repetitive process. This is usually seen in the sheer drudgery of counting words, which the computer does many times faster, and a great deal more accurately than a manual operation, thereby releasing the researcher for more productive work. Similarly the computer's ability to store and work with large numbers of complex classifications is of great help, especially when these may be related to each other by processes which are difficult to remember. The placing of material on an input medium means that repeated passes of the data may be used, saving a great deal of replication manually. On the other hand there are circumstances in which it would be unwise to go to the time and expense of setting up a computer system. The most notable is where the study is likely to be used only once, and in this instance the costs of preparation of the data are likely to be prohibitive. Also, the material, even for a limited content analysis by computer, often assumes vast proportions for little intellectual reward. Data must be selected carefully and analysed extensively for its preparation to be worthwhile computationally. Other problems may be more effectively solved by manual than computer means. This is particularly true where the entire item, such as a book or complete articles, is the unit of analysis. It may also be less time consuming to search for complex themes (thematic analysis) at some stage by hand, where specification of the relationships in computing terms would involve a great deal of additional card punching and program development.

Before describing particular systems it is advisable to point out some of the difficulties in this area, which make the formation of an effective, and economic, program, or set of programs, so difficult. There are *coding problems* which must be overcome. Coding must be based on a logically adequate and theoretically relevant classification, and, it must be said, at present there is a distinct absence of widely recognised standard categories. There are also *sampling problems*. Very rarely is it possible, for the reasons stated above, to analyse all the data considered relevant to a particular project, and therefore some form of sampling must be devised. This is especially problematic where source documents are difficult to obtain as with policy-making documents in the study of Politics or International Relations. A unit of analysis must be chosen, perhaps words or phrases, and, even more important, the context of such a unit, for increasing or decreasing the context radically alters the results. Other problems are those of *reliability* and *validity*. In a sense the accuracy of computers has solved the problem of reliability of calculation, but really at the expense of placing the problem one stage back in the process, where the formation of the categories for analysis is tackled. Validity is difficult to demonstrate in content analysis, the main tests being those based on predictive validity and construct validity. The former is concerned with the predictive capacity of the process in a situation where evidence is not initially available. This was used, for example, after the Second World War to examine Nazi documents and to see whether predictions made previously about German actions were accurate (George, 1959). Construct validity is concerned with the establishment of the theory underlying relationships, rather than with relationships themselves. This implies that relationships should be generalisable to a number of situations, rather than be limited to a single study or situation.

These basic considerations, which are applicable to all content analysis, manual or computer based, have important implications for the structure of computer programs. In one respect the advent of computers has had a beneficial effect on content analysis research, for it has forced decisions in respect to the definitions which are employed, and has provided a means of testing, at least in part, various assumptions.

Two main kinds of content analysis programs have been used. They are first, word count programs, and second, programs based on the use of a dictionary, in which the data are referred to listed 'meanings' then processed accordingly. The word count program is simpler in form than the dictionary-based program, but is widely used. In many ways it can be seen as an extension of the KWIC type of indexing program, in which the data are processed, listed, and counted at the same time. A simple program of this type is seen in Fig. 5.3 where vowels are counted in a given piece of text. This could be modified so as to use words, and not individual characters, as the basis of analysis. Indeed this is what many programs are exclusively geared to achieving. One impetus for the development of word count programs has come from psychiatry, and psychotherapists in particular, for frequency of word usage has been a major concern of some psychotherapeutic practitioners. One

```
←CALL 'AEIOU' THE VOWELS.
←RESERVE SPACE FOR 5 ELEMENTS IN A FREQUENCY LIST.
←SET THE FREQUENCY LIST TO 0,0,0,0,0.
←PRINT '/THE FOLLOWING TEXT IS INPUT/'.
←READ A TEXT.
←SET L TO THE LENGTH OF THE TEXT. SET I TO 1.
←(OUTER LOOP) SET K TO 1.
←(INNER LOOP)
←IF THE I-TH CHARACTER OF THE TEXT IS THE SAME AS THE K-TH
←CHARACTER OF THE VOWELS INCREASE THE K-TH FREQUENCY BY 1,
←AND CONTINUE WITH THE END OF THE INNER LOOP.
←IF K IS LESS THAN 5. INCREASE K BY 1, AND REPEAT FROM
←THE INNER LOOP.
←(END OF THE INNER LOOP)
←IF I IS EQUAL TO L CONTINUE WITH THE OUTPUT.
←INCREASE I BY 1. REPEAT FROM THE OUTER LOOP.
←(OUTPUT)
←PRINT '/ THE FREQUENCIES OF A,E I,O,U ARE/'
←THEN THE FREQUENCY LIST THEN '  RESPECTIVELY'.
←TERMINATE. EXECUTE.

THE FOLLOWING TEXT IS INPUT


←THE HISTORY OF ALL HITHERTO EXISTING SOCIETY IS THE HISTORY/-
←OF CLASS STRUGGLES. FREEMAN AND SLAVE, PATRICIAN AND PLEBEIAN/-
←,LORD AND SERF, GUILDMASTER AND JOURNEYMAN, IN A WORD,/-
←OPPRESSOR AND OPPRESSED, STOOD IN CONSTANT OPPOSITION TO ONE-/-
←ANOTHER, CARRIED ON AN UNINTERRUPTED, NOW HIDDEN, NOW OPEN/-
←FIGHT, A FIGHT THAT EACH TIME ENDED EITHER IN A REVOLUTIONARY/-
←RE-CONSTITUTION OF SOCIETY AT LARGE, OR IN THE COMMON RUIN/-
←OF THE CONTENDING CLASSES.


 THE FREQUENCIES OF A,E I,O,U ARE
 27, 38, 30, 36, 8  RESPECTIVELY


HALTED  PROGRAM TERMINATED
←
```

Fig. 5.3 An example of a search procedure. This program determines the frequency of vowels in a piece of text, and is written in a language called SNAP, which is a stylised form of natural English. The example shows the listing obtained when using SNAP from an 'on-line' terminal (Housden and Kujawa, 1971). Lines beginning ← are input by the user, the remainder being the system's replies. The method used is a simple sequential search.

of the most sophisticated of the word count packages uses a large series of interlinked programs which delete irrelevant words (i.e. prepositions and so on) subsume closely related words under a single generic title and analyse by the relationships between the remaining words (Iker and Harway, 1965). This procedure has been extended to deal with associations between various literary works, particularly dealing with authorship problems, and to print out concordances (alphabetic indexes of words in context) of books or articles. Other researchers have used word count programs for specific purposes, such as compiling lists of particular word groups. A good example is the attempt to trace the authorship of the Federalist Papers by Mosteller and Wallace (1964). The Federalist Papers, essays written to support the adoption of the American Constitution, were published anonymously, but known to be written individually either by Hamilton, Jefferson or Jay. By plotting the frequencies of both common and infrequently used words they were able to trace with more, or less, probability the authorship of the individual Papers. Some word count programs of greater sophistication allow a selection of the words to be counted, which is dependent on the difference between *expected* and *actual* frequency. This is often much more useful where, for instance, there may be a common vocabulary for many areas of computer science (e.g. 'file', 'input', 'output', etc.) but a researcher is interested in particular deviations from this vocabulary such as 'information retrieval' or 'content analysis' (Meadow, 1967). This endeavour has largely been applied to the humanities rather than the social sciences (Parrish and Painter, 1963) but it is possible that particular 'classics' in the social sciences could be analysed by means of concordance programs.

The major problems with word count problems are first, that there must initially be a great deal of time and effort applied to the construction of machine-readable data, and second, the generally limited use of these data. This difficulty can be seen particularly in psychotherapeutic interviews, when a large number are analysed. Difficulties of analysis in *context* are also acute and lead to concern with the reliability and validity of the material. The implication is that a wider and deeper analysis of the data input might prove more acceptable. This in turn led to a growth of dictionary-based programs, our second type of content analysis program.

The most well-known and sophisticated of these is the 'General

Inquirer' system (Stone *et al.*, 1966, 1968). This is seen as a way of transforming what are normally intuitive judgements about the content of text into explicit rules whilst ensuring reliability and speed of coding. In this process several things are needed: the specification of the content characteristics to be measured, and the rules to be used for identifying and recording these characteristics when they appear in the text. The 'General Inquirer' system was designed to be sufficiently broad that it could cope with content analysis in a large number of fields and subjects. In practice it performs a number of operations: identifies within the text, words and phrases specified by the investigator, counts occurrences of these words and phrases, prints and graphs the tabulations, performs statistical tests, and sorts and regroups sentences on the basis of specified categories.

Initially the information is input by means of punched cards but is then stored on magnetic tape for ease of access and storage. The text can be input 'straight', that is as it was originally written, but as we noted earlier one of the key problems in text analysis is the context of the word or phrase to be analysed. The 'General Inquirer' has special facilities for 'tagging' words with a number or letter to indicate certain features which then can be recognised by the computing system. At a minimum this might include proper name and pronoun identification, which have been found to require separate facilities. In a more sophisticated way the system has made use of certain syntactic principles. This idea is based on the difficulty of investigating complex texts without tracing relationships between words and phrases in any given sentence. Two features were found to require particular emphasis, the analysis of the position of a word which may change its meaning, and the tracing of 'subject' and 'object' relationship, for example, 'who is saying what to whom' is important in many texts. These problems were tackled with the addition of numbers describing such things as subject and position, verb position, object position and so on. An example is given below:

MARX/8 SAID/9 TO LENIN/0 THAT THE WORLD/1 IS RIPE/3 FOR REVOLUTION/5

which equals . . . (Marx said to Lenin that)+(the world is ripe for revolution).

Where /1 = subject position
/3 = verb position
/5 = object position
/8 = attributive subject
/9 = attributive verb
/0 = attributive object

The process of content analysis is started by relating the text input by means of punched cards, or magnetic tape to a 'dictionary' (also on magnetic tape) which includes the main categories which the investigator wishes to link together. The dictionary includes both words and phrases and has instructions about which words to relate together, and to look for specific combinations of words which constitute some significant characteristic. The size of the dictionary is reduced by just using the 'root' of a word rather than all suffixes so that, say, 'develop' would be treated as equivalent to 'development' or 'developing' and all words not found by means of the dictionary are printed out as 'leftovers'.

The set of programs add up the 'tags' on the words, print out sentences and also the relevant syntactic information. They also reorder the information by tags so that the text can be analysed across categories, produce graphs and perform various statistical and ordering operations.

Figure 5.4 is a diagrammatic representation of the 'General Inquirer' set of programs in which the flow and sequence of operation is designated.

A number of dictionaries have been used in the 'General Inquirer' process, relating to various subject areas of psychology, sociology and politics. Stone *et al.* (1966, page 140) noted that there are 17 dictionaries in current use ranging from dictionaries for need-achievement scores to the Stanford political dictionary and a number of anthropological dictionaries. Their size need not necessarily be large for it appears, from empirical analysis, that a small number of words generally account for a large percentage of the text, and many dictionaries do not exceed more than a thousand or so words. These dictionaries cover basically different areas. However, because they relate to the same program, it means that the same text can be analysed under different dictionaries thereby making maximum use of the text.

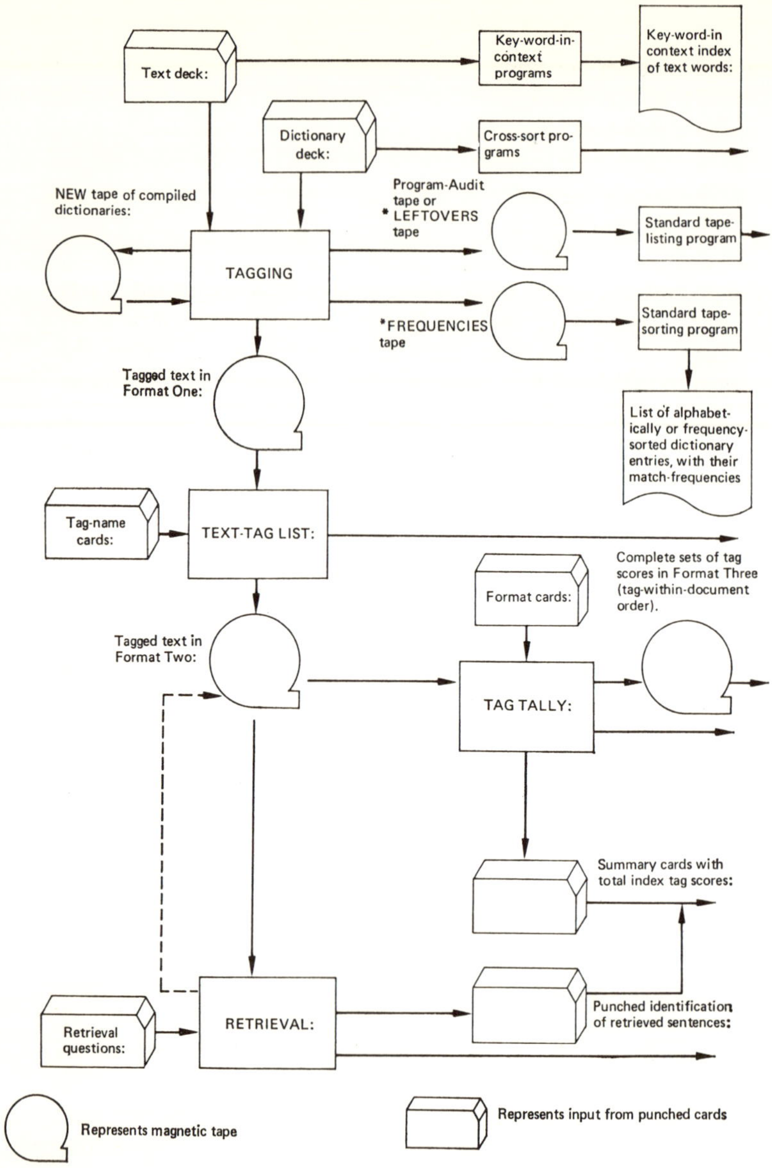

Fig. 5.4 The General Inquirer System. Solid lines indicate the flow of data in the

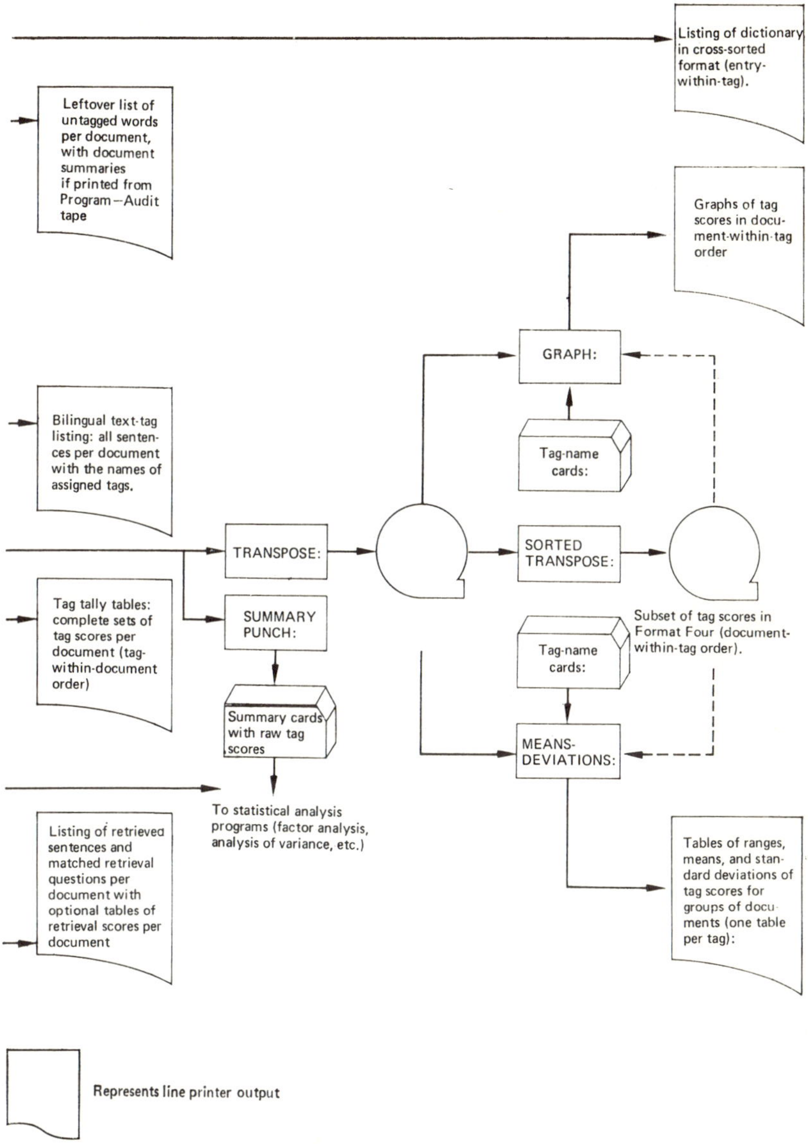

system. Broken lines indicate feedback or second application of a program.

Problems with the 'General Inquirer' are basically those which bedevil all work with text handling, namely the high cost of data preparation, and the complex relationships between pieces of text compared with relationships between numerical data (Psathas, 1968). This in turn involves complex processes of definition, and in computing terms the need to make the storage of the data and search procedures as efficient as possible. Difficulties of definition in the 'General Inquirer', and also problems of contextual meaning, are partially met by extensive manual coding and tagging beforehand. However, this involves in itself a great deal of time in addition to the computing process itself. But the major problem, certainly where the installation is a relatively small one, is the one of storage, and then making efficient searches of the text for the required analyses. Storage problems are effectively lessened by sampling a long text (although this has its own drawbacks) rather than repeating it in full and by keeping a dictionary to as limited a size as possible.

Storing text in the main memory of the computer is obviously the way to achieve the quickest access time but is usually impracticable. Therefore the main alternatives are magnetic tape, or magnetic disc storage, and given these alternatives, the maximum possible efficiency of computer use must be achieved. Content analysis, even by computer, without any refining of the search process, is generally a slow process. If a dictionary is used the 'normal' procedure might be seen as follows. A word is picked out of the text by the 'cycling' method mentioned earlier, this word is then taken and compared systematically to each dictionary word, usually arranged in alphabetical order, say on a magnetic tape, until the same word is found and then the matched characteristics are printed out. This process is then repeated with every word of the text. Assuming that the text itself is analysed progressively, then at the minimum a (more or less) complete tape rewind is required each time the dictionary is used. The rewind is a slow process, and hence it is evident that this should be kept to a minimum. We have here assumed that the text will be analysed progressively, which is not usually the case. Indeed the 'General Inquirer' has specific provisions for the analysis of phrase structure which may be important for the examination of words in context, and which requires reference back to the preceding text to check for a number of conditions which might give a word a different meaning

Other ways of reducing the time spent in searching the text data may be employed. One of these is to use a number of separate programs simultaneously, which is achieved by the 'General Inquirer', and another is to limit the context, and unit of analysis, to the smallest possible one. The problem essentially is that a balance has to be struck between the speed of the process in computing terms, and the extraction of as much information as possible from the text. However, with any given text translation there are ways of achieving a more or less efficient use of facilities.

Sort and search techniques

So far we have looked very generally at the uses and some of the problems of storage and retrieval of information on the computer. It is obvious that these have presented special technical difficulties, and given rise to particular solutions in computing terms. The two aspects of the procedure, storage and retrieval, are closely linked. Generally the better ordered the storage of data is, the more efficient the searching programs can be. The complexity of each operation, however, depends largely on the content of the stored data, and the sophistication of the search procedure required. Sorting data is a basic procedure in the storage and retrieval process. This technique, which consists of putting a file of data in sequence, is necessary before most search procedures can be used. There are a number of ways of sorting data often dependent on the means used to store the data preliminary to a sort. For example, using peripheral devices is slower than using the main memory. One common method is to sort data into order by successively merging it together. Each record has one or more 'keys' by which it is sorted. These may be reference numbers of records in a social survey, book numbers, ages of personnel and so on. The object is to furnish the sorting operation with a string of numbers in order. The merging process is illustrated in the table on page 156.

In the process of sorting, the length of each string of numbers doubles at each successive merge, until the string is complete and in order (the bars below the numbers indicate the length of the string at any stage). There are a variety of other sorting techniques not mentioned above which may be employed in particular situations (Meadow, 1967, pages 256–257; Flores, 1969).

Ages in Random Order	Stage 1 Tape I	Stage 1 Tape II	Stage 2 Tape III	Stage 2 Tape IV	Stage 3 Tape I	Stage 3 Tape II
46	46	57	46	21	21	22
57						
21	21	33	57	33	33	34
33						
34	34	45	34	22	46	45
45						
59	59	22	45	59	57	59
22						

Stage 4 (Final Stage) Tape III
21
22
33
34
45
46
57
59

The importance of searching procedures for the use of certain types of content and text analysis, and the constraints on computer time available, have led to a number of attempts to speed the process of searching records. The basic process has always been that of a 'linear' search. This involved a search for a one-to-one match between a specified value input to a search program, and a value in a list of characters being searched. These characters (numeric or alphabetic) were initially not ordered, and therefore the search process was very cumbersome, with every item checked if the appropriate value was not present. The next development was the ordering of the data in some sequence, perhaps highest to lowest value, if numeric characters were used, or alphabetic order. This speeded up the process of searching, but has led to some of the difficulties described in relation to the 'General Inquirer' programs. 'Binary' search techniques substantially cut the time taken to locate values. This process depends on a numerically ordered table. Comparisons between the items being searched for and items in the table, are first made in the middle of the table. If the new item precedes this value, then the first half of the table is searched; if the item follows on from this value, then the second half of the table is searched.

Again the search starts in the middle of the appropriate section of the table, with half of each section being eliminated as the values are compared. An example of the efficiency of this process is given below:

Linear Search—Table contains: 1048576 ($=2^{20}$) items
Average number of items searched—
$\frac{n}{2}=524288$ comparisons

Binary Search—Table contains: 1048576 items
Average number of items searched—
$\log_2 n=\log_2 2^{20}=20$ comparisons.

In any similar situation, the binary search will obviously be much quicker. However, there are limitations about incorporating new items into the table, and problems when the length of the table is not a power of two, which have to be taken into account when using binary search procedures.

A technique known as 'hashing' (Coffman and Eve, 1970) has been developed to deal with situations where only a small number of a range of locations is used for storing significant characters. In this case, rather than search through all locations to find the characters wanted, a procedure has been developed to search more economically. If say of 100000 stored values only 100 are non-zero, then by dividing all the stored values by 1000 and noting the remainder (which would take values between 0–99) a new table could be produced presenting the significant characters, with which comparisons could then be made. Again a number of problems arise with this method. For example, it would be normal practice to increase the 0–99 values by 1 to eliminate the zero (which of course would comprise the majority of the 100000 values). The other major problem is that caused by *collisions.* That is situations where two or more different numbers have the same remainder, and hence the same final storage location. For example, the three numbers 256, 1256, 2256 would all have the same locations based on the remainder '56'. It may be wise therefore to combine the hashing process with a linear search in which these numbers are differentiated. The hashing technique may also be used in conjunction with binary search procedures, but the logistic problems become increasingly complex. The most successful occasions on which hashing can be used are where the significant values are sparsely distributed over a large number of locations, and where collisions are unlikely.

Most of the above procedures are more effective when used with numeric data because on the whole alphabetic character strings are more difficult to manipulate, and compare. This is compounded when the context of an alphabetic character string changes its meaning (as in more sophisticated content and linguistic analysis). If these strings are few in number, and are known before the program is written then a linear search may be the most effective and least complicated technique to search a given series of character strings. Since this is not normally the case, various techniques have been adopted to produce more efficient storage of structures, and hence more effective retrieval. Three ways of organising such data are particularly applicable. These three rely on certain relationships between each piece of data. The use of a 'stack' for storage has become increasingly common. A stack is usually a list of items which are stored in a certain sequence, and then retrieved in reverse order. In this case a series of items would be stored in sequence ('pushed down on the stack') and the last item in the stack removed first ('popped up'). A 'queue' is another method of storing data in which a similar storage sequence to that of the stack is employed. However, in this case the retrieval is by the *same* sequence as the data is input (first in—first out). A queue may be *double-ended* when items may be retrieved from either or both ends of the stored sequence of data. These two methods are particularly useful in text handling where one character string is used in relation to several others. An example might be the KWIC index mentioned earlier, or any concordance where one word is placed centrally in a piece of text, and a fixed sequence of words is required. One grave disadvantage of stacks and queues is the fact that no additional information can be stored in the middle of the existing list, or retrieved from any other point than the beginning or end of the list.

The third, and possibly most flexible, method of storing and retrieving information is that of 'list-processing', which was introduced in Chapter 3. We will return to the idea of general data structures again in the following chapter.

For economy, several examples in this book use different algorithms for the related process of sorting, and the reader can compare

SORTING LISTS IN POP2

```
VARS SEED;  10 -> SEED;

FUNCTION RANDOM L;
COMMENT  THIS SELECTS A RANDOM ELEMENT FROM THE LIST L;

L; INTOF(LAMBDA;(125*SEED+1)//16384; ERASE() -> SEED;
                SEED/16384;END   .APPLY*LENGTH(L)) ->.L;
COMMENT  INTOF IS A STANDARD FUNCTION GIVING THE NEAREST INTEGER TO
         A REAL EXPRESSION. THE OPERATOR '//' GIVES TWO RESULTS
         ONE OF WHICH IS DESTROYED BY THE FUNCTION 'ERASE', SO THAT
         THE VARIABLE 'SEED' BECOMES THE REMAINDER FROM THE DIVISION.
         THE SECTION 'LAMBDA' TO 'END' DEFINES A TEMPORARY FUNCTION
         TO GENERATE A RANDOM NUMBER AND IS APPLIED TO THE LENGTH
         OF THE LIST TO GIVE A VALUE BEWTEEN 1 AND L.;
LOOP:   IF L>0 THEN L-1 -> L; TL(); GOTO LOOP  CLOSE;
        HD();
COMMENT  THIS LOOP FINDS THE L-TH ITEM OF THE ORIGINAL LIST, WHICH
         WAS PLACED ON THE STACK AT THE BEGINNING OF THE FUNCTION
         DEFINITION;
END;

FUNCTION JOIN X Y;
COMMENT  THIS JOINS THE LISTS X AND Y TOGETHER;

VARS Z;
IF NULL(X) THEN Y EXIT;
X;
LOOP:  TL(X) -> Z; IF NULL(Z) THEN Y -> TL(X) EXIT;
       Z -> X; GOTO LOOP;
END;


FUNCTION ORDER LIST SORT;
VARS Z Y A V W S; 0;
LOOP1:   IF NULL(LIST) OR NULL(TL(LIST)) THEN GOTO SPLIT CLOSE;
          NIL -> S; NIL -> Y; NIL -> Z;
         RANDOM(LIST) -> W;
LOOP2:   DEST(LIST) -> LIST -> V;
COMMENT  THE FUNCTION DEST PLACES THE HEAD AND TAIL OF A LIST
         SEPARATELY ON THE STACK;

    IF SORT(W,V)  THEN V::Z -> Z;
         ELSEIF SORT(V,W)  THEN V::S -> Z;
         ELSE V:: Y   -> Y; CLOSE;
         IF NULL(LIST) THEN Z; Y; 1; S -> LIST; GOTO LOOP2 CLOSE;
         GOTO LOOP 2;
SPLIT:   -> A; IF A = 0 THEN LIST EXIT;
          ->Y; IF A = 1 THEN -> Z; JOIN(LIST,Y); 2; Z -> LIST;
         GOTO LOOP1 CLOSE;
         JOIN(Y,LIST) -> LIST; GOTO SPLIT;
END;


COMMENT  REFERENCE: BURSTALL ET.AL. (1971) PROGRAMMING IN POP2
                              EDINBURGH, THE UNIVERSITY  PRESS,
                                 PP. 124-126;


ORDER ([WORKING PEOPLE OF ALL COUNTRIES UNITE],ALPHA) =>


**  [ALL COUNTRIES OF PEOPLE UNITE WORKING]

ORDER([12 5 19 14 11 13 25],NONOP >) =>


**  [25 19 14 13 12 11 5]
```

Fig. 5.5 Sorting lists in POP2. This example illustrates the generality of POP2, compared with other languages in widespread use. The list can be sorted according to any function given as one of the arguments of the function ORDER and can contain any kind of information. Two applications are illustrated, one using a lexicographic sorting function ALPHA, not shown here, and the other a numerical sort. 'NONOP>' causes the operator to be treated as a function. Output from the program is prefaced '**'. The sorting method chooses an item at random and partitions the list into subsets to which the same process is applied in turn. Compare this with the method of the FORTRAN subroutine in the Appendix to Chapter 7.

Notes on POP2

Programs consist of function definitions, which can be applied as shown in the example. Values are placed on a pushdown storage stack, and removed when needed (for example, A; places the current value of A on the stack: —> B; takes the first item from the stack and assigns it to B: = > prints the current stack contents). The example uses list processing functions, HD, TL and NULL as described in Chapter 3, and a function LENGTH which gives the size of a list. Functions shown with no arguments (an example is HD();) operate on the stack.:: appends an item to a list. VARS defines new variable names for 'global' use.

them for relative efficiency. In Fig. 5.5 list processing functions are used in a general sorting function in the POP2 programming language. Lists may be *double-chained* by having links not only from one cell forwards to the next one, but working backwards as well, which gives additional flexibility. The branching tree structure is achieved by having a sequence of three cells, one holding the value and two having pointers forward to the next sequences of three cells. Each cell therefore has two forward branches. This procedure can give rise to extensive 'tree' structures (Windley, 1960). Further complexities can be introduced by increasing or decreasing the number of pointers at any point in the tree structure, although this needs careful programming.

The list-processing method detailed above could considerably shorten the search process, using hierarchies of, say, words from given texts. However, this does assume that the theoretical structures of any problem considered for processing (and hence the concepts and definitions used) are amenable to hierarchical ordering. This may be true where concepts are well developed, but it is not necessarily useful in either simple word count programs, or others where key ordering concepts are not specified, or subjected to radical modification. There are instances in the social sciences where the list processing procedure can operate very successfully. An often-quoted example is that in some branches of psychology certain organising words and phrases are discovered to have a series of related and lower-order words associated with them. In this case there might be a dictionary associated around the concepts of aggression and sexuality, with sequences of lower order, and dependent words arranged in a list-processing tree structure.

This brief description gives some idea of the range of techniques for the storage and retrieval of non-numeric data (Day, 1972). The complexity of these procedures varies widely, according to the sophistication in the search process and the exact nature of the data to be stored and analysed. It is obvious that the more developed data-analysis techniques become the more widely will they be used not only by the social sciences still largely concerned with numerical data but also those concerned with text handling.

Machine translation and syntactic analysis

The importance of language processing and machine translation lies in the attempt to equate computer language with natural language. This would bring benefits in terms of communication and solve many problems in producing universally programmable languages accessible to all.

The basic process of syntactic analysis involves the classification of words in categories, the use of a theory of grammar which is translatable into machine terms, and the transformation of the data into suitable means of input and output. While it is not possible in this book to give more than a brief indication of the theoretical basis of work on automatic language processing, we can give a few examples of the problems involved and a simple illustration of the basic computation involved.

Much interesting work originates in modern linguistic theory and has been devoted to attempts to provide machine translations of natural languages and to grammatical analyses of interest to specialists in language (Lyons, 1970; Borko, 1964). There is no reason why the social sciences in general should not be able to benefit from the techniques of this kind of work and apply them to the extension of existing methods of content analysis for other theoretical purposes.

Many concepts employed in computer-assisted linguistic analysis can be expressed in terms of the work of Noam Chomsky, whose terminology and theories have become recognised as the basis of a major reorientation of the study of linguistics. Although many of his ideas appear naturally suited to computer application, and have indeed found very faithful application in the theory of computer languages as well, they were, in fact, developed quite independently as a theory of the syntax of natural languages. The basic idea concerns the existence of a transformational grammar which, from a finite set of rules, is capable of generating the infinite set of utterances which are possible in any living human language. Chomsky has also graphically illustrated his early distinction between syntactic and semantic criteria of acceptability in some, by now, well-known examples. 'Colourless green ideas sleep furiously' is grammatically correct but is equally as nonsensical as natural English as the syntactically incorrect sentence 'Furiously sleep ideas green colourless'. Similarly 'the book seems interesting' and 'the child seems sleeping' are equally semantically similar in structure but the latter is not really acceptable syntactically (Chomsky, 1957, page 19). It used to be thought that this distinction could provide a sufficient basis for machine translation but in fact the rigorous separation of syntax and semantics in a computer algorithm is much less satisfactory in practice than the application of both techniques more or less together to develop a self-consistent interpretation. However, nobody would claim that the problem has been solved adequately, and it may be that natural language will always prove essentially un-computable, although there has been some success with limited linguistic models.

To be able to apply a computer to the problem of 'understanding' a language, other than its own, it is, of course, necessary to define it fully. If the language is very simple, as for example with the control commands for a packaged program as discussed earlier, it may be quite sufficient to list all meaningful alternatives. Then any communication can simply be matched against the stored vocabulary by a searching algorithm, and appropriate action taken when an item is found. This can rapidly become a wasteful procedure, and in the case of any interesting language, in the proper sense, it is impossible. Designers of computer languages, however, are at liberty to choose their syntactic rules for their computing convenience, although the techniques for defining these or natural languages are similar.

In both cases, the problem of parsing a sentence is fundamental. The trouble with natural languages is that they are often ambiguous syntactically. For example, a set of rules which makes an acceptable English grammar must be capable of producing two separate semantic descriptions of the sentence 'They don't know how good meat tastes' (Chomsky, 1965, page 11). Whereas the FORTRAN expression

A+B*C*D**E ('**' stands for exponentiation)

is rapidly parsed without ambiguity by the insertion of brackets to indicate the order of evaluation

(A+((B*C)*(D**E)))

Computer languages can be designed so as to provide an unambiguous interpretation for the unbracketed expression, which is expressed in the order of priorities assigned to the various operators. It may be that the problem of ambiguity in natural language is not of major difficulty for application in the social sciences. Indeed, so long as it is possible to recognise and specify ambiguities automatically, the computer can be a very useful aid in the objective study of communications, in which the frequency of redundant or ambiguous phrases can be in itself of theoretical interest. This is particularly true, for example, of the study of the content of diplomatic exchanges. An early attempt at construction of a syntactic analysis applied to the Nuclear Test Ban Treaty found at least one ambiguity which could not be resolved easily by consideration of the context. The analyser in question unavoidably output numerous nonsensical paraphrases which could be discarded by a human reader. It did, however, pin-point a loose sentence dealing with the majority required for amendment of the Treaty (Langevin and Owens, 1964).

To achieve such a parsing, computer language design relies upon the linguistic concept of a context-free phrase structure grammar, consisting of the rules which can generate all syntactically correct statements. These define *sentences* in terms of *words* by means of *classes* or intermediate groups of symbols for each of which are defined a set of possible alternative structures, or productions. The following example uses a type of notation common to this kind of definition. We will use some arbitrary capital letters to denote the classes defined, and vertical bars to separate the possible alternatives.

(1) S→VP NP CON NP
(2) VP→there are

(3) NP→N N ADJ N ADJ N
(4) N→lies statistics
(5) ADJ→damned
(6) CON→and

Notice the hierarchical arrangement of these productions, which can be considered in order as rules for rewriting the different classes. This very limited definition could be used to generate, among other valid sentences, the well-known aphorism shown by the steps now illustrated:

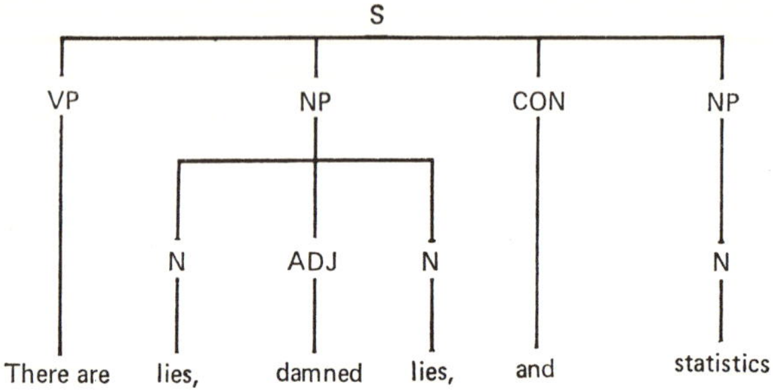

Other possible statements in this grammar include:

There are damned statistics and lies
There are statistics
etc., etc.

It is a simple matter to write out every possible valid sentence which can be generated, since there are obviously a finite number of these. Each class definition contains at least one production which leads to a termination of the generation process, indeed in this example only classes involve alternatives at all. There should be no productions of the kind

N→N
or N→ADJ N

since if these are the only alternatives the process would never terminate.

Such finite grammars are of comparatively little interest, but the presence of one or more recursive definitions causes the set of syntactically valid sentences to be infinite. In our example, the production

N→lies statistics ADJ N

would introduce a recursive alternative into the system.

The object of parsing a statement is to fill a conceptual triangle whose vertex is the highest level of class, the sentence and whose base is assumed to be a valid sentence.

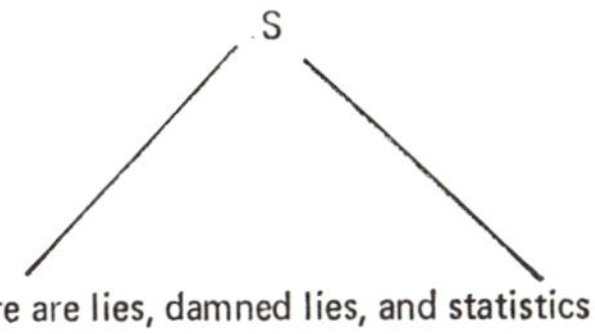

Whether we think in terms of a tree structure or the bracketed notation used earlier, the task is to find a self-consistent set of derivations for a particular sentence and grammar. The individual steps in any method applied to the problem consist of trying to find a production which fits the level of the parsing tree currently under consideration. The object in seeking an automatic method for computer use must be to avoid so far as possible false starts which do not yield a self-consistent result with a consequent need to restart from a lower level. A variety of parsing methods are in use for compiling computer languages, for which both the definition and the parsing algorithm can be designed with computing efficiency in mind (Foster, 1970). In fact, context-free grammars are in general too broad for this application, and have to be restricted carefully to be efficient in use. In an indirect way, this helps to indicate the special difficulty of applying computers to natural language.

Chomsky's refined theory, published in *Aspects of the Theory of Syntax* (Chomsky, 1965), relates syntactic rules to both a surface structure of a particular language, and to a deep structure which represents the common semantic content of all human communication. The basic conception of transformational grammar was that syntactic rules must include definitions for the valid transformation of one expression into its semantic equivalent, for example, for turning a sentence using an active verb into one which uses a passive verb to convey the same meaning. The later theory incorporates a syntactic generative element, operating at both deep and surface levels and two interpretive components. The semantic component is conceived as operating for the deep structure and the phenological component for the surface level. Moving from the deep structure to the surface involves a combination of lexical rules which associate words and meanings with categorical rules, similar to the phrase-structure rules illustrated earlier, which help to select from lexical structures. The lexicon itself is required to solve an important inadequacy of transformational rules when applied to natural languages. This arises because rewriting rules cannot reflect the cross-classifications inherent in lexical subcategories. For example, nouns in English may be classified as proper or common, and as human or non-human. An attempt to express these two cross-cutting dimensions by the kind of rules we have used so far causes one such classification to dominate over the other and produces tortuous definitions of functionally equivalent operations (Chomsky, 1965, pages 79–80).

Even this brief account should suggest the complexity of the full theory, and it is not surprising that it has been applied only in limited ways. But language definitions making use of these ideas are the basis for attempts to devise parsing systems for natural languages. The system has itself received successful expression as a computer model which is capable of testing attempts at the definition of transformational grammars by generating sentences from them and giving an account of the process as it goes. This is done by defining separately a lexicon, a phrase-structure grammar, and transformational rules in a notation which is not far from Chomsky's own.

In experiments with machine translation, it has long been recognised that an ideal system requires accurate grammatical descriptions of both the source and the target languages. Reflection on the example in Fig. 5.6 will quickly suggest that a simple word-for-word translation would require a very large dictionary indeed. German translation would require the full specification of a wide range of inflected forms in addition to compound words and idiomatic expressions which would probably need full specification anyway. Both the dictionary and the kind of pragmatic contextual rules which a teacher might use to help pupils to understand German in a

	Process	Test
(1)	Read in a sentence	'Die Geschichte aller bisherigen Gesellschaft ist die Geschichte von Klassenkampfen'
(2)	Grammatical analysis of source language	(((Die Geschichte) (aller bisherigen Gesellschaft)) ist ((die Geschichte) (von Klassenkampfen)))
(3)	Look up equivalents in a dictionary	The (history) / (story) of all (hitherto existing) / (present) society is the (history) / (story) (of) / (from) / (by) / (concerning) class-struggles
(4)	Grammatical analysis of target language (for example, determination of likely structure, and 'natural' English order of the sentence; use of context to resolve any ambiguity)	(This example needs little revision)
(5)	Rearrange and output translation	One outcome *should* read: 'The history of all hitherto existing society is the history of class-struggles'

For reasons discussed in the text, theoretical problems of stages (2) and (4) are unresolved, although some pragmatic solutions exist

Fig. 5.6 Stages in Machine Translation.

fluent left-to-right scan would require considerable empirical work on the language itself (Marchand, 1961). Fortunately, a pragmatic approach is helped by the 50% semantic redundancy of natural language, while the replacement of literal translation with some rules for local contexts can resolve structural and semantic difficulties in 85% of cases. It has been possible to construct unsatisfactory but working systems which considerably reduce the work required of human translators when assisted by machine output. Machine translation produced in this way may not make use of a detailed syntax. Such systems are the origin of such, probably apocryphal, renderings as

The vodka is potent but the meat has gone bad
for
The spirit is willing but the flesh is weak
and
invisible idiot for *out of sight, out of mind*

However, as we suggested earlier, even imperfect attempts at translation or parsing may be of interest to social scientists in their study of the content of human communications.

References

E. D. Barraclough *et al.* (1971) 'The Computer/Library Interface; an Introduction' in C. K. Balmforth and N. S. M. Cox (Editors) *Interface*, Bath, Oriel, pages 73–92.

A. B. Blackney and M. Scatcherd (1970) *Information Retrieval in the U.S.A.*, London, Ministry of Technology.

H. Borko (Editor) (1967) *Automated Language Processing*, New York, John Wiley.

N. Chomsky (1957) *Syntactic Structures*, The Hague, Monton.

N. Chomsky (1965) *Aspects of the Theory of Syntax*, Cambridge, Mass., MIT Press.

E. G. Coffman and J. Eve (1970) 'File Structures using Hashing Functions', *Communications of A.C.M.*, **13**, pages 427–436.

A. C. Day (1972) *FORTRAN Techniques with Special Reference to Non-numerical Applications*, Cambridge University Press.

I. Flores (1969) *Computer Sorting*, Englewood Cliffs, N.J., Prentice-Hall.

J. M. Foster (1970) *Automatic Syntactic Analysis*, London, Macdonald; New York, American Elsevier.

J. F. Friedman *et al.* (1971) *A Computer Model of Transformational Grammar*, New York, American Elsevier.

A. L. George (1959) *Propaganda Analysis*, Evanston, Ill., Row Peterson.

O. P. Holsti (1968) *Content Analysis for the Social Sciences and Humanities*, London, Addison Wesley.

R. J. W. Housden and R. T. Kujawa (1971) 'EASNAP—an on-line system for Arts students', *Computer Bulletin*, **15**, 8, pages 295–299.

M. P. Iker and N. I. Harway (1965) 'A Computer Approach towards the Analysis of Content', *Behavioral Science*, **10**, pages 173–182.

International Computers (1969) *'Find 2' Inquiry System*, London, ICL.

A. Kaplan (1943) 'Content Analysis and the Theory of Signs', *Philosophical Science*, **10**, pages 230–247.

A. Kent (1971) *Information Analysis and Retrieval*, New York, John Wiley.

R. A. Langevin and M. F. Owens (1964) 'Computer Analysis of the Nuclear Test Ban Treaty', *Science*, **146**, pages 1186–1189.
H. P. Luhn (1959) *Keyword in Context for Technical Literature* (*KWIC Index*), IBM, New York (amongst other publications).
J. Lyons (Editor) (1970) *New Horizons in Linguistics*, Harmondsworth, Penguin.
J. W. Marchand (1961) 'German Syntax Patterns' in H. P. Edmunsen (Editor), *Proceedings of the National Symposium on Machine Translation*, London, Prentice-Hall International.
C. T. Meadow (1967) *The Analysis of Information Systems*, New York, John Wiley.
F. Mosteller and D. L. Wallace (1964) *Inference and Disputed Authorship: The Federalist Papers*, Reading, Mass., Addison-Wesley.
S. M. Parrish and J. A. Painter (1963) *A Concordance to the Poems of W. B. Yeats*, New York, Cornell University Press.
G. Psathas (1968) 'The General Inquirer—Useful or Not?', *Computers and the Humanities*, **3**, pages 163–174.
A. M. Rees and D. G. Schultz (1967) 'Psychology and Information Retrieval' in G. Schechter (Editor) *Information Retrieval—a critical view*, London Academic Press, pages 143–150.
P. J. Stone *et al.* (1966) *The General Inquirer—A Computer Approach to Content Analysis*, Cambridge, Mass., MIT Press.
P. J. Stone *et al.* (1968) *The Users Manual for the General Inquirer*, Cambridge, Mass., MIT Press.
A. S. Tauber (1967) 'The Facts of Life about Man-Machine Interaction' in A. Kent *et al.* (Editors) *Electronic Handling of Information*, London, Academic Press.
B. C. Vickery (1968) 'The Raw Material of Retrieval' in K. Samuelson (Editor) *Mechanised Information Storage, Retrieval and Dissemination*, Amsterdam, North Holland.
P .F. Windley (1960) 'Trees, Forests and Arranging', *Computer Journal*, **3**, pages 98–88.

Further reading

The collections of papers edited by E. A. Bowles (1967)—*Computers in Humanistic Research*, Englewood Cliffs, N.J., Prentice-Hall and R. A. Wisbey (1971) *The Computer in Literary and Linguistic Research*, London, Cambridge University Press, provide useful introductions to some of the applications covered in this chapter.

For extensive basic treatments of the computational techniques involved see Kent (1971) and Meadow (1967).

I. Flores (1969) is a more advanced treatise which includes the detailed problems of using tapes and discs efficiently.

O. R. Holsti (1968) provides a comprehensive review of applications of quantitative text analysis.

D. E. Hays (1967) *Introduction to Computational Linguistics* (London, Macdonald; New York, Elsevier) is an excellent and clear introduction to this field.

6 Computer simulation

The previous two chapters have introduced the computer as an assistant to work which is predominantly inductive in character. As a third area of application, we now turn to the use of computers in theory development, as a means of representing and manipulating models of social processes. In this way the social sciences can gain a facility for a kind of experimentation, using theoretically derived models, which renders redundant many previously held positions regarding the desirability or possibility of cumulative empirical theory.

The term 'simulation' has been loosely used as a means of grouping a variety of gaming and modelling methods as a 'tool' of research (Guetzkow, 1962). Here we are concerned with the use of the physical system of the computer to represent some model of the real world, however conceived. The more general role-playing exercises to which the same generic term is often applied are beyond our scope here, as are models which find expression in other media than by running a computer program. While not denying their use in social science, we contend that computer models are usually more rigorous and consequently more fruitful. This is because a model must be fully specified to be computable, and its successful construction is an indication of the self-consistency of the theory on which it is based. Computerisation forces a holistic conception of the problem in question, yet the effort of model-building can also illuminate deficiencies in conceptualisation of detailed relationships.

In general, simulation may be used deductively, as a means of testing the consistency of a given theory, or heuristically, as a guide to inductive theory-building. Finally, some computer models are more easily and explicitly manipulated than others.

Model-building

Formally, we can say that some system A is a *model* of another system B, if some theory of A, $T(A)$ is also a theory of B. Models are abstractions of the theoretically important characteristics of the real system to be studied, and vary considerably in detail according to the degree of accuracy with which they are required to approximate to reality. The first basis for classifying models is thus their degree of abstraction. Representations can be thought of as ranged along a continuum between one-to-one correspondence between the theoretical and real systems, or *isomorphism*, through degrees of similarity to the general behaviour of the real system, or *homomorphism*. We can broadly distinguish 'iconic' models, which attempt a direct representation, as with an architect's wooden scaled-model town, and 'analogue' or 'symbolic' models which use abstract symbols to achieve an equivalent effect (Ackoff and Sasieni, 1968; Chapter 3). It may be satisfactory to include 'black boxes' in the model too, to represent processes which are either little understood except in behavioural terms, or which are unimportant to a particular study of the overall system. For most purposes homomorphism is sufficient as a basis for simulation experiments, and isomorphism is practically unattainable for complex or weakly conceptualised systems. In any case, it is easily shown that the accuracy of an aggregated model is not necessarily much less than that of an isomorphic one (Ashby, 1956; Section 6/16).

In Chapter 2, we noted the use of analogue computer components to provide a direct physical form for a theoretical system. The various digital simulation languages mentioned in Chapter 3 also provide for the linking together of standard components, this time of a software kind, and some are effectively similar in use to the 'patching' of an analogue computer to represent a model. Digital computers cannot match the speed of analogue machines in simulation, but may well be used for tasks in which analogue or hybrid hardware would be strictly more suitable. This is because of their availability, and relative ease of programming for a non-mathematical user.

One of the attractions of a modelling approach is that even if little or no experimental or observed data are available about a certain kind of social behaviour, it is still quite feasible to begin at a conceptual level. If consistent predictive propositions can be formulated from a suitable set of assumptions, the behaviour of a model can be studied using a computer program. Some applications to mathematical modelling discussed below are of this kind. Most situations are, however, intermediate. Some kinds of behaviour in the real system to be simulated are reasonably well documented and understood. Others may be subject to speculation. The great advantage of computer modelling is the possibility for experimentation with the speculative parameters to study the behaviour of a complex conceptual system under different assumptions.

A second useful distinction is between closed and open systems. The components of a system, its variables, may be conceived as endogenous, if they are entirely interdependent, or exogenous, if they are determined by factors outside the scope of the particular model. Simulated systems may thus be more or less open, according to the extent to which their variable values are generated inside the system itself, or subject to external manipulation.

In addition, variables can be related together in a deterministic or a stochastic, or probabilistic, way. Which conception is applicable depends very much on the state of knowledge and theory about a particular relationship. Computer modelling is probably the only medium which can represent really complex probabilistic relationships for systematic study, especially when relationships are recursively defined and evaluated over simulated time. The behaviour of such models is often in principle unpredictable until a simulation program is run on the computer.

We will consider next how such variables can be treated using a computer, and then return to the representation of dynamic systems in which time is a variable.

Monte Carlo technique

Certain problems are found to defy attempts at rigorous mathematical analysis, but can be shown to be adequately solvable by the introduction of a concept of randomisation. From this, particular numerical solutions can be obtained even when direct experimental methods would not be feasible. For example, queuing theory is a branch of the mathematics of probability which studies the characteristics of congestion in systems which are subject to random flows. The same mathematical concepts cover queues for service at the post office counter as traffic delay or waiting periods at the car-wash. Ideally, a mathematical solution might be preferred, but since the theory still does not extend beyond a few idealised systems, in practice a decision to provide more facilities would have to depend on a simulation or on work-study. This type of problem is not common in the social sciences, but can be handled very conveniently by the IBM General Purpose Systems Simulator (GPSS) described briefly in Chapter 3. This provides for the direct modelling of processes which involve the movement of units of traffic through a network of transactions, and could readily solve otherwise intractable queuing problems by recording what happens to the simulated flow.

In the most general case, estimates of the limiting behaviour of a physical system can be evaluated by averaging a series of repeated events in which variations are assumed to be random. The term 'Monte Carlo technique' was coined in 1944 by John Von Neumann and S. Ulam to express an approach to some computational problems associated with the atomic bomb project at Los Alamos laboratory, but a similar idea is encountered in classical probability theory in the Buffon needle problem. If a needle is dropped 'randomly' on a floor made up of parallel boards, the proportion of times it hits one of the cracks between boards will be $2/\pi$ if the length of the needle is exactly half the width of each board. Another example, for which the derivation can be more briefly explained, supposes that darts are thrown 'at random' at a circular board of one foot diameter, inscribed in a square with side also one foot. In the long run, darts should hit the board itself with a frequency proportional to the ratio of areas. That is, the proportion will be the area of the circle ($\pi \times \text{radius}^2 = \frac{1}{4}\pi$) divided by the area of the square ($=1$). The expected proportion of darts inside the circle is therefore $\frac{1}{4}\pi$ (Sahlin, 1968).

All this depends on a rather problematic concept of randomness, which must be better specified. Von Neumann and Ulam applied the roulette wheel analogy, from which we could re-define the dartboard example by drawing co-ordinate pairs for the notional darts from pairs of runs of a suitably divided wheel. The application of computers to this conception made possible a high-speed electronic realisation of such a process, and served to reawaken interest in the theory of probability on which it is based. A recent textbook on elementary statistics has even used Monte Carlo simulation to attempt an intuitively satisfying demonstration of several concepts of sampling and statistical estimation (Lohnes and Cooley, 1968).

Pseudo-random numbers

Analogue computers can contain electronic generators of 'white noise', and the machine used in Britain for monthly premium bond number selection is a purpose-built electronic random number indicator (Tocher, 1963; pages 50–67). Two possibilities are open when only digital hardware is available. Either a set of numbers tabulated by other specialised equipment can be input as required, or some form of deterministic 'psuedo-random' number generation must be used to produce sequences which will satisfy statistical tests based upon appropriate assumptions about randomness and probabilities.

A method suggested by John Von Neumann in early Monte Carlo applications takes the middle digits of an initial number, squares them, and repeats the process in sequence to produce successive terms of a sequence. For example, if a series of three-digit 'random' numbers is required, an initial value of, say, 397 is squared to produce 15920. The middle three digits are taken as the first number in the generated sequence, 592, and are squared to yield the next, and so on in an iterative process.

A simple FORTRAN program using integer arithmetic might read

```
N=M**2/10
K=N/100
M=N-K*100
```

This takes an initial value of M, squares it and removes the first and last digits to give the next value of M in the sequence. But the middle-square method is clearly unsatisfactory when any very small number is generated, since the sequence is in danger of reaching a limiting value of zero. The process will begin to cycle as soon as the same number as the initial value is generated. It can, in fact, be shown that for a given radix r a maximum of r^{2p} possible p-digit numbers can be generated before cycling.

The reproducibility of these sequences makes it possible to re-run a computer model for the same set of pseudo-random behaviour but with different parameter values. It is as though an historical process could be repeated changing only the factors in which significant alternatives seem to exist, to investigate in a quasi-experimental way the causal structure of the past. This feature of digital simulation introduces the possibility of controlled experimentation on a social science model of any kind. Events which can be regarded statistically as randomly generated can be reproduced exactly by taking the same initial value as the start of a pseudo-random sequence.

Most experiments employ a congruential method to generate pseudo-random sequences. The general form of a commonly used multiplicative generation rule is

$$x_{n+1} = L \,.\, x_n \text{ (Modulo } M\text{)}$$

in which the modulus M is used to truncate or scale the next term of the series to a suitable size, and the multiplier L can be selected to maximise the number of terms of the series (K) before repetition begins since

$$L^K \text{ is the same as } 1 \text{ (Modulo } M\text{)}$$

(x_n Modulo M stands for the remainder after x_n has been divided by P giving the largest possible integral result)

FORTRAN instructions for a multiplicative congruential series might read

```
X=125·0*X+1·0
X=AMOD(X,16384·0)
X=X/16384·0
```

which is equivalent to the function used in the POP2 example in Fig. 5.5. Here, the standard function AMOD is used to give the remainder of the division of the first of its arguments by the second. Given a suitable initial value for X, successive applications of these instructions would produce a series of pseudo-random real values uniformly distributed between 0 and 1·0. The choice of multiplier and modulus usually depends on the particular computer used, if the period is to be maximised (Naylor *et al.*, 1966; pages 47–57).

Sequences of numbers generated in this way satisfy many statistical tests for 'randomness' of behaviour. These include uniformity of distribution, the relative absence of autocorrelation over various intervals, and the absence of sequences or 'runs' of various lengths which might constitute unwanted influences on simulated behaviour. In general, congruential methods behave well under such tests, although their investigation continues. Their important advantage is their reproducibility and mathematical definition, combined with behaviour which passes most requirements for 'randomness'.

Uniformly distributed values can be converted to other kinds of distribution by suitable transformations. Discrete probabilities to correspond to some empirical distribution are easily obtained by testing the range of a generated number. To simulate a dice throw, for example, this is divided into six equal intervals, and the resultant value depends upon the division into which the particular value falls.

Continuous probability distributions are sometimes more difficult to obtain, although there are convenient expressions for most commonly encountered statistical distributions (Naylor *et al.*, 1966; pages 68–118). One general method is to obtain the cumulative frequency distribution, and apply its inverse as a transformation to a set of uniformly distributed values, to produce a set of numbers with the required distribution. This is because, using P to stand for probability and $F(y)$ for the cumulative frequency distribution,

$$P(F^{-1}(x) \leqslant y) = P(x \leqslant F(y)) = F(y)$$

Two illustrations

As an initial example, Fig. 6.1 is a flow chart for a simulation of a version of the board and dice game Snakes and Ladders. The simulation is completely determined by the board structure, and moves from square 1 to square 100 are made according to throws of a dice. The probability of landing on any particular square at a given move also depends on the penalties and rewards of the snakes and ladders which connect certain pairs of squares. A Monte Carlo simulation of the game illustrated in Fig. 6.1 terminated after a mean of 51 moves in 100 runs. Figure 6.2 is a histogram of these

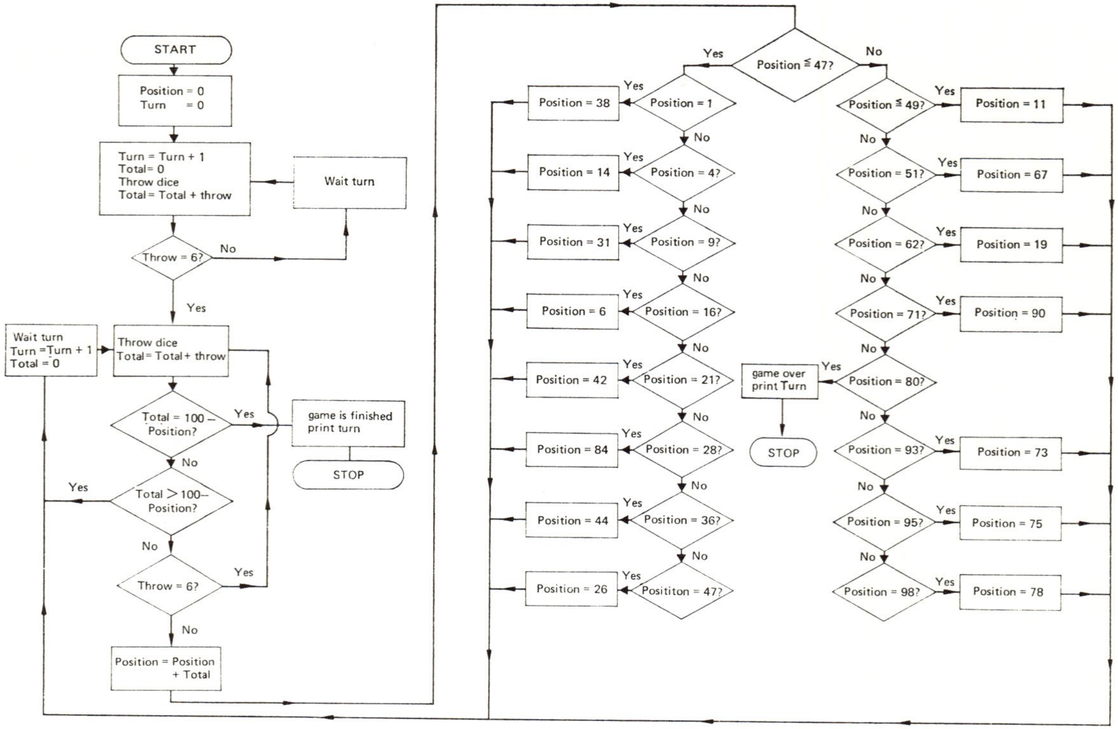

Fig. 6.1 Flow chart for the simulation of 'Snakes and Ladders' Notice the reduction in work achieved by the first decision box of the tests for the presence of snakes or ladders at the current positions. Further similar subdivisions of the test logic would produce a more efficient program. The version shown here generated the game frequencies shown in Fig. 6.2.

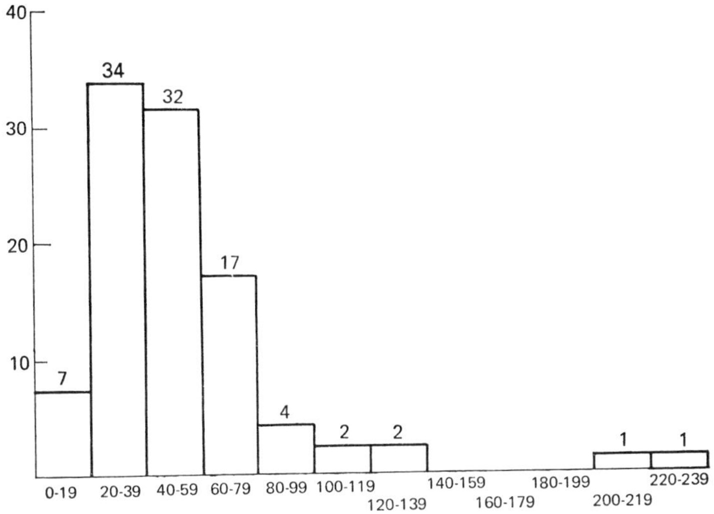

Fig. 6.2 Results of 100 simulated games of snakes and ladders. A histogram of the distribution of 100 repetitions of the simulated game outlined in the flow chart of Fig. 6.1. Games ranged between 11 and 24 moves, with a median of 44.

results, in which the shortest game was 11 moves and the longest 224. While 100 games is not sufficient for very accurate estimation, it is clear that a game on this board is most likely to take between 20 and 39 moves, which should be within the patience of its players, and this conclusion, at least, suggests a use for the investigation.

In fact, because the game is completely determined, an analytical solution can be calculated for any particular board design, and suggests a most likely game of 26 moves for a similar example to ours. The histogram for the simulation method also approaches the theoretical distribution obtained by analysis (Bell, 1972; pages 175–181).

As this example suggests, simulation can sometimes be found to serve as mathematics for the man in a hurry, and as a rather inelegant, if often convenient, substitute for analytical rigour.

Monte Carlo techniques become indispensable when the problem considered still eludes mathematical analysis. A well-known problem in the theory of voting and social choice involves the situation in which the individual preference orders of those engaged in voting yield a cyclical result. To illustrate the difficulty, suppose there are three people voting on three different policies, x, y, z and that xp_iz means that the i-th person prefers policy x to policy z. Then if the three preference orderings are

$$x\,p_1\,y\,p_1\,z$$
$$y\,p_2\,z\,p_2\,x$$
$$z\,p_3\,x\,p_3\,y$$

simple majority voting between pairs of issues could produce a collective vote of two to one in favour of any of the three issues, depending upon the order in which they are presented. The theoretical difficulty is that no clear collective choice can be reached if individual preferences are all to be respected. This is, in fact, a special case of Kenneth Arrow's 'general possibility theorem' in social choice, which proves the existence of similar intransitivity for any system of determining collective preferences by the aggregation of complete individual preference orderings. Among many attempts to avoid the difficulty caused by such cyclical majorities, the suggestion has been made that their probability may not, in practice, be very great, so that the theoretical possibility of deadlocks need not be taken too seriously. Nevertheless, despite the existence of some specific results, achieved by the enumeration of possible combinations of orderings for different numbers of voters and issues, no general formula has yet been found to express those probabilities. For this reason, Pomeranz and Weill have applied Monte Carlo methods to the enumeration of what can be regarded as samples of possible preference patterns, generated at random. Theirs is not the first attempt to model this particular process, but seems to be the most accurate when compared with some of the known exact probabilities (Pomeranz and Weill, 1970). From 15000 simulated preference orders they estimated the probability of cyclical majorities for voting patterns involving between three and thirty-seven voters choosing between up to forty issues. It appears, for example, that the probability of deadlock rises from ·05, for the case described above, to ·80 for the largest combinations of voters and issues in this simulation. However, when thirty-seven vote on three issues, the estimated probability was still only ·09, which is probably a tolerable level in practice.

In this way the Monte Carlo method, applied to an otherwise

intractable problem, helps to support one possible pragmatic argument for reducing the scope of the Arrow theorem (*cf.* Pattanaik, 1971).

Dynamic behaviour

Computer simulation also provides a convenient method of studying the dynamic behaviour of system models. We earlier discussed the essential difference between analogue and digital computers, in the representation of mathematically continuous variations in value. Although a digital computer cannot perform exact numerical differentiation and integration of functions over time, an adequate approximation can usually be achieved by making the discrete time intervals involved as short as a particular problem requires. In a large-scale model with many interactions of variables, problems of the stability of digital discrete-function approximations sometimes arise. We will return to this after considering some simpler kinds of application.

A common element in a simulation is the inclusion of some kind of time-counter, which is incremented during a computer run by units representing the minimum periods which are of theoretical interest. In the next example, a simple count was kept of a series of iterations, each representing the activity of one day. The selection of incremental values and the specification of the particular model determine whether the time-scale approaches 'real-time' or is only a scaled version to represent time units in a simulation run. If an exact parallel in time-scale is intended between the computer model and some process in the real world, it must be regulated according to the internal clock which most computers contain. This can be interrogated by a program instruction as necessary. Clearly, though, if scaled time is used in the model, a few seconds of computer time can be used to study years of simulated events.

The following example again applies the Monte Carlo method, this time to a simple business problem which involves a kind of time-scale. It is a variant of the newsboy problem (McMillan and Gonzalez, 1965; Ackoff and Sasieni, 1968; pages 63–64) for which a simple complete solution exists by maximising expected profits under an estimated demand distribution. A shopkeeper sells at 25 pence per box fresh strawberries which he purchases from a grower at 5 pence per box. Unsold strawberries deteriorate and are a total loss. By taking demand over a period of 20 days the empirical distribution is calculated as follows:

Sale	Frequency	Probabilities
0	1	0·05
1	3	0·15
2	6	0·30
3	5	0·25
4	3	0·15
5	2	0·10
Total	20	1·00

The mean daily sale is 2·6, but the distribution is skewed. By calculating a matrix of conditional profits, multiplying by the assumed demand probabilities and then summing the expected values for each stock purchase strategy, it is quite simple to calculate the greatest expected value under uncertainty as 42·5 pence per day. This corresponds to a daily purchase of four boxes (Smith *et al.*, 1969; pages 53–61).

The maximum profit under certainty is 52 pence, so that perfect information is here worth an extra 22% profit. However, the strawberry season is short, and the shopkeeper is accustomed to a decision rule which avoids this calculation. He simply buys one box more than he sold the previous day, and never more than five boxes a day. How much does this cost him in lost profit, assuming demand is still distributed as estimated previously? A simulation model is not difficult to construct, and can easily be used to test the sensitivity of different decision rules to changes in the actual demand distribution.

Profit depends upon sales and the number of boxes purchased for sale each day, so that these relationships determine the model:

$$\text{Cost} = \text{Purchase} \times 5$$
$$\text{Profit} = \text{Receipts} - \text{Cost}$$
$$\text{If Demand} > \text{Purchase, Profit} = (\text{Purchase} \times 25) - \text{Cost}$$
$$\text{If Demand} \leqslant \text{Purchase, Profit} = (\text{Demand} \times 25) - \text{Cost}$$

In our simulation, Demand values are generated from a pseudo-random sequence, and the decision rule is that

$$\text{Purchase} = \text{Yesterday's Demand} + 1$$

However, If Yesterday's Demand = 5, Purchase = 5

The mean profit for a thousand simulated days was 38·6 pence on a mean outlay of 17·4 pence, compared with 41 pence for the optimal policy of buying four boxes every day, which requires a daily outlay of 20 pence. The strawberry season is short, so the shopkeeper may well be quite satisfied with a buying rule which stands up quite well. Other policies and other demand distributions could be tried by changing the parameters of the simulation.

Experimental design

The results of simulation experiments can be analysed in a similar way to the results of any other kind of experiment. Controlled variation in different parameters of a computer model can be used to test the sensitivity of the model to those changes, and can uncover causal relationships between variables. In this work, established principles of experimental design apply, and need not be discussed here.

However, one point of using a computer model is to study systems of a complexity which makes other approaches uneconomic or otherwise not feasible. In this case, it is frequently found that simple experimentation is too costly in computer time to permit exhaustive examination of the behaviour of the model. In some of the examples to be discussed later, this aspect of the problem has proved intractable, and results are reported which do not permit of detailed causal analysis in the traditional sense. Guidelines can be found in sampling theory to permit the kind of trade-offs between computing costs and acceptable degrees of accuracy in statistical estimation using the results with which social scientists are already familiar in the field of social surveys. At the simplest level, statistical theory can be applied to determine the number of computer runs, regarded as independent samples, which would be needed to obtain a required degree of accuracy of estimation of a given parameter. Monte Carlo methods can be very expensive of computer time, since the accuracy of an estimate is generally proportional to the square of the number of computer runs made. For a series of n independent samples, the estimates obtained for the mean M of a given quantity have a variance of σ^2/n where σ^2 is the variance of the parent population. If the sampling process can be stratified in terms of some attribute of known theoretical relevance to a later analysis, it is possible to reduce the overall sample variance by the exclusion of the variance between strata for which sample means are different. This improvement in the accuracy of the estimate of the population mean from a total sample of the same size n is approximately equal to

$$\frac{\sum n_i(m_i - m)^2}{n^2}$$

where n_i and m_i are strata sample sizes and means. Thus, the greater the spread of the values of strata means, the better is the estimate obtainable.

A useful alternative is the method of *antithetical variables* in which a succession of pairs of computer runs is used to estimate the mean of a response variable. The second run of each pair uses the exact inverse of the pseudo-random number sequence used in the first. Because the variances of pairs of sample responses are equal, their means can be used directly to estimate the overall mean value:

$$M = \frac{1}{2n} \sum_{i=1}^{n} (m_i + m'_i)$$

This illustrates further the advantage of using uniformly distributed pseudo-random numbers to represent stochastic variables.

These and similar methods are necessary to try to reduce the number of computer runs in a simulation experiment to an economic level (Naylor, 1969; Tocher, 1963).

Varieties of simulation

The structure and notation of models varies according to the area of study and the ingenuity and imagination of the modeller. Some further illustrations in the next few pages will indicate something of the range of possibilities which have already been explored.

1. Models using transition probabilities

A number of computer modelling attempts in social science have treated their problem as a stochastic process of some kind. That is, one in which the model changes its behaviour in a series of discrete steps, in a probabilistic way. The model itself is specified in terms of the probabilities of transition from one state to another, and its simulation requires the evaluation of these to trace its long term behaviour.

Among the simpler processes studied in this way is the flow of accused prisoners through the various steps of a judicial system, for which the transition probabilities from one type of court or trial hearing to another are empirically measurable. This kind of model was constructed for the U.S. President's Commission on Law Enforcement and Administration of Justice, and based on delays in the court system of the District of Columbia for the year 1965. Simulated offenders can be generated according to known probabilities for different classes of offence, and their course through the model judicial system can be recorded. On the basis of the results or of experimentation with the model to improve the rate of flow at identifiable 'bottlenecks' in the system, the recommendations can be made for the reduction of delays in the real system for dispensing justice (Martin and Norman, 1970, page 112).

The project called Simulmatics attempted to simulate the behaviour of the American electorate in the presidential elections of 1960 and 1964 (Pool *et al.*, 1965). The behaviour modelled was conceived as fully determined and no random variables were involved, but a computer was needed to make possible a very large number of individual calculations. Since the work involved initially some projections of past behaviour into the future, a popularisation of the attempt in *Harper's* magazine termed it 'make-believe on mathematical principles'.

The idea was relatively simple. For the 1960 election, the electorate was simulated using a classification of voter types based upon seven background variables: region, city size, socio-economic status, sex, religion, ethnic group, and political identification by party. This led to 480 different voter types who were found to occur with sufficient frequency in the 50 and in some cases 65 national sample surveys covering the period 1952–1958 which were available to the project. For each significant voter type 52 'issue clusters' were also identifiable from the same aggregated opinion polls, so that the distributions of attitudes were known for such dimensions as Anti-McCarthyism, Pro-Labour attitudes and attitudes to Catholicism and Communist China. The distributions of the 480 voter types was also known for the 32 states outside the South, so that simulated state electorates could be constructed with the correct statistical compositions. Models of the behaviour of each voter type were constructed under assumptions about their probable reaction to issues which were thought likely to arise in the election campaign. The consequences for voting behaviour were then calculated. The most notable investigation, given the candidacy of J. F. Kennedy, applied the theory of 'cross pressure' to the effect of anti-Catholicism among the voters. If the Catholicism of the Democratic contender became a campaign issue, as it later did in fact by Kennedy's own choosing, what consequences could be foreseen?

The theory predicts that those who find themselves torn between competing claims upon their loyalties, Protestant Democrats, for example, in this situation, will withdraw from the situation by abstention to resolve the problem. Others may change their political allegiance if the attraction of another factor were strong enough. For each of the 480 voter types, it was possible to identify nine different cross-pressure situations, made up of the combinations of two threefold classifications, into Catholics, Protestants and others, and into Republicans, Democrats and others. Taking two of these cases, for Protestant Republicans it was assumed that the following relationships would hold in the absence of cross pressure.

V_K (the vote for Kennedy) = 1956 preference for Stephenson x correction for non-voting

V_N (the vote for Nixon) = 1956 Eisenhower preference x correction for non-voting

The non-voting correction was expressed as $(1-P_{35})$, where P_{35} is the known proportion of non-voters for the voter type.

For Protestant Democrats, estimates were needed of the following proportions by voter type:

	Anti-Catholic	Not Anti-Catholic
Democrat	*a*	*b*
Republic	*c*	*d*

The ratio ad/bc was known to be approximately 0·6. Denoting the party preference proportions from the 1958 opinion polls as P_{58} and Q_{58} and using a double non-voting correction because of the hypothesised cross-pressure, the model defined

$$V_K = (P_{58} - a)(1 - 2P_{35})$$
$$V_N = (Q_{58} + a)(1 - 2P_{35})$$

An estimate for a was obtained by solving the equations

$$a+b=P_{58}$$
$$a+c=P_{14}(P_{58}+Q_{58})$$
$$ad/bc=0{\cdot}6$$

in which P_{14} is the total Anti-Catholic proportion. Since only relative percentages were required, the multiplier d could be arbitrarily chosen. It was also necessary to estimate the proportion of Catholic Democrats who were Republican voters in 1958, but could be expected to switch to Kennedy, together with Catholic Republicans and Independents.

The computer was used to solve these and similar equations for the simulated state electorates. One finding was that the gains of making religion a campaign issue outweighed the losses. The adequacy of the simulation could be judged later by the correlation of ·82 between the simulated and actual proportions voting for Kennedy in the 32 states, compared with ·53 between these results and the latest opinion polls used which were taken in October 1958. Clearly there had been some success in modelling the changes which took place over two years, but the methods used for this and the following presidential election raise difficulties of interpretation. Even in an apparently simple theoretical model it is very difficult to tell which assumptions are essential and which dispensable to the results achieved. However, the use of a limited number of different assumptions and estimated values did reveal the relative effectiveness of the use of the simple religious cross-pressure model we have briefly discussed. The advice given by the simulation group to Kennedy's staff conceivably influenced the course of the campaign they set out to simulate.

Cross-pressure theory formed the basis for another simulation of individual behaviour, in which the interest was likely response to reward or punishment for social actions. A simulation called HOMUNCULUS (Gullahorn and Gullahorn, 1965) generated 'answers' to a questionnaire about preferred behaviour, based on the mean values obtained from an actual survey and a theory about the generation of the real data. Monte Carlo methods were applied to produce the behaviour of simulated individuals. Three reference groups were assumed to exert conflicting pressures on members of an organisation. These were the executive committee of the relevant trade union, the members' of the employees' social club, and the management. The hypothetical question posed attempted to uncover the point of relative pressure at which an employee who is both an officer of the employees' club (a channel to job promotion) and the union members' chief steward will resign one job. Both cannot be done properly in the time available. The model constructed allowed for different combinations of encouragement from the three reference groups. Taking average values for the Monte Carlo simulation drawn from survey data using the same questions, HOMUNCULUS used a simple theory of decision rules based on expected costs and rewards to produce results close to the answers given by the actual employees. Its construction was thus an attempt to demonstrate and validate a theory of role conflict by producing simulated questionnaire data for comparison with observed results.

A similar but more general computer system has recently been described in which artificial data could be generated, or existing data could be 'explained' by trying to match them by simulation. The method can be used to produce simulated social survey data based on models of a structural or causal kind. The separate components considered are population growth and change, sampling procedures, opinion formation, opinion change and opinion measurement. Random errors of measurement can be simulated, so that the effects of different methods of statistical analysis can be tried out on a generated data set. The system's designer tried initially to meet a challenge to produce simulated survey answers which would be undetectable as such, but suggests a wide range of possible applications to the study of research designs and statistical models (Harper, 1972).

More interesting results are achieved when more than one transition between possible states is possible, and the stochastic process is simulated over a succession of time intervals. We are then dealing with a discrete state approximation to a continuous dynamic system.

As a general notation, consider the transition probability matrix

$$\mathbf{p} = \begin{bmatrix} \mathbf{p}_{11} & \mathbf{p}_{12} & \cdots & \mathbf{p}_{1n} \\ \mathbf{p}_{21} & \mathbf{p}_{22} & \cdots & \mathbf{p}_{2n} \\ \cdot & \cdot & \cdots & \cdot \\ \mathbf{p}_{n1} & \mathbf{p}_{n2} & \cdots & \mathbf{p}_{nn} \end{bmatrix}$$

in which n is the number of possible states of the system,

$$\mathbf{p}_{ij} \geqslant 0 \text{ and } \sum_{j=1}^{n} \mathbf{p}_{ij} = 1{\cdot}0$$

A special type of stochastic process, which can be simply analysed, is called a Markov process. This is a sequence of events with outcomes defined by an initial probability distribution, determining the initial states, and a stochastic matrix as defined above. If $\mathbf{p}_t$ and $\mathbf{p}_{t-1}$ are row probability vectors at times t and $t-1$, in a Markov process

$$\mathbf{p}_t = \mathbf{p}_{t-1}\,\mathbf{P}$$

that is, the transition probabilities at any time depend on the immediately prior state of the system and a fixed stochastic matrix.

Of course, processes can be conceived in which the matrix **P** changes over time, but the main method of studying them consists of reducing them to the simpler Markov form.

In a two-state system, with the probability matrix

$$\begin{bmatrix} 0{\cdot}3 & 0{\cdot}7 \\ 0{\cdot}4 & 0{\cdot}6 \end{bmatrix}$$

the changes of moving from state 1 to state 2 in one step are 7 in 10 and of staying in state 1, 3 in 10. Similarly, the probabilities of these moves after two steps can be shown as follows:

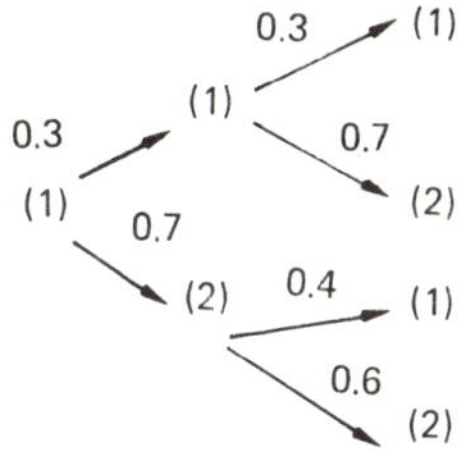

so that the probability of moving from (1) to (2) after two steps is

$$0{\cdot}3 \times 0{\cdot}7 + 0{\cdot}7 \times 0{\cdot}6 = 0{\cdot}63$$

This matrix might represent the prospects for Mr T. Leaf, a house-breaker, of being caught or evading detection in a series of his criminal activities. The more offences he commits, the greater his chance of arrest.

Readers familiar with matrix multiplication will recognise that the second-order transition probabilities are given by

$$\mathbf{P} \times \mathbf{P} = \mathbf{P}^2$$

and in general the probabilities after r steps are given by $\mathbf{P}^r$ for a Markov process.

Some Markov processes tend to limiting probabilities after a large number of steps, in which case there exists a matrix $\mathbf{Q}$, with identical row vectors, such that $\mathbf{P}^r \to \mathbf{Q}$ as r becomes large. If all row vectors are the same, it ceases to be important which state is the starting point for a transition, and the process is in equilibrium. For a particular process, attempting to solve the matrix equation

$$\mathbf{Q} = \mathbf{QP}$$

which must, by hypothesis, hold for the matrix $\mathbf{Q}$ if it exists, gives the limiting values for a particular case (Mapes, 1971; pages 28–32). For the two-state process above, these are

$$\begin{bmatrix} 0{\cdot}36 & 0{\cdot}64 \\ 0{\cdot}36 & 0{\cdot}64 \end{bmatrix}$$

so that in the long run just over one-third of all Mr Leaf's activities will result in his apprehension by the police. A further state would, of course, be needed to account for his chances of conviction and punishment.

If some $p_{ij} = 1{\cdot}0$, the relevant state is said to be absorbing, since no further transition is possible once it has been reached. For example, a stochastic matrix of the general form

$$\begin{bmatrix} p & q & 0 & 0 & \dots & 0 & 0 \\ 0 & p & q & 0 & \dots & 0 & 0 \\ \cdot & \cdot & \cdot & \cdot & \cdots & \cdot & \cdot \\ 0 & 0 & 0 & 0 & \dots & p & q \\ 0 & 0 & 0 & 0 & \dots & 0 & 1{\cdot}0 \end{bmatrix}$$

can represent a 'random walk' through a series of states, ending eventually in the last. Such states can be incorporated into a Markov model as destinations of items in a theoretical process. Simple models of this kind have been used in physics to describe the random motion of particles which are subjected to a number of collisions with known probabilities. In sociology, they have also been applied to the study of career patterns and labour mobility. Here the predicted probabilities of promotions after a given number of years have been fitted quite successfully to observed patterns in organisations.

Transition probability models are particularly suited to the limited level of measurement often achieved in the social sciences. Often, all that can be done is to count the number of people held to have a particular attribute at a given time, and to develop hypotheses about the probability of their changing from one state to another. By taking observations at arbitrarily fixed intervals, some quite simple mathematics can be applied to modelling dynamic systems and computers can be used where necessary to investigate the properties of large matrices in Markov processes.

Hayes-Roth and Longabaugh have recently described a computer system designed to facilitate work on sequential interpersonal interaction in these terms. This enables the construction of Markov models to any required order, and investigates the components of predictability in the resultant situation. The original application of REACT has been to modelling the interaction of a nurse and a schizophrenic patient as a second-order process. The system applies multivariate uncertainty statistics which determine for a nominal criterion variable what for continuous variables is discovered by analysis of variance. Again, the computer is used as an aid in the refinement of theoretical models which can be related to observed human behaviour (Hayes-Roth and Longabaugh, 1972).

2. Models of 'continuous' dynamic processes

As an example of an approach to dynamic systems modelling using the mathematics of continuous variation, the work of Forrester, Meadows and others for the Club of Rome Project on the Predicament of Mankind attempts nothing less than the simulation of the world's ecology. We will consider this in terms of the general method developed by Jay Forrester for the study of 'system dynamics', which is not suited to queuing problems, but can be adapted to a range of economic and other problems to which a differential equation notation has usually been applied.

Sets of equations can represent continuously variable systems in terms of the rates of change, or differential coefficients, and the

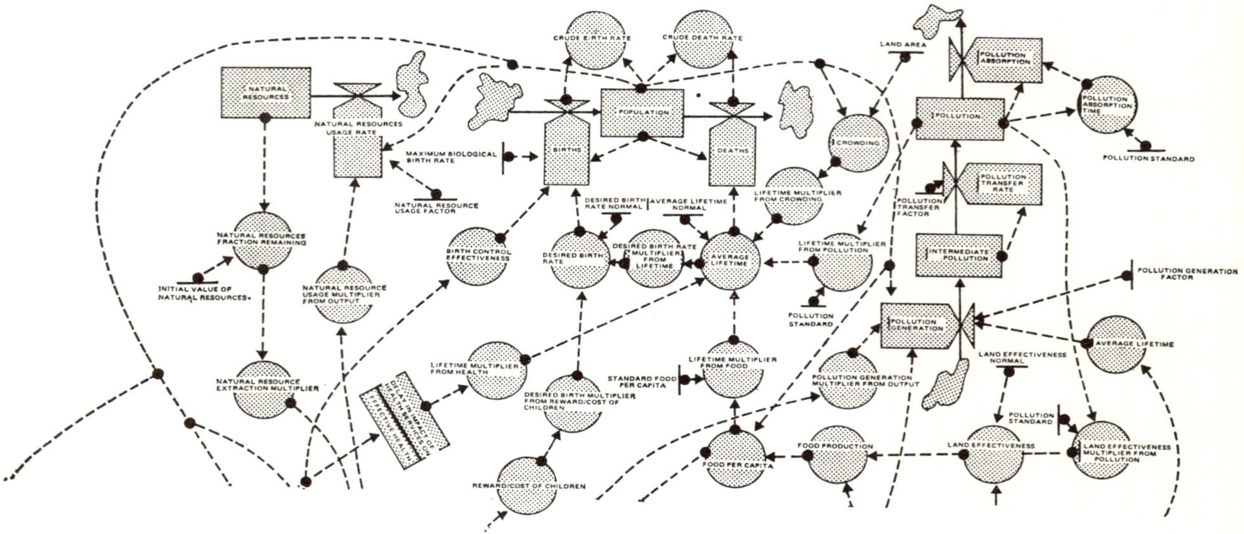
NATURAL RESOURCES
NATURAL RESOURCES USAGE RATE
MAXIMUM BIOLOGICAL BIRTH RATE
NATURAL RESOURCE USAGE FACTOR
NATURAL RESOURCES FRACTION REMAINING
INITIAL VALUE OF NATURAL RESOURCES
NATURAL RESOURCE USAGE MULTIPLIER FROM OUTPUT
NATURAL RESOURCE EXTRACTION MULTIPLIER
DELAY IN IMPACT OF HEALTH SERVICES ON EFFECTIVE HEALTH
CRUDE BIRTH RATE
CRUDE DEATH RATE
POPULATION
BIRTHS
DEATHS
BIRTH CONTROL EFFECTIVENESS
DESIRED BIRTH RATE NORMAL
AVERAGE LIFETIME NORMAL
DESIRED BIRTH RATE
DESIRED BIRTH RATE MULTIPLIER FROM LIFETIME
AVERAGE LIFETIME
LIFETIME MULTIPLIER FROM HEALTH
DESIRED BIRTH MULTIPLIER FROM REWARD/COST OF CHILDREN
REWARD/COST OF CHILDREN
STANDARD FOOD PER CAPITA
LIFETIME MULTIPLIER FROM FOOD
FOOD PER CAPITA
LIFETIME MULTIPLIER FROM CROWDING
CROWDING
LAND AREA
LIFETIME MULTIPLIER FROM POLLUTION
POLLUTION STANDARD
POLLUTION GENERATION MULTIPLIER FROM OUTPUT
FOOD PRODUCTION
POLLUTION ABSORPTION
POLLUTION
POLLUTION ABSORPTION TIME
POLLUTION STANDARD
POLLUTION TRANSFER RATE
POLLUTION TRANSFER FACTOR
INTERMEDIATE POLLUTION
POLLUTION GENERATION FACTOR
POLLUTION GENERATION
AVERAGE LIFETIME
LAND EFFECTIVENESS NORMAL
POLLUTION STANDARD
LAND EFFECTIVENESS
LAND EFFECTIVENESS MULTIPLIER FROM POLLUTION

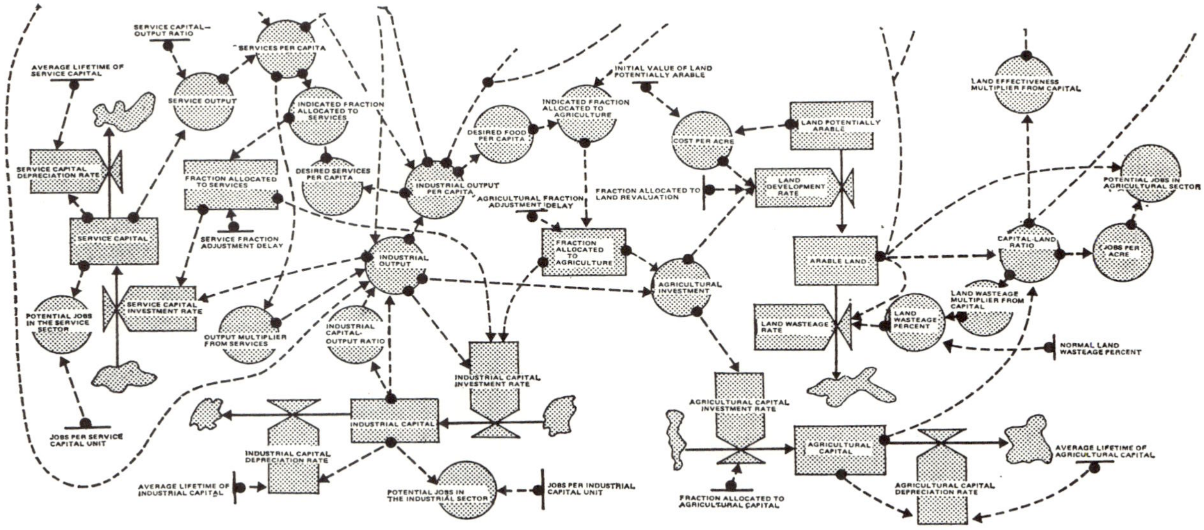

Fig. 6.3 The Dynamo World 3 Model. This flow chart uses the Dynamo system conventions. The rectangles represent 'levels' (population, pollution, etc.). Valves (figures suggesting fire extinguishers) are 'rates' (birth rate, death rate, etc.) which directly determine levels. Circles are 'auxiliaries', used in the calculation of rates. Clouds (irregular figures) represent levels which are not considered in the simulation (e.g. the source of human life before birth and its destination after death). The chart is adapted from a version in *The Futurist*, August 1971, pages 140–1, and is in fact an intermediate model between Forrester (1971) and Meadows *et al.* (1972).

interdependencies of variables over time. Equivalent equation sets can be constructed for any system which can be shown as a flow diagram, and their numerical solution reveals the behaviour of the system. The flow diagram approach is simple to understand, but a mathematical notation is needed for an analytical solution (Tocher, 1963; Ashby, 1956). But for those who find the more conventional use of differential equations mathematically forbidding, Forrester's notation is a rigorous yet simple alternative.

It uses a computer system called DYNAMO (Pugh, 1963) which allows for the modelling of dynamic information-feedback systems in sets of finite difference equations. Simulated system behaviour can be displayed as a plot as shown in Fig. 6.4. The two basic concepts are the 'level' and the 'rate'. Rates are measured over time and depend only on levels, or system variables, and constants. Level equations are integrations of relevant rates over a given solution time-interval. This system is indifferent to the relative difficulty of linear and non-linear equations, since it produces only specific numerical solutions and is not concerned with a general mathematical analysis.

Figure 6.3 uses simplified DYNAMO flow-chart conventions to specify the third World Model developed by the M.I.T. system dynamics group. This embodies statements, observations and assumptions about the world system interrelating concepts from the study of demography, economics, agriculture and technology to produce a multiple feedback model. The basic variables concerned are population, natural resources, capital investment, agricultural production and pollution.

As an illustration of the reasoning and notation involved, we can consider an earlier specification of the population sector of the model (Forrester, 1971; pages 19–30). The diagram below uses DYNAMO conventions for the basic feedback loops concerning population. Uncontrolled positive feedback loops produce exponential growth, that is a curve with a constant rate of increase, while negative feedback results in an eventual convergence on a limiting value, in this case zero population. The dynamic effects of multiple feedback relationships of any complexity are essentially unpredictable except in particular numerical solutions.

This flow diagram indicates that the population level is in a negative feedback loop with the death rate and a positive loop with the

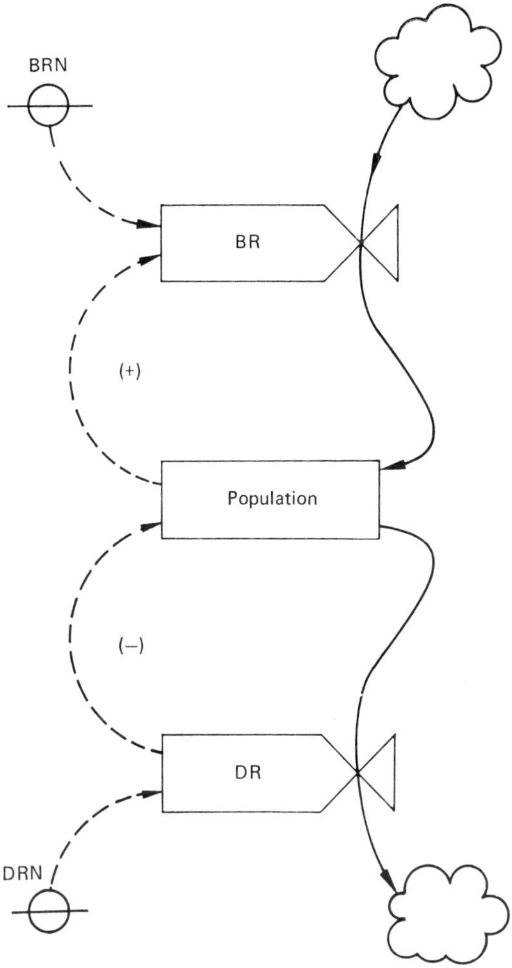

birth rate. These rates in turn depend on constant population norms and the current level of population. Other controls are not shown here. Translating this into equation form, we get for population (p) the 'level equation'

$$P.K = P.J + (DT)(BR.JK - DR.JK)$$

and for the birth rate the 'rate equation'

$$BR.KL = (P.K)(BRN)(\times \text{ some multipliers not shown here}).$$

Since DYNAMO is a digital simulation system, it clearly cannot be evaluated continuously. Instead the equations are numerically solved, beginning from some initial values, by evaluating rate equations and level equations in alternation, for the duration of simulated time required. The accuracy of this approximation to continuous variation depends partly on the solution interval *DT*, which Forrester recommends as less than half the shortest first-order feedback delay in the model, but for computing economy not less than 0·2 of this period. Depending on the transfer functions involved, too large an incremental value causes instability in digital simulation. Variables which should display smooth change curves, instead oscillate around their 'true' values, and the compounding of such effects destroys the value of the simulation. Digital simulations must therefore be designed very carefully, to reduce the possibility of this source of error (Forrester, 1968; Section 6.2).

BRN, the 'Birth Rate Normal', is measured as a fractional increase per annum. Guesses at *BRN* and *DRN* were made using the observed world population increase from 1900 to 1970, values of 0·04 and 0·028 were used (consistent with a net increase of 1·2% per annum), but the model proved relatively insensitive to the precise assumptions used. The values chosen for constants of this kind seem not to be very critical. Here, the characters are subscripts indicating time periods, and these relationships are both first-order feedback loops. Longer delays are used in some other equations. The multiplier *DT* represents the minimum solution interval, and in this case was taken as one year of simulated time. Quite simply, the level equation denotes that population at time *K* is population at time *J* times the difference between births and deaths in the interval *JK*. The usefulness of the model clearly depends on the adequacy of each of its constituent definitions and assumptions.

The behaviour of this model has been fully described elsewhere (Forrester, 1971; Meadows *et al.*, 1972), but we should note some of the conclusions reached from its partial analysis as an indication of the reasoning applied. The model itself was based on current opinions about the constituent relationships. In its unmodified form, it has been used to demonstrate the consequences of exponential growth curves in a finite world. As soon as the limits to growth are reached in the simulation, the same behaviour which for centuries has been regarded as acceptable or even desirable becomes, in a space of 50 years or so, disastrous for the system. Various 'obvious' solutions were also simulated, without materially changing the nature of this behaviour. Given much improved birth control, a population collapse is caused by increased pollution from industrialisation. Controlling pollution emission by itself produces a similar collapse through exhaustion of food supplies or raw materials for industry. In each case, the collapse seemed to be followed by the beginning of another period of rapid growth in population and economic activity. The time-scale shown in Fig. 6.4 is of little

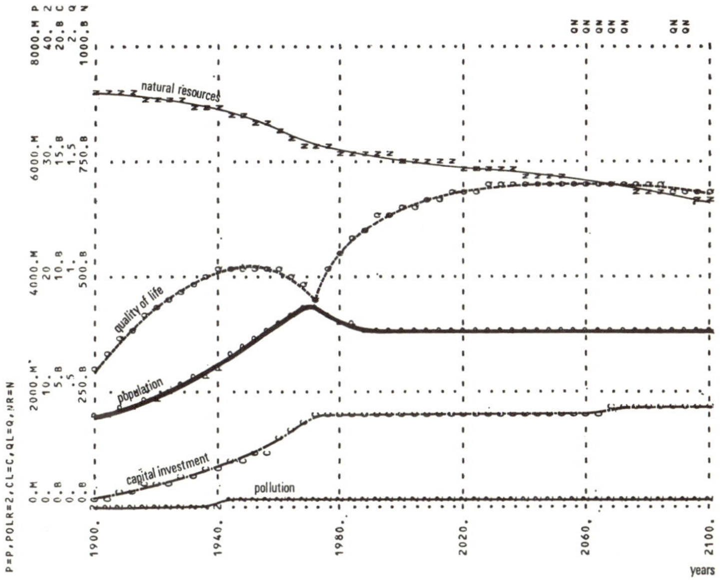

Fig. 6.4 Equilibrium conditions in the World 3 Model. This figure reproduces a typical DYNAMO system plot of a dynamic simulation. Different 'levels' are superimposed on the same grid to show system behaviour in graphic form. The overlap of curves is indicated in the margin at two points.

This simulation of the World 3 Model, shown in Fig. 6.3, assumes that in 1970 the capital investment rate is reduced by 50%, pollution generation is reduced by 50%, natural resource usage is reduced by 75% and food production is reduced by 20%. These conditions leave a stable population to enjoy a high quality of life. The abrupt change in population level is clearly visible, as unchecked exponential growth is halted.

The print-out is adapted from *The Futurist*, August 1971, page 150.

importance, compared with the demonstration in other runs that partial changes in one sector of the model did not prevent the characteristic oscillation of the population level. Figure 6.4 shows one computer run which produced a reasonably stable world system. By reducing the birth rate, together with the level of industrial activity and pollution generation, the world crisis displayed by other simulations is replaced by a very gradual decline in the system's activity, which appears to be in relative equilibrium for the foreseeable future.

Experience with this dramatic world simulation tends to reinforce Forrester's contention that the behaviour of complex social systems is often counterintuitive, and that verbal or partial models can prove seriously misleading about the true pattern of system behaviour. However, using these flow diagrams and computer language, any social scientist can begin to relate this type of model to his own area of interest. Even at this global level of aggregation, it is possible to interpret some levels already incorporated in terms of theories of social mobilisation, political participation, modernisation, and the growth of governmental activity (Harbordt, 1971). The model illustrated here already makes use of a measure of 'the quality of life' which is somewhat persuasively defined in terms of the economic surplus for consumer goods and leisure. Whatever the merits of this particular work, the methods used do seem to offer a very powerful tool for some kinds of social science modelling.

Criticisms of the World Model are twofold. First, some of the assumed constants or feedback structures may be criticised. The very broad 'pollution' level is not very clearly conceptualised, but has been modified to make some rather generous concessions to technological optimism. In the work so far reported, objections of this kind do not seem to alter the fundamental mode of behaviour of the simulated system. Nor do those engaged in the project claim theirs is the only possible set of equilibrium conditions. They do take their experiments to illustrate how little time mankind has left to take some kind of corrective action before the crisis to which the system appears to be headed. The continuing search for 'better' alternatives seems a reasonable answer to those critics who suggest that the analysis of causal links in the model has been incomplete, subjective, and therefore unscientific. To change the basic 'crisis' behaviour of the model seems to require that its assumption of finite world resources be modified to allow for continued economic growth indefinitely (Freeman, *et al.*, 1973).

A more serious source of objections to these findings is the high level of aggregation of the model. The version of Fig. 6.3 has disaggregated some sectors from a preliminary model which contained only five global variables. More recent work in a similar vein for the International Labour Organisation in Geneva has abandoned the pollution and natural resources sectors, but represents population structure in a much more sophisticated way. The age structure is simulated in this work, as are rural/urban distributions and some complex fertility assumptions.

It is still very difficult to interpret the results in policy terms. This again stems from the global nature of the simulation. Some investigations have been made of the effects of phased changes in, for example, birth control policy, but the level of aggregation clearly masks politically very important distinctions between the rich industrial nations and the rest. A graphic demonstration of the behaviour of the world system is a relatively poor guide to the consequences of only partial geographical application of the recommended policies.

More formally, the effect of a high level of aggregation of variables is to increase the bandwidth time delays in a particular channel of flow in the model. The greater the diversity of items in the channel, the wider is the range of the individual delays, and the less sharply defined is the response to any individual delay source. This provides a basis for arguing that the overall behaviour of an over-aggregated model may be misleading, depending, of course, on the purpose for which it is intended. In the area of the world system simulation, there is unlikely to be much agreement anyway about estimates of some poorly measured or conceptualised relationships.

3. *Man/machine simulations*

Some uses of a computer in simulation involve one or more human actors in the system. The object may be either to provide a simulated environment for a study of human behaviour or to train a subject to perform a simulated task. These two aims are often combined in an exercise which is justified by its heuristic value, in a field which is not sufficiently understood or is otherwise unsuitable for an all-computer model. The best known and most dramatic applications are aircraft flight simulators, in which computer graphics and computer-controlled full-scale models are used to train pilots or investigate aircraft behaviour (Fetter, 1965; pages 46–69). Here, computer control of a 'real-time' simulation makes it possible to replicate situations at a fraction of their cost using actual aircraft. In the official enquiry into the BEA Trident crash near London Airport in June 1972, the Commissioner, Mr Justice Lane, who was a former Squadron Leader in Wellington bombers, took the controls of a simulator as part of his investigation of evidence. In reconstructed runs using flight data from the crashed plane, he was able to 'save' and 'crash' the aircraft by different pilot action.

In the social sciences, a number of conceptually similar simulations have been constructed, with similar possibilities for use. Some have an explicit instructional purpose. At the Institute of Development Studies of the University of Sussex, for example, a development game has been devised to simulate economic decisions in a developing country. The core of the game is a mathematical model of the economy which is affected by international trade but not by interactions among the players. The economy produces five sorts of goods, food, raw materials, a manufactured consumer good, machinery and land reclamation. The primary factors of production available are labour, land and machines. These and other population and economic parameters are defined at the outset of a particular 'play', as is the structure of ownership in the different sectors of the economy. Players may attempt to control the development of the defined economy by manipulating 23 different variables, including taxation changes and prices paid by marketing boards for various raw materials and primary products. Over a couple of days, decisions can be simulated for ten to twelve sets of allocations ('years') during which time the players experience the limitations of the structure given to them initially, and the results of their own actions. A computer is used to calculate the consequences of each set of economic decisions. In common with other similar simulations, the development game is intended to refine the basic economic model as well as to provide a convincingly complex environment for training decision-makers (Bell, 1970; Williamson 1970; Coplin, 1970).

Computers have also played parts in games based on more structured role-playing by the participants. Characteristic of these are exercises derived from the Inter-Nation Simulations at Northwestern University, directed by Harold Guetzkow (Guetzkow *et al.*, 1963). These originally involved controlled role-playing by pairs of players representing the decision-makers of five competing 'nations'. Of each pair, one represented internal and the other external concerns. The national government made economic allocations to consumption investment and defence from resources given at the outset. Resource use was subject to given rules which defined the effect of each allocation. Constitutional and political constraints were placed on decision-makers, to represent limits to the government's tenure of office and ability to take decisions. These were quantified into variables expressing the people's satisfaction with the level of national security provided, and the threshold below which there was risk of revolution. Chance intervened at several levels, in the form of calculations made by those running the simulation, after each play period. For example, the probability of staying in office was given by the expression

$$l - R = (l - S)(l - \alpha)$$

in which R stands for a retention-of-office function, S for satisfaction and α the decision latitude allowed. Later developments of the INS approach have introduced improved computer models of domestic economic and political processes, and added a level of international diplomacy to the human role-playing. Each team later included a 'citizen', who might develop international contacts of a non-political character independently of the national government (Smoker, 1968).

4. Behaviour simulation and artificial intelligence

We have been concerned so far with computer models designed to represent behaviour which is, at least in principle, thought to be replicated by some real system. In this case a simulation model is intended to make sense in itself as well as produce reasonable behaviour. In some approaches the object is mainly to produce useful outputs, in which case the theoretical status of the model as a strict simulation of some real system is not of interest (Apter, 1970). The difference is well summarised by the different objectives of machine intelligence and simulation of human behaviour. In the first, the aim is to construct a problem-solving machine in the most efficient way possible, but in the second the processes used to produce the desired behaviour are related much more directly to theories about human thinking. For example, a computer programmed to play a game of chess will employ a problem-solving algorithm which is probably of a very different kind from the methods used by a chess master, although both play chess to a very high standard. The computer program usually conducts an elaborate evaluation of all available moves and possible responses projected as far into the future as the machine's capacity and speed will allow, and then chooses what appears to be the best move at the time. Human players work more intuitively and in terms of overall positions of relative advantage. It would be surprising if no human insights were transferred into designs for intelligent machines, but even in the simple case of the game of noughts and crosses an efficient machine algorithm bears little resemblance to any conscious human behaviour in making decisions about moves (Bell, 1972). On the other hand, a well-known computer problem-solving system, the General Problem Solver (Ernst and Newell, 1969) was intended to embody theories of human thought processes to produce generally 'intelligent' behaviour. The object was not only to obtain convincing solutions but also to study the precise stages by which a solution is achieved.

The General Problem Solver carries out a constrained search for possible manipulations of objects in its task environment which will help to reduce the difference between the current state and a desired goal. It requires definitions of objects and states, together with rules for recognising the difference between two states. Transformation rules must also be defined which can be applied to objects to bring them closer to the specified goal. The program essentially breaks down objectives into sub-goals and systematically searches for a beneficial transformation until a higher goal is reached or the process fails. It reports each stage of its reasoning for later study. Unlike some problem-solving programs, GPS does not 'learn' from its mistakes but works within a definitional system to solve logical problems in a general way. It has been able to find algorithms to solve such apparently unrelated problems as the game of noughts and crosses and the generation of magic squares. Other systems have successfully solved algebraic equations and produced logical proofs of some originality.

The theoretical status of such computer programs is of major interest. Although determined by the program instructions, their behaviour, whether it is regarded as simulation or artificial intelligence, is essentially unpredictable each time they are run. Unless its construction is closely related to theories of actual behaviour, it is very difficult to interpret what has happened when a heuristic program succeeds in reaching a given goal of performance (Simon, 1971).

The overall distinction drawn here is perhaps not very clear-cut. Some earlier examples may have suggested that it would be difficult to sustain if the terms of a theory of behaviour are not easily operationalised, except by simulations. This would be true of psychological models which derived behaviour from psychoanalytic propositions instead of more conventional variables and relationships drawn from experimental psychology. Even if the results of a simulation of this kind related well to available empirical data, the nature of the constructs used in the model would still raise criticisms of its credibility (*cf.* Moser *et al.*, 1970; Blackmore 1972).

The scope of computer simulation

The great attraction of simulation clearly lies in its ability to handle otherwise intractable models as a matter of routine. For large models, a computer is also indispensable. It would not be particularly helpful in a short introduction to develop a more exhaustive categorisation of models, many elements of which would find no representation in social science work to date. Instead, we will draw on some more general concepts in the study of systems, to suggest something of the power and potential range of computer simulation as a research method.

Systems-thinking of varying degrees of precision now pervades the social sciences. While the origins of all concepts which are based on some notion of system are not always the same, the success of a general mathematical systems theory in control engineering has clearly reinforced attempts to adapt its terminology in other fields. Even though, for example, functional explanation in sociology and anthropology is of different intellectual descent, the tendency is nevertheless, in areas originally influenced mainly by their concept of system, to adapt ideas of feedback and control from the more developed theory (Emery, 1969; Russett, 1966; Kuhn, 1966, Chapter

3; Cohen, 1968). James G. Miller has recently drawn together a wide range of research findings on human organisations in terms of the concepts of general systems theory, which at least demonstrates the possibility of a transfer of terminology (Miller, 1972). Leaving aside questions of the plausibility of verbal theories of this kind in particular formulations, it does seem that even many radical positions which are severely critical of the 'technocratic' implications of a systems approach nevertheless share many of its holistic and synthetic characteristics (Roszak, 1970). If systemic relationships can be suitably specified, computer modelling can provide a method of studying their consequences. In this sense, given an appropriate awareness of the relevant techniques, simulation becomes as ethically neutral as any other research apparatus.

One major problem to be overcome has already been discussed in connection with the World Dynamics studies. Interesting theoretical designs which can be given some kind of verbal treatment tend to be too complex for available computational resources unless conceptual units are aggregated. The extent of aggregation in a mathematical or symbolic model offers consequent opportunities for critics to argue that the sense of an originally less precise verbal formulation has been distorted in the process. Computer models in themselves, if they are fully explained, need not prove more controversial in this respect than any others. Some further support can be drawn from the theory of decomposability of systems, which suggests that partial models can still retain important behavioural characteristics when treated in isolation. A system which is in reality made up of functionally independent subsystems can be called completely decomposable, since any subsystem can be adequately studied in complete separation from the others. Beginning from this definition, Simon and Ando have shown that a system which nearly approximates to complete decomposability will in the short run behave as if its subsystems were quite independent. More important, in the long run, the relative behaviour of a subset of variables will still be preserved by using an assumption of complete decomposability. The lesser property of decomposability is defined as the existence of an ordering of variables, so that those in any given subset are functions of their own past values and of variables in any lower-order subset, but not of any higher. For a system which only approximates to this condition it can again be shown that the relative dynamic behaviour of a subset of variables can be studied without reference to higher-order subsets and taking into account the influence of the lower (Fisher and Ando, 1962). This provides a rationale for the study of partial systems.

Nor need we consider simulation as confined to numerical variables, or to systems whose states are defined in numerical terms. Numbers can of course be attached to structures which are not theoretically numeric in conception. We have seen how some plausible sociological propositions and consequences can be incorporated into the MIT World Model without departing from the use of numerical variables as indicators of the behaviour of the system.

Analogues of human perceptual models of their environment are of major interest in the investigation of problem-solving and artificial intelligence. Any attempt to model cognitive and evaluative processes thus involves the use of some stored configuration of symbols as a data structure. Some notations may use matrices of the distances between perceived objects over Euclidean or some scaled attitude space to manipulate such structures. Equally, recent work in psycholinguistics has been concerned with the mapping of domains of meaning by the construction of a 'subjective lexicon'. Here the structure of interest is a verbal one, expressed in terms of semantic attributes and relationships.

A more general notion of system can now be stated, where variable states are conceived as data structures, which may be expressed in any form which the subject of study seems to require. Peter Abell has expressed the characteristic form of the functional proposition in social theory in the following way. The assertion X has a social function Y in system S, involves three related entities, the function serving variable X, the served function variable Y, and the system S, which is itself composed of variables of these two types, and can be referred to as a functional system (Abell, 1971; pages 134–136). A functional proposition asserts more than a mere statistical co-variation between X and Y, but introduces an assertion of negative feedback into its explanation of a sequence of events. In a formal sense, served functions cannot (generally) be identified, but in cases where *intention* is involved a feedback model can be constructed to link goal states, purposes and the associated behaviour. In this way the task of explanation becomes one of specifying the nature of a set of two or more system states and the rules of transition between them. Abell himself has pursued the idea of structured social relationships in terms of the mathematical theory of graphs, and as a basis for a theory of structural balance and strain (Abell, 1970). The conditions for stability can still be investigated even if it is not possible to look at served functions in terms of intentions, but here we will pursue the case of the purposive system.

Explanations in terms of purpose may be broadly distinguished as 'teleological' if the behaviour is held to be goal-seeking or 'mnemic' if it is held, as in the case of the exercise of memory, to be a reaction to some prior events mediated by a conscious act of recall (Braithwaite, 1953; pages 319–341). Probably the most common treatment of these kinds of answer to the question 'Why?' has been to demonstrate that they achieve nothing which cannot otherwise be subsumed under causal laws and chains of events given a causal interpretation. Teleological explanation is quite widely held to be redundant, on these grounds, and the implication is that researchers should preferably seek causal relationships in the phenomena they study. This attitude has led to continuous controversy in various social sciences about the appropriateness of what is seen as a mechanistic view of behaviour. Many social scientists find explanations inherently unsatisfying which are necessarily partial and are not expressed in terms of human consciousness.

Ackoff and Emery have recently argued that there is no need to adopt this position, nor to regard causal explanation as the only form worthy of scientific consideration. If it is possible to deduce the results of a teleological argument from an equivalent set of causal arguments, it is equally possible to deduce sets of causal arguments from teleological theory. In general, it seems that economists have preferred to construct causal theories, which they then overlay and interpret with teleology. Sociologists and political scientists have concentrated more on the goal-seeking and subjective aspects of various system approaches. The idea of purposefulness in a system must be given a behavioural definition, but is still a more fruitful general approach than reliance on causality or less rigorous concepts of system (Ackoff and Emery, 1972).

In applying simulation methods to purposeful systems, we can clearly make use of some of the ideas about data structures encountered in the previous chapter. Some of the methods of representing structures in the computer's storage are equally adaptable as notations for the representation of non-numerical system states. Again, a computer programming language which can accommodate as a matter of routine some complex structures such as lists and trees of 'nested' lists is of great value. The POP2 language, for example, which was developed as a tool for work on machine intelligence, is based on a general concept of a data structure, with associated 'characteristic functions' for its manipulation. These include constructor, destructor, selection and updating routines defined for their class of structure. Standard language functions are available to manipulate lists, arrays, and pairs as a special case of a two-element list, as well as individual computer words. Other structures can be defined as required, together with their associated functions, while a standard function, 'DATAWORD', produces a value, usually a text word, which identifies the class of data structure associated with a particular variable name (Burstall *et al.*, 1971). A language with this capacity makes it possible to model very general information structures, and provides a notation for system states which are conceived in structural form and not as single-valued numerical variables.

Computers can also be applied directly to the elucidation of such structures. G. R. Kiss of Edinburgh University has developed a computer-controlled routine for 'recursive concept analysis' which employs some of the techniques discussed in the last chapter for the representation of structure in natural language information processing. The system is similar to 'free association' methods in which subjects identify concepts in a semantic or cultural category by responding to selected stimuli. The computer's questions are guided by the replies received to determine the next stimulus (Coxon and Jones, 1972).

In these ways, the highly rigorous tool of computer modelling can also be applied to investigations of subjective structures. Of course, the definition of their theoretical form ultimately depends on the creativity of the theorist who can make use of these methods.

The problem of validation

We have argued that a system which has been successfully modelled in a computer program has in a useful sense been 'explained', and that there is no reason to regard a set of causal laws as the only means of formulating an acceptable explanation. Also, in so far as the 'uniqueness' of social events has often been regarded as an objection to the possibility of systematic prediction in social science (Winch, 1958), simulation does seem to offer a means of exploring, by modelling and experimentation, just those features of particular events which are sometimes regarded as beyond justifiable speculation. Monte Carlo or other estimates of features of system behaviour are adequately rigorous and precisely defined, yet may permit investigation of otherwise inaccessible aspects of social probabilities in the broadest sense. It is not, then, an insuperable objection that the uniqueness of each event prohibits causal explanation except of a trivial kind.

As a means of convincing others of the 'explanation' offered by a model, there is a major, if rather trivial, problem of the comparative unintelligibility of the source of the model. The language of the explanation offered may be, in the strict sense, the language of the computer program which embodies it, since to replicate findings it might be necessary to re-create the exact configuration of computer and program from which the original set of results were obtained.

The greatest difficulty which must be acknowledged remains that of the acceptable *validation* of simulation results. It is quite easy to suggest that good simulation practice might include the following steps:

1. Formulate the problem and gather appropriate data on the real system.
2. Formulate the mathematical model. The computer program should not, ideally, be the only representation available of the theoretical relationships.
3. Write and test the computer model to remove program errors. Here, effects due to the particular program or machine must be eliminated, if possible.
4. Check the computer model against the real data to validate the model. The behaviour of the model must correspond to some known characteristics of the real system.
5. Use the computer model to make some predictions about the real system, which may later be tested or form a basis for policy decisions. This is necessarily an act of faith. British Petroleum, for example, used a model of 800 equations to maximise profit at all stages of its operation from extraction

to marketing. This worked so well to reduce the size of its tanker fleet that the company was badly hit by the closure of the Suez Canal and by the Six-Day War of 1967 (Calder, 1969; page 206).

Some of these stages would be inappropriate to some purposes, but concentration on the computer model without an attempt at specifying validation criteria would be seriously incomplete. The creative attractions of programming must not in the end be allowed to be a distraction from theory construction. Problems arise when the state of available theory, or measurement difficulties, makes the sequence outlined above impossible to carry out.

This is well illustrated by a large-scale simulation of international relations called TEMPER (Technological, Economic, Military and Political Evaluation Routine) (Clemens, 1968; Gordon, 1968; Forward, 1971, pages 100–104). This was developed between 1961 and 1965 on a military contract by the Raytheon Corporation, and provided for the simulation of relations between states ranging from Cold War manoeuvres to nuclear war. The model concentrates on international interactions, and makes no attempt to incorporate the effects of domestic political constraints on foreign policy. There are, however, a series of 'trade-offs' between military and other foreign and domestic expenditure of available resources, and the balance is determined by perceptions of the international situation. Within the military budget, allocations are made between different projects, in which quality can be weighed against quantity, and development against production costs. Military actions are further determined by the state of the model, and by 'enemy' actions.

States enter into alliances, depending on their past histories as allies as well as upon current conditions. TEMPER assumed a three-bloc world covering 13 land-conflict regions, so that the nations of the real world could be simulated in up to 39 nation-groups, according to their location and alliance sympathies. Sub-models represented the structure of psychological, economic, military and decision-making behaviour of nations, reacting in a rational way to events in a world situation which changed each week of simulated time. Each submodel contained subroutines to simulate quite complex processes within the state-decision process. For example, the psychological group covered communication distortions in perceptions and evaluations of possible threats in the current world situation. The model can be criticised at a number of levels, notably for its reinforcement of the three-bloc 'Cold War' outlook which seemed reasonable enough when the work began in 1961 but was soon overtaken by world events. Its purpose as a demonstration of the logical consequences of certain verbal theories has also been questioned, because the relation of simulated behaviour to the scenarios used as initial settings for simulations is still highly ambiguous. TEMPER provides a striking example of what can happen to a fully computerised simulation in an area where theory and criteria for validation are weakly defined. Apart from some readily admitted technical and financial difficulties in achieving a working simulation on this scale, its size and complexity make it difficult to study.

In much of its reported development the model seems to have been modified when its behaviour was thought unreasonable by the designers. When a run involving the United States intervention in a dispute between Cuba and a Latin American neutral nation found the USSR refusing aid to Cuba, the rules governing assistance to allies were reconsidered. Similarly, when an incident in the Arctic produced nuclear war between the USA and USSR, it was attributed to a 'distortion' in the model, which was consequently modified. Some 'unreasonable' effects were held to result from faulty translation of verbal propositions into the computer model, as when aggressive nations were found to be able to subdue others before they had time for military mobilisation.

The data base for TEMPER included some perceptions of the world situation gathered by questionnaire from a small sample of actual decision-makers in the United States. But judgement of its behaviour remains problematic, both in its internal structure and its correspondence with the real world.

Similar consequences can be expected when a model is very complex, or is constructed at the limits of the speed and memory capacity of the available computer. We have already noted that Monte Carlo methods can be very expensive if used too liberally as a substitute for mathematics, and it is not difficult to design simulation models which are prohibitively expensive to analyse in full. Indeed, the non-experimental nature of much social research virtually ensures that a convincing model will be expected to contain many variables and generate complex behaviour patterns (Beshers,

1968). If the cost of full analysis of the simulation model is consequently high, testing and validation must suffer. It may then be asked: What has been achieved by the effort of its construction? It is, after all, possible that use of a computer program instead of mathematics can introduce greater difficulties of analysis than those it was hoped to overcome (Diesing, 1971; pages 95–100). If all that we can conclude is that the behaviour of a model looks plausible, its explanatory power is rather limited.

The model may, of course, be said to have heuristic value, but ultimately validation in the real world must be the object. Two further purposes can, however, be served by a partial analysis of some kinds of model. One is to test the sensitivity of certain kinds of system behaviour to changes in some of its parameters. If the computer model is felt to be an accurate simulation of the real system a validly estimated set of input parameters can yield arguably valid results. This is a method to which econometricians have given a great deal of attention (Zellner, 1968). The other is to concentrate on the broad features of dynamic behaviour. Jay Forrester's work outlined earlier exemplified this approach, and Forrester has elsewhere developed the idea of basic modes of system behaviour which he holds to be the major object of study (Forrester, 1968; Ashby, 1956). Complex dynamic systems with multiple feedback loops can still exhibit broad behavioural features, such as equilibrium, the oscillation of some variables or the rapid growth and collapse of others.

Despite these difficulties we hope to have shown something of the potential of rigorous simulation in social science. There is a danger that some theories may be trivialised to achieve a computer version, but enough has been said to demonstrate the challenge to ingenuity and imagination which the computer's facility for simulation presents.

References

P. Abell (1970) 'Some Problems in the Theory of Structural Balance: Towards a Theory of Structural Strain' in M. Lane (Editor) *Structuralism—A Reader*, pages 389–409, London, Jonathan Cape.

P. Abell (1971) *Model Building in Sociology*, London, Weidenfeld and Nicolson.

R. L. Ackoff and F. E. Emery (1972) *On Purposeful Systems*, London, Tavistock Publications.

R. L. Ackoff and M. W. Sasieni (1968) *Fundamentals of Operations Research*, New York, John Wiley.

M. J. Apter (1970) *The Computer Simulation of Behaviour*, London, Hutchinson.

W. R. Ashby (1956) *An Introduction to Cybernetics*, London, Chapman and Hall.

A. G. Bell (1972) *Games Playing with Computers*, London, George Allen and Unwin.

C. Bell (1970) 'A Development Game: Decision-Making in a Simulated Less Developed Economy' in R. H. R. Armstrong and J. L. Taylor (Editors) *Instructional Systems in Higher Education*, Cambridge Institute of Education, pages 127–134.

J. M. Beshers (1968) 'Substantive issues in models of large scale social systems' in J. M. Beshers (Editor) *Computer Methods in the Analysis of Large Scale Social Systems*, 2nd edition, Cambridge, Mass., MIT Press, pages 121–129.

W. R. Blackmore (1972) 'Some comments on "Computer simulation of a model of neurotic defence processes" ', *Behavioral Science*, **17**, pages 232–234.

R. B. Braithwaite (1953) *Scientific Explanation*, Cambridge University Press.

R. M. Burstall, J. S. Collins and R. J. Popplestone (1971), *Programming in POP2*, Edinburgh, The University Press.

N. Calder (1969) *Technopolis*, London, McGibbon and Kee.

W. C. Clemens Jr. (1968) 'A Propositional Analysis of the International Relations Theory in TEMPER—A Computer Simulation of Cold War Conflict' in W. D. Coplin (Editor) *Simulation in the Study of Politics*, Chicago, Markham, pages 59–101.

P. S. Cohen (1968) *Modern Social Theory*, London, Heinemann.

W. D. Coplin (1970) 'Approaches to the Social Sciences through Man-Computer Simulation', *Simulation and Games*, **1**, pages 391–410.

A. P. M. Coxon and C. L. Jones (1972) 'Occupational Cognition: Representational Aspects of Occupational Titles'—Project on Occupational Cognition, Working Paper No. 1, Edinburgh University, Department of Sociology.

P. Diesing (1971) *Patterns of Discovery in the Social Sciences*, Chicago and New York, Aldine Atherton.

F. E. Emery (Editor) (1969) *Systems Thinking—selected readings*, Harmondsworth, Penguin.

G. Ernst and A. Newell (1969) *GPS: A Case Study in Generality and Problem Solving*, New York, Academic Press.

W. A. Fetter (1965) *Computer Graphics in Communication*, New York, McGraw-Hill.

F. M. Fisher and A. Ando (1962) 'Two theorems on *ceteris paribus* in the analysis of dynamic systems', *American Political Science Review*, **56**, pages 108–113.

J. W. Forrester (1968) *Principles of Systems*, 2nd Preliminary Edition, Cambridge, Mass., Wright Allen Press.

J. W. Forrester (1971) *World Dynamics*, Cambridge, Mass., Wright Allen Press.

N. Forward (1971) *The Field of Nations*, London, Macmillan.

C. Freeman *et al.* (1973) 'The Limits to Growth Controversy', special issue of *Futures*, vol. 5, No. 1.

M. Gorden (1968) 'Burdens for the Designer of a Computer Simulation of International Relations' in D. B. Bobrow and J. L. Schwartz (Editors) *Computers and the Policy-Making Community*, Englewood Cliffs, N.J., Prentice-Hall, pages 222–245.

H. Guetzkow (Editor) (1962) *Simulation in Social Science: Readings*, Englewood Cliffs, N.J., Prentice-Hall.

H. Guetzkow, C. Alger, R. Brody, R. Noel and R. Snyder (1963) *Simulation in International Relations: Developments for Research and Teaching*, Englewood Cliffs, N.J., Prentice-Hall,

J. T. and J. E. Gullahorn (1965) 'Computer Simulation of Human Interaction in Small Groups', *Simulation*, **4**, pages 50–61.

J. T. and J. E. Gullahorn (1965) 'Some Computer Applications in Social Science', *American Sociological Review*, **30**, pages 353–365.

S. C. Harbordt (1971) 'Linking socio-political factors to the world model', Cambridge, Mass., Club of Rome Project on the Predicament of Mankind, System Dynamics Group, Massachusetts Institute of Technology (mimeo).

D. Harper (1972) 'The Computer Simulation of Sociological Surveys', *Behavioral Science*, **17**, pages 471–480.

F. Hayes-Roth and R. Longabaugh (1972) 'REACT: A Tool for the Analysis of Computer Transitional Behavior Matrices', *Behavioral Science*, **17**, pages 384–394.

A. Kuhn (1966) *The Study of Society—A Multidisciplinary Approach*, London, Tavistock Publications.

P. R. Lohnes and W. W. Cooley (1968) *Introduction to Statistical Procedures with Computer Exercises*, New York, John Wiley.

C. McMillan and R. F. Gonzalez (1965) *Systems Analysis: A Computer Approach to Decision Models*, Homewood, Illinois, Irwin.

R. Mapes (1971) *Mathematics and Sociology*, London, Batsford.

J. Martin and A. R. D. Norman (1970) *The Computerized Society*, Englewood Cliffs, N.J., Prentice-Hall 1973 edition: Harmondsworth, Penguin.

D. H. Meadows, D. L. Meadows, J. Randers and W. W. Behrens (1972) *The Limits to Growth*, London, Earth Island, New York: Universe Books.

J. G. Miller (1972) 'Living systems: the organization', *Behavioral Science*, **17**, pages 1–182.

U. Moser, I von Zeppelin and W. Schneider (1970) 'Computer simulation of a model of neurotic defense processes', *Behavioral Science*, **15**, pages 194–202.

T. H. Naylor, J. L. Balintfy, D. S. Burdick, K. Chu (1966) *Computer Simulation Techhniques*, New York, John Wiley.
T. H. Naylor (Editor) (1969) *Symposium on the Design of Computer Simulation Experiments*, Durham N.C., Duke University Press.
P. K. Pattanaik (1971) *Voting and Collective Choice*, Cambridge University Press.
J. E. Pomeranz and R. L. Weill Jr. (1970) 'The Cyclical Majority Problem', *Communications of the Association for Computing Machinery*, **13**, No. 4, pages 251–254.
I. de S. Pool, R. P. Abelson (1965) *Candidates, Issues and Strategies: A Computer simulation of the 1960 and 1964 presidential elections*, Cambridge, Mass., MIT Press.
A. L. Pugh (1963) *DYNAMO Users' Manual*, Cambridge, Mass., MIT Press.
T. Roszak (1970) *The Making of a Counter Culture—Reflections on the Technocratic Society and its Youthful Opposition*, London, Faber and Faber.
C. E. Russett (1966) *The Concept of Equilibrium in American Social Thought*, New Haven, Yale University Press.
H. Sahlin (1968) 'The Monte Carlo Method' in D. B. Bobrow and J. L. Schwarz, *Computers and the Policy-Making Community. Applications to International Relations*, Englewood Cliffs, N.J., Prentice-Hall, pages 253–269.
H. A. Simon (1971) 'The theory of problem-solving', IFIP Congress Papers, **I**, pages 249–266.
C. W. Smith, G. P. Mead, C. T. Wicks and G. A. Yewdall (1969) *Management Information*, London, Pan Books.
P. Smoker (1968) 'International Processes Simulation: A Man-Computer Model' (Mimeo) Northwestern University.
K. D. Tocher (1963) *The Art of Simulation*, London, English Universities Press.
J. Williamson (1970) 'A Computer-Based Economics Game for Social Studies Instruction: International Balance of Payments', *Journal of Educational Data Processing*, **7**, pages 181–192.
P. Winch (1958) *The Idea of a Social Science*, London, Routledge and Kegan Paul; New York, Humanities Press.
A. Zellner (1968) 'Estimation of parameters in simulation models of social systems' in Beshers (Editor) *Computer Methods in the Analysis of Large Scale Social Systems*, 2nd ed., Cambridge, Mass., M.I.T. Press, pages 137–157.

Further reading

The most comprehensive introduction to simulation applications in social science are the papers edited by J. M. Dutton and W. H. Starbuck

(1971) *Computer Simulation of Human Behaviour*, New York, London, John Wiley. Similar collections which relate to more specific areas of study are Coplin (1968), S. S. Tomkins and S. Messick (Editors) (1963) *Computer Simulation of Personality*, New York, London, John Wiley, and B. G. Hickman (1972) *Econometric Models of Cyclical Behavior*, 2 volumes: N.B.E.R. Conference on Research in Income and Wealth—Studies in Income and Wealth No. 36—New York, Columbia University Press. See also T. H. Naylor (1971) *Computer Simulation Experiments with Models of Economic Systems*, New York, John Wiley. A good sampling of man/machine simulations is provided in Armstrong and Taylor (1970) and the same authors' *Feedback on Instructional Simulation Systems* (1971) Cambridge University, Institute of Education.

Further examples of general interest will be found in recent issues of the journals *Simulation and Games* and *Behavioral Science*.

On techniques, several fairly accessible textbooks are available, of which Tocher (1963) and Naylor *et al.* (1966) are probably the most useful. The latter draws its illustrations from economic and business applications.

Some impressions of the impact of computer simulation in other fields may be gained from S. H. Hollingdale (Editor) (1967) *Digital Simulation in Operational Research*, London, English Universities Press, and J. McLeod (Editor) (1968) *Simulation: The Dynamic Modelling of Ideas and Systems with Computers*, New York, John Wiley.

Two other books by Jay Forrester which incorporate the system dynamics approach are *Industrial Dynamics*, Cambridge, Mass., M.I.T. Press, New York, John Wiley, 1961, and *Urban Dynamics*, Cambridge, Mass., M.I.T. Press, 1969.

7 FORTRAN: an introduction

Earlier chapters have been concerned more with applications common to the social sciences than with the practical details of writing your own programs when necessary. Although increasing availability of packaged programs can take care of most problems calling for established statistical procedures, there are still many occasions when they will not be sufficient. As we noted in Chapter 4, problems arise if data have been coded for computer input in a format which is unacceptable to any of the programs to be used. It is, of course, always possible to record the data manually, at considerable time and expense, but much simpler to program the computer to do it. Cautionary tales are probably quite numerous. In one major research project of the authors' acquaintance, survey data were less than fully utilised for the temporary lack of a suitable program to accept their card format. The difficulties are greater but not insuperable if large amounts of data are held on magnetic tape files in an awkward form for access at the user's own installation. Underutilisation of data, is, of course, quite common in some kinds of social research, as in social surveys in which the amount of information gathered is simply too great for complete analysis. However, in the age of large-scale computer systems there is no reason why any researcher should be hindered by purely technical considerations, given some elementary programming skills. A large number of problems of file organisation or tabulation can be dealt with quite easily and efficiently by users with some knowledge of a higher level programming language, even if they have no intention of experimenting with their own more advanced applications.

This chapter is an introduction to programming in the most widely available language for scientific and mathematical applications. It is intended to offer some encouragement to further study by offering a short description of FORTRAN, together with some example programs illustrating its use. For aspiring computer scientists, the present approach is likely to be much too schematic to convey the full potential of the language, but for readers with more limited requirements, the range of instructions and syntax described should be sufficient for most purposes. The need for concise explanations means that we rarely repeat comments on any language features. The reader should try to be sure he has understood every example fully before he continues, turning back if necessary to revise earlier sections of the text. References are given for topics of which some prior knowledge is assumed.

As with most practical skills, FORTRAN programming is most easily learnt by practical experience, since the only way, in the end, to check whether a program will achieve the desired results is to try to compile and run it on a computer. The present account will, we hope, satisfy the curiosity of general readers interested in 'how it's done', and should otherwise be regarded as a preliminary to a practical course with computer access. A compiler with a good error-listing system will very effectively expose gaps in knowledge and confirm what has been learned.

Versions of FORTRAN

The FORTRAN project began in 1954 at IBM with the aim of producing a high level language suitable for mathematical and scientific applications on that manufacturer's hardware systems. The resultant language, FORTRAN II, was subsequently adapted, with many variations, in so many installations of different kinds that the need was felt for some authoritative standardisation, and a basic language definition was issued as standard X 3·9—1966—'FORTRAN IV' of the American Standards Association (since 1969, the American National Standards Institute). This version also formed the basis for the International Standards Organization's Draft

Recommendation 1539—Programming Language Fortran. Fortunately, it is possible to obtain glosses on these difficult definitions (National Computing Centre, 1970) which are invaluable as reference sources on the exact interpretation of statements in the language, and as a supplement to a particular manufacturer's or installation's own language description.

But because FORTRAN is a very widely implemented language, many different compilers exist which admit a variety of different variations in the form of estimations, which perform error diagnostics on source programs in a variety of ways and with varying efficiency, and which contain a large number of additional facilities to make the language more flexible and easier to write. Fortunately most compilers, whatever their own modifications to the vocabulary of the language, will admit a basic standard form as a subset of their own versions. Acceptance of the sometimes rather irritating restrictions imposed by using standard forms does carry the considerable advantage of making the transfer of programs between machines much more straightforward. While it is comparatively easy to write a program which will compile satisfactorily on a number of computers, it is much more important to ensure that its execution is the same everywhere, and is as intended. This is where standard FORTRAN conventions are a particularly useful safeguard against expensive errors when transferring programs between one machine and another.

Some preliminaries

FORTRAN was designed to use a very limited set of characters corresponding to the basic typewriter keyboard, plus a few special characters, commonly available on card or paper-tape punching equipment. In standard FORTRAN only the following characters may be used:

A to Z } alphanumeric characters
0 to 9 }

+	(
−	)
*	,
/	.
=	space

Note that, in some circumstances, a space is counted as a character. No other symbols can be used, except as part of character strings used only for purposes such as table headings. Additional symbols must, of course, be selected from those recognised by a particular computer and compiler.

Some conventions are useful when writing programs by hand or in ordinary type and these are suggested.

Ø = letter O to distinguish from 0 = zero
Ƶ = letter Z to distinguish from numeral 2
▽ = space

(I should always be distinguished clearly from 1 and the 'continental' 7 instead of 7 aids clarity)

Quantities

Quantities in FORTRAN are distinguished as variables and constants, according to whether they take a number of possible values during execution of the program or only one. A fundamental distinction must be made between different types of values, which can be mixed together only in very restricted circumstances. This difference of type arises from provision for holding data in different ways in the computer's store, mainly because it is more economical of storage use to allow a distinction than to treat all data in the same way internally.

The main types of quantities likely to be encountered are:

INTEGER
REAL
LOGICAL
TEXT

Some examples of constants of these basic types will show the difference.

INTEGER: The simplest type of numerical value, occupying one storage unit in the machine (that is, usually two bytes or one computer word); this is used for storing whole decimal numbers, for example, 10, 5020874. In FORTRAN these are distinguished from numbers having an integer *and* a fractional part, which are termed *real* numbers.

REAL: Real values are interpreted as decimal numbers with an integer part a decimal fraction part and an exponent part, sometimes not all explicitly expressed when writing constants. They may take a number of forms, each of which must be signed if the value is negative, and may be signed if it is positive. The most familiar form of a real decimal constant as it is written in calculations is 10·123. If the number is less than one, the integer part may be omitted, so that 123 is equivalent to 0·123. When writing constants, both of these forms may be followed by an exponent part, giving the power of ten to which the number is to be raised, e.g.

+0·123E3 is equivalent to 123·0
and −1·23E-2 is equivalent to −0·0123

Real values are held in the computer in two storage locations in a floating-point format, in which all numbers are reduced to a standard form equivalent to a decimal fraction and an exponent power of ten.

These restrictions of REAL and INTEGER types to one or two storage locations establish the maximum size of number which a machine is capable of holding in store without the occurrence of a condition called overflow, and this determines the degree of accuracy involved in any arithmetic performed. These limits have already been discussed in Chapter 2, which should be consulted again if this section is not understood. As an example, a machine holding numbers in 24-bit computer words could hold a maximum integer value of around $\pm 2^{23}$, or 8,388,608 assuming the first bit of the word is used for the sign of a number. For greater accuracy in numerical work a DOUBLE PRECISION type utilising twice the storage of an ordinary REAL value is also defined. Working with variables declared as DOUBLE PRECISION in type helps to reduce the effects of rounding errors in arithmetic, at the cost of using twice as much storage as is needed for the corresponding REAL values.

LOGICAL: Logical values represent either 'true' or 'false'. As constants specified in the course of a program, they are written in the form: .TRUE. and .FALSE. where the fullstops are part of the constants themselves and not just punctuation. The use of logical variables and expressions is discussed later.

TEXT: Text values are strings of characters which may be processed only in limited ways, and should not be used by a beginner in arithmetic statements. There is, however, no provision for a separate type of variable to hold character strings, and text may be stored in variables of type real or integer, as required. How they are held will depend in practice on the number of characters to be held in a string and the number of characters which can be the basic unit contained in the storage in a particular computer.

In examples in this chapter, we make no use of TEXT constants in the course of programs, since the ways of comparing and processing character strings in FORTRAN are beyond the scope of a simplified introduction. The only use of text in this chapter is to input and output characters to improve the identification of values in a printed table.

Names

All variables used in a program must be distinguished by separate names, which become associated with individual storage locations on execution, and are used to refer to the contents of a location when performing operations on variable values. Every variable must therefore have a distinct name of its own. All names must begin with a letter of the alphabet, and should be up to six alphanumeric characters long in standard FORTRAN. For example,

```
DATA1   V1   ALPHA       INT 3
```

Note that spaces are ignored in names, a fact which can be exploited to improve the layout of listings of programs. It also helps other readers of a program if names are selected to convey some understanding of the values they represent.

The *type* of a variable is distinguished intrinsically by its first letter, which conveniently avoids the bother of making every variable type explicit in a program. (All LOGICAL variables must be declared as such. Declarations consist of the type name, followed by a list of variable names, separated by commas.) But names beginning with I, J, K, L, M or N are understood as INTEGER, and those with any other initial letter are REAL, unless the convention is overridden by declarations of the form

```
REAL        INT 1,    INT 2,    INT 3
INTEGER     DATA
```

Arithmetic statements and expressions

The basic element in numerical calculation in FORTRAN is the assignment statement. As its name suggests, this assigns to a named variable a value equal to a given arithmetic expression. A statement such as

A=B+C−D

although it resembles an algebraic equation, is thus no more than a means of associating the variable name A with the value of the given expression. The symbol = represents an operation, not an equality, and could be read as 'becomes' to avoid confusion.

An arithmetic expression in its simplest form consists of a single element, for example, the values assigned may be a single variable or constant:

A=B
or PI=3·14159

More complicated expressions may be formed by combining individual variables or constants (or, as will be seen later, array element names) with a series of arithmetic operators. These operators express the familiar arithmetic symbols in a slightly unfamiliar form, and enable complex algebraic expressions to be written in a single line statement. The FORTRAN symbols are as follows:

+	addition (or positive sign)
−	subtraction (or negative sign)
*	multiplication
/	division
**	exponentiation (i.e. raising a number to a power)

It is important to realise the difference between division where the divisor, dividend, and result are integers, and division of real numbers by real numbers. The result of integer division is defined as the nearest integer whose absolute value does not exceed the mathematically correct value of the term:

Thus 7·0/2·0 is calculated as 3·5
but 7/2 becomes 3

Most of the rules for the use of arithmetic operators are fairly obvious intuitively. Two operators must not be adjacent, the operators + and − must be followed by an element, and the other three must be both preceded and followed by an element. No other form of expression is permitted, for example, multiplication must be written A*B and never AB or A.B. Inadmissible expressions are termed 'illegal' and their inclusion in programs will result in failures of compilation. The intrinsic order deals first with exponentiations, then multiplications and divisions, and finally additions and subtractions. With this order of precedence, expressions are evaluated from left to right.

To avoid ambiguity, or to override this order of evaluation, brackets can be introduced, and expressions in parentheses are given the highest order of priority. Note that a plus or minus sign before a constant is part of the expression and not of the constant, so that X** −2 cannot be written for X**(−2).

The expression A**B**C is clearly ambiguous (as well as illegal) and must be written (A**B)**C or A**(B**C).

B**2−4·0*A*C−B/2·0*A is equivalent to the algebraic expression

$$b^2-4ac-\frac{ab}{2}$$

whereas (B**2−4·0*A*C−B)/(2·0*A) is equivalent to

$$\frac{b^2-4ac-b}{2a}$$

Finally, where a series of parentheses within other parentheses are employed, evaluation starts with the inner-most set and works outwards. Thus the effective order of evaluation of the expression (A*B−C**2/(D+E))*F+G**(H+I) is in the following stages:

1. D+E $=E_1$
2. C**2 $=E_2$
3. E_2/E_1 $=E_3$
4. A*B−E_3 $=E_4$
5. H+I $=E_5$
6. G**E_5 $=E_6$
7. E_4*F+E_6

Types of variables in expressions

There are limitations on the combination of types of constants and variables, which can be used in arithmetic expressions. In general it is unwise to mix types of values in calculation, although some combinations are permitted in standard FORTRAN. Of the arithmetic operations, only exponentiation is permissible with bases and exponents of different types. An expression of the form REAL**INTEGER produces a result of type REAL, but the form INTEGER**REAL is illegal. All other operations cannot be used to combine elements of different types (except for real and double precision values which are interchangeable). The assignment of values takes care of most mixed type expressions by converting their numerical value to the type of the variable to which they are assigned, as in the table below.

Effect of Arithmetic Assignments

Variable type		Expression type	Effect
INTEGER	=	REAL	Value is floated before assignment (becomes a real value with decimal point and trailing zeros retaining as many digits of integer as possible)
REAL	=	INTEGER	Value is fixed before assignment (the fractional part is removed)

Statement structure

FORTRAN statements have a fixed form in order to be understood by a compiler and any departure from this format will have disastrous consequences for the program. The layout of a statement is probably best explained in terms of a punched card record, but it should be realised that FORTRAN statements prepared on paper tape, magnetic tape, or a direct input console still must conform to the same layout. The sequence of instructions is also very important, since compilation of most statements can only proceed in the order in which they are given.

A single statement consists of an initial line and up to 19 con-

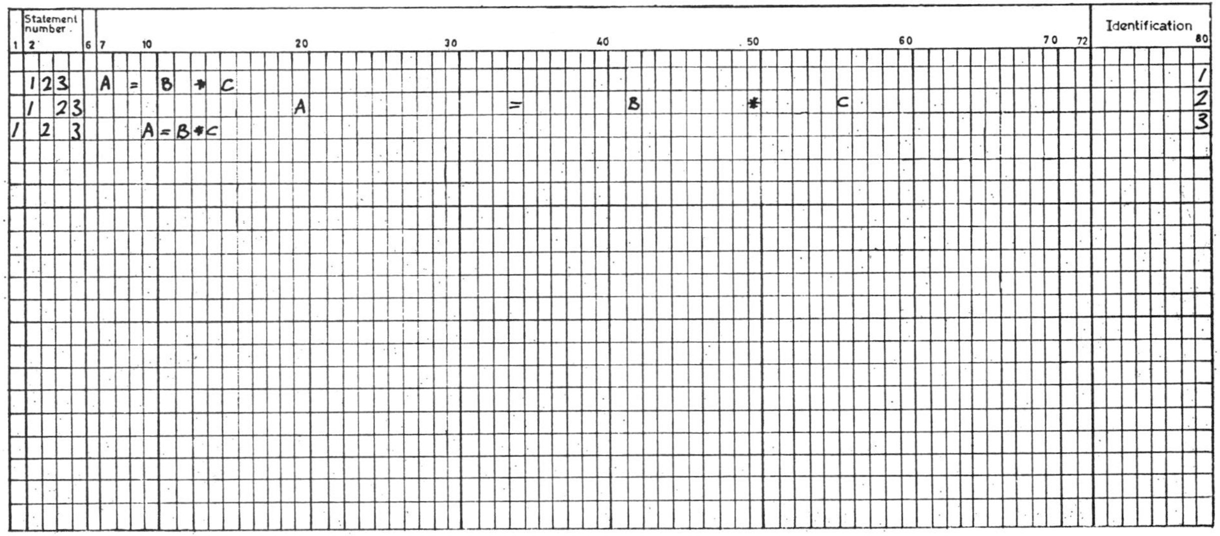

Fig. 7.1 FORTRAN statement format.

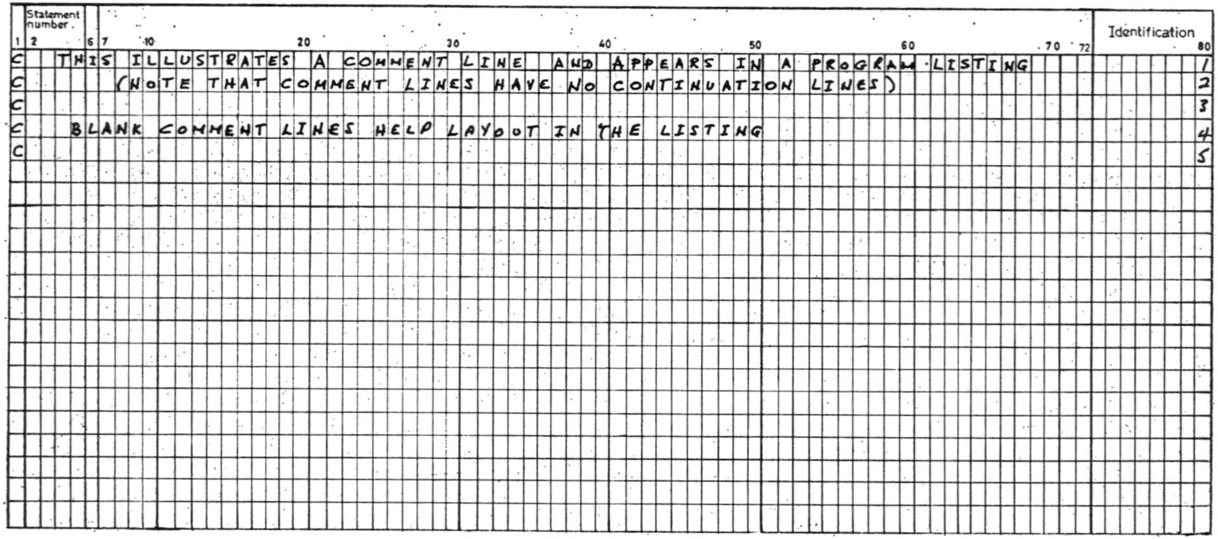

Fig. 7.2 Comment lines.

tinuation lines. Each line contains 80 character-positions, corresponding to the 80 columns of a standard punched card, of which the first 72 are used for language statements, the remainder being ignored. It is a good idea in a long program on punched cards to use characters 73–80 for card sequence numbers, to make sorting easy in the event that the deck of cards is ever shuffled or dropped.

The FORTRAN statement proper occupies any character positions between 7 and 72 inclusive, and positions 1 to 5 are reserved for statement labels used in the course of a program. Labels are sequences of digits, which may also include spaces, and are understood as decimal numbers. They need only be included when logically necessary to the program, but when used must be unique to a particular statement within the current program unit. (The last point is explained later in the chapter.) Figure 7.1 shows a series of equivalent statements with labels. The flexibility allowed by including optional spaces can be exploited to produce program listings on the line-printer which are easier to read than if every statement begins in the same place in the line.

If a statement cannot be completed on a single line, it may be continued on up to 19 continuation lines, which are numbered and identified as such by the appearance of alphanumeric symbols in character-position 6. An initial line may optionally contain a zero in position 6, after which continuation lines must contain a character other than zero at this point. In the example given, a zero in position 6 would thus *not* form part of the statement label 123. Some further illustrations of the use of continuation lines will be found in later examples.

As an aid to understanding a program after it has been written, any number of *comment* lines can be included between statements. These are ignored by the compiler and simply included in any listing of the program. Any line with the character C in the first position will be treated in this way, so that the remainder of the line may contain any remarks which help interpret the action of the program.

Input and output

Before giving an example of a short program, we must deal briefly with the method defined in FORTRAN for obtaining values needed in calculations from an input peripheral and giving output from a program. The basic rules are quite simple, and we will postpone consideration of some more complicated facilities until a little later.

Peripheral units are identified by logical unit numbers with each program, allocated to available hardware in various ways which we must here take as given. These unit identifiers are called channel numbers, and in the basic READ and WRITE statements indicate which peripheral is to be used. It is also necessary to state the form which an input or output record will take, since the computer recognises only a string of characters and must be told how to interpret them by the programmer. This is done by means of a FORMAT statement, associated by its statement label with the corresponding READ or WRITE instruction, and giving the layout of the data values. Unformatted READ and WRITE statements are sometimes permitted, and are useful in conserving space on magnetic tape files, but should be used with some caution by a beginner.

The structure of READ and WRITE instructions is the same. Thus

```
READ  (1,100) ITEM1, ITEM2
WRITE (2,100) ITEM1, ITEM2
```

reads the values of the given list of variables from an input peripheral associated with program channel number 1 and outputs them to the peripheral associated with channel number 2. 100 is the label of the corresponding FORMAT statement, which may be anywhere else in the program. In the present chapter, channel number 1 can always be taken to correspond to a card reader, or any other input device, and channel number 2 to a line-printer.

The general form of formatted input and output statements is

```
READ (u,f) list
WRITE (u,f) list
```

where *u* is the channel number and *f* the label of the corresponding format statement. The list may be a single item, or a series of items separated by commas. A WRITE statement output list may be omitted if the corresponding FORMAT specification contains only text to be output, for example as a table heading. Every READ or WRITE statement begins a new input or output record, so that the corresponding lists must include every item to be contained in at least one record. FORMAT statements have the following general form:

label FORMAT (format specification list)

The basic format specification list contains a coded description of the form of the input or output, with a separate field descriptor to correspond to each item in the input or output list of the READ or WRITE statement. These descriptors must be suitable for transmitting the correct *type* of value indicated in the list, or the statement is in error.

A field descriptor must contain a character signifying the field type, and a decimal numerical code to indicate the field width, that is, the total number of character positions occupied by the value to be transmitted, and the number of decimal places to be recognised, if appropriate. It may be preceded by an optional repeat count digit, which saves explicit repetition of the same descriptor a large number of times.

The most common descriptors are given in Table 7.1, with an indication of their effect.

Whatever the fixed format of a value as input, once it is stored in the computer as a variable value it should be considered as having leading and trailing zeros added to bring it up to the total number of digits held in the appropriate number of storage units for the variable type. On output, values are rounded to the accuracy specified in the format description, and leading zeros are suppressed.

In format specifications, these field descriptors are separated by commas, single slashes (/) or a series of slashes, with different effects on evaluation. A comma or slash indicates the end of a field, but a slash also denotes the end of a record, for example the end of the useful information contained on the punched card currently being read, and the next record is then considered. A series of n slashes, used as a separator, causes $n-1$ records to be ignored on input, or outputs $n-1$ blank records. In the case of output to the line-printer,

Table 7.1

Field descriptor	Form	Meaning	Used for
I	rIw	r integers of w digits	INTEGER values
F	rF$w.d$	r real numbers of w characters overall (*including the decimal point*) with d digits to the right of the decimal point. The point may be implied on input but always appears on output	REAL values or input of whole numbers as REAL values in Fw.O
X	nX	A field of n space characters	Missing n character positions on input or output
A	rAw	A field of w characters	Input and output of TEXT values held in variables
H	nH$c_1c_2...c_n$	A string of n characters to be output as stated	*Output only* of a given character string

r is the optional repeat count
n, r, w and d are integer constants; r and w must be non-zero
Allowance must be made in w for the possible appearance of a negative sign, and for a decimal point in real values, as part of the value
Positive signs are always suppressed

the effect is to move the paper on $n-1$ lines. On input, a single slash causes a skip to the next input record, whether or not there is information remaining unread on the current record.

Format specifications are repeatedly scanned from left to right until all values for all items in the corresponding input/output list have been transmitted, and, on output, no further *H*-format strings of characters remain to be output. Each repetition of a parenthesised format description also begins a new record. When this has been done, the next statement in the program is carried out.

For example

```
    READ(1,100) DATA1, DATA2, INT, DATA3, DATA4
100 FORMAT (F7.4, 4X, F10.0/I4)
```

will read two real numbers from the first input record, an integer from the second, and two more real numbers from the third. Inner parentheses in FORMAT statements may be used to repeat groups of format descriptors within the main FORMAT description. Repetition begins with the rightmost inner parenthesised group and the next group to the left is used if and when this group is exhausted. Descriptors contained in inner parentheses may be preceded by a repeat field parameter but need not be. Without a specified report parameter, they are repeated indefinitely until the input list is completed, beginning a new record at each repetition. With suitable input lists in a READ statement,

```
100 FORMAT (2I3/(2F10.5))
```

will read two three-digit integers, skip to the next input record, and read a sequence of real numbers, two at a time, each pair being contained in a separate input record.

In FORMAT statements intended for output to a line-printer the initial character of each output record is always used for carriage control, even if it is part of a numerical value. Because of this it is a good idea to make the carriage control character in these circumstances quite explicit.

The standard control characters for the line-printer are as follows:

1	throw to a new page
▽ (blank)	new line, with single spacing
0	new line, with double spacing
+	leave paper in the same position, so that the new line overwrites the old

The effect of using any other character is undefined in standard FORTRAN, and varies from machine to machine. These control characters are best given in H format, as in the example below. Line throws can also be achieved, as noted earlier, by using slashes in the course of a format specification.

Thus if program channel 2 is a line-printer, the statements

```
 10 WRITE (2,100) N,DATA
100 FORMAT (8H1RESULTS//1H▽,I4,3X,F10.7)
```

will send the printer to a new page, write the heading RESULTS, leave a blank line, and output a four-digit integer, three spaces and a real value in fixed format, with ten character positions in all, of which the third will be a decimal point. The second carriage control character could also have been given in the form 1X, with the same effect.

Two conventions help to make FORMAT statements easier to read and understand, which is always a good objective since the majority of simple programming errors occur in input and output formats. Labels of FORMAT statements within a program are more easily distinguished from other statement labels if they have a different number of digits, for example as in this chapter, where they are always of three digits, starting with 100. It is also useful to give carriage control characters for the line-printer in 1H format, since this clearly identifies output format description and more readily shows up errors and omissions.

Example 7.1

Enough detail has now been given to consider a short example.

The program shown is complete as it stands although not very useful since it can deal with only one input record at a time. Nevertheless, it could with some modification form part of a FORTRAN program for simple data processing. The statement STOP must appear at least once in any program to terminate the operation, and the statement END signifies the end of the program code. Some versions of FORTRAN also require a statement to show where a program actually begins, but this is not part of the standard language specification.

Example 7.1 is of no great use in itself but illustrates the minimum requirements to write correct FORTRAN. To make it repeat the process defined with a second and subsequent data, corresponding to further stock purchases by the dealer in question, it would be necessary to repeat the same set of instructions, without the STOP, as many times as repetition is needed. Although it is quite admissible, this would soon become an uneconomic process, while gradually filling the computer store with repetitious program code. It would also soon become very tedious to have to specify by a separate and distinct name a series of input values containing very many more

```
C
C        AN EXAMPLE TO ILLUSTRATE BASIC FORTRAN STATEMENTS,
C        THESE INSTRUCTIONS CALCULATE AND TABULATE ITEM COSTS AND
C        RESALE PRICES FOR A GIVEN QUANTITY PURCHASE
C        THERE IS A MINIMUM PROFIT OF 20% AFTER STANDARD OVERHEADS
C        ARE INCLUDED,
C
       READ(1,100) ITEM,COST,QTY
  100  FORMAT(I5,1X,F6,2,1X,F10,0)
C
C        NOTE THE USE OF F - FORMAT TO INPUT  THE WHOLE NUMBER 'QTY'
C
       OHEADS=QTY*0,15 + 50,0
       COST  = COST + OHEADS
       PROFIT=COST  * 1,20
       PRICE = PROFIT/QTY
       PROFIT= PROFIT - COST
       COST=COST/QTY
       DISC  = PRICE
       PRICE = PRICE/0.85
       WRITE(2,101) ITEM,COST,PROFIT,PRICE,DISC
  101  FORMAT(1H1,5HITEM ,I10,12H UNIT COST £,F6.2,17H MINIMUM PROFIT £,
      1F14.2//14X,14HRETAIL PRICE £,F6,2,5X,20H15% DISCOUNT PRICE £,F6,2)
       STOP
       END
```

INPUT DATA

```
1 2   6 7  10        20        30        40        50
12345 250.75        300
```

EXAMPLE PRINTOUT

```
ITEM      12345 UNIT COST £  1,15 MINIMUM PROFIT £         69,05

             RETAIL PRICE £  1,62     15% DISCOUNT PRICE £  1,38
```

Example 7.1 Basic FORTRAN statements.

elements than the three in the example. Imagine, for example, a string of 20 or 200 different names for single variables.

FORTRAN loops and arrays deal with this kind of problem in a less repetitious and more elegant way than would be possible with the repertoire of instructions discussed so far.

Arrays and their uses

It is a very common form of abbreviation when writing mathematical or statistical formulae to use a symbol with a subscript to represent any series of values of the same or an equivalent quantity or variable. For example, the sum of n numbers is quite often represented as $\sum_{i=1}^{n} x_i$, as a shorter form of the expression $x_1+x_2+x_3 \ldots +x_{n-1}+x_n$. Here x is termed a subscripted variable with individual values x_i. In a similar way, elements of a matrix of r rows and c columns can be conveniently referenced using a system of double subscripts, as follows:

$$\begin{matrix} x_{11} & x_{12} & x_{13} & \dots & x_{1c} \\ x_{21} & x_{22} & x_{23} & \dots & x_{2c} \\ \dots & \dots & \dots & \dots & \dots \\ x_{r1} & x_{r2} & x_{r3} & \dots & x_{rc} \end{matrix}$$

A short notation for column sums is thus available in terms of elements x_{ij} $(i=1, r; j=1, c)$, so that the sum of the nth column is denoted $\sum_{i-1}^{r} x_{in}$. In this kind of notation, the convention is that the second subscript changes most rapidly, that is, the subscript which corresponds to the columns of the matrix.

In FORTRAN, a similar subscripted notation is adopted to permit reference to a series of elements making up an ARRAY. Arrays may be of one or two dimensions corresponding in conception to the subscripted variables above, according to the number of independent subscripts employed. If it is helpful to the layout of a program, arrays may also be defined with three dimensions. However, since all FORTRAN arrays are stored in the computer as a series of consecutive locations ordered so that the *first* subscript varies most rapidly (the equivalent of storage by columns of a matrix if the array is of two dimensions) the use of more than one set of independent subscripts, or expressions evaluated as subscripts, is purely of conceptual convenience for the programmer. The number of dimensions employed may be chosen to suit the solution method employed in the program or to make for ease of understanding the process involved. Alternatively, so long as the maximum number of elements is the same, a two-dimensional array, representing a matrix, can easily be rearranged into a one-dimensional array, in which it may be more efficiently processed. This greater efficiency derives from the means of calculating the address of an array element in store, which is always shorter for a single dimension alarray in FORTRAN (see National Computer Centre, 1970; pages 30–32).

As with any other variable quantities, arrays must have distinct names, and may be of any permitted type, depending on the initial letter of the name or a type declaration explicitly overriding the implied type. Array elements are referred to by names, made up as in the following examples:

```
ARRAY(10, 4, 3)
ARR(4, 2)
INT(I,J)
XY(I*J)
```

All subscripts or subscript expressions must be evaluated as integers, for obvious reasons, but since standard FORTRAN places restrictions on the type of compound expressions which may be used in place of integer constants or variables, these should be used cautiously. The reader should first consult a more comprehensive treatment to check on the full range of permissible forms.

Arrays will not be recognised as such by a compiler unless they have been listed at the beginning of a program, and storage reserved for their elements by means of a DIMENSION statement (they will otherwise be taken as an erroneous type of function reference). The word DIMENSION is followed by a list of array names, with the corresponding array size given in brackets after each name. The size is specified as a set of bounds to the size of the subscript elements, which correspond in order to the three permitted dimensional subscripts already described, or as many of these are are needed. So that

```
DIMENSION X(100), Y(10,12), INT(4,2)
```

would have the effect of setting up three arrays. The first is single dimensional and may contain up to 100 real values. The second has 120 elements, providing the equivalent of a ten rows by twelve columns matrix. The third holds up to eight integer values, and is written as though of two dimensions.

The most useful application of arrays occurs when a large number of values are to be processed in an identical way by a program. By varying the value of a subscript expression the same set of arithmetic assignment statements, such as

```
1 J=J+1
  I=I+1
  A(I)=B*C/2*D(I,J)
```

can be made to perform calculations which would otherwise need a large number of repetitious statements. The arrays A and D should, of course, have been declared and given dimensions at the head of the program containing these instructions, and a means must be found of branching back to the statement labelled 1 when each single calculation is complete.

DO loops

One way of causing a program to perform 'loops' of repeated instructions in FORTRAN is to use a DO statement. This defines the range of statements to be executed a number of times, and an integer variable to act as a counter for the number of loops performed. The values which this control variable may take are defined in three ways. It must be given an initial value and a terminal value, that is the maximum value to be attained before control in the program proceeds to the next statement after the loop, optionally, an incrementation value may be given representing the amount by which the control parameter increases on each repetition of the DO loop. If no such value is specified, the compiler assumes that the control variable will increase in steps of 1, so that in practice it is only necessary to state exceptions to this rate of incrementation.

The general form of the DO statement is

$$\text{DO } l \text{ i} = \text{M}_1, \text{M}_2, \text{M}_3$$

where l is the label of the terminal statement, i is the control variable, and M_1, M_2, M_3 are the initial value, terminal value and incrementation value of the control variable. Since i is an integer variable, clearly M_1 and M_2 (and M_3 if included) must be positive integer constants or names of variables holding values of this kind.

The instructions to be repeated in the loop are defined by reference to the label of the last statement to be executed. This *terminal statement* marks the *range* of the DO, and the effect following a DO statement is to repeat all subsequent instructions up to and including that point in the program, subject to the range and specified rate of incrementation of the control variable. A terminal statement may be one of the executable program statements, provided that it makes logical sense with the program to use it in this way, or it may be the dummy statement

CONTINUE

This is used simply as a means of having a label at an appropriate point in a program, but can be effectively employed to clarify the structure of a DO loop, even if it is not strictly essential to the sense of the program.

Thus

```
      X=0
      DO 10 I=1,4
      X=X+1
   10 Y(I)=X
```

or

```
      X=0
      N=4
      DO 10 I=1,N
      X=X+I
      Y(I)=X
   10 CONTINUE
```

are equivalent sets of statements. This example also shows how a control variable may be used as a value in the loop it controls.

In addition, further DO loops can be 'nested' each within the range of an outer loop. In this case, separate loops may share the same terminal statement. An inner loop will always be completed before the control variable of the next outer loop is incremented. So that the statements

```
      DO 10 I=1,10
      DO 11 J=1,10
      A(I,J)=I*J
   11 CONTINUE
   10 CONTINUE
```

are equivalent in effect to

```
      DO 10 I=1,10
      DO 10 J=1,10
   10 A(I,J)=I*J
```

and set up a multiplication table in the square matrix A. The reader should verify this, and try the effect of incrementation values greater than one.

DO-implied input/output lists

When reading in or writing out arrays it is very convenient to use a form of expression in which a DO loop is implied, rather than to express a set of DO instructions in full. Since this is used in examples in this chapter, some equivalent sets of instructions are given here, together with the forms of implied DO lists applicable to arrays of one, two or three dimensions.

```
          DO 10 I=1,10
          DO 10 J=1,10
       10 READ (1,100) A(I,J)
      100 FORMAT (10F12.6)
```

and

```
          READ (1,100)((A(I,J),J=1,10), I=1,10)
      100 FORMAT (10F12.6)
```

will each read in a 10-by-10 matrix of real values given a row at a time on separate input records. Note particularly the manner of nesting of parentheses for arrays of two and three dimensions:

```
          DIMENSION X(10), Y(4,10), Z(3,4,10)
          READ (1,100) (X(I), I=1,10)
          READ (1,100) ((Y(I,J),J=1,10), I=1,4)
          READ(1,100) (((Z(I,J,K), K=1,10), J=1,4), I=1,3)
      100 FORMAT (10F12.6)
```

Standard functions

In the next and subsequent example programs, we take advantage of some facilities defined in Standard FORTRAN to avoid writing out instructions of our own to evaluate some common mathematical functions. The subject of functions is dealt with more fully later, but the use of standard functions, that is operations automatically included by *any* compiler, is very easy to understand. A very frequent requirement is to calculate the square root of a variable or expression, and for this we have a standard function SQRT. The function name is followed by an *argument* in brackets, the effect being to evaluate the square root of the *argument*, and substitute this value in the statement calling the functions.

```
X=SQRT (Y/Z)
```

is the FORTRAN equivalent of evaluating $x=\sqrt{\frac{y}{z}}$ in algebraic notation. The argument for SQRT *must be* of type real. Some frequently used standard functions are given in the table.

NAME	PURPOSE	Number and type of arguments	Type of function (i.e. type of result *returned*)
AMAX1	Find largest of *n* values	More than one, less than nine; real	Real
SQRT	Square root	one; real	Real
ALOG	Natural logarithm ($\log_e a$)	one; real	Real
EXP	e^a	one; real	Real
SIN	Trigonometric sine	one; real	Real
COS	Trigonometric cosine	one; real	Real

Example 7.2

We are now in a position to consider an example of greater power than the earlier program. Example 7.2 calculates the product-moment correlation coefficient for up to 100 observations of the two variables x and y, making use of the formula

$$r_{xy}=\left(\frac{1}{N}\sum_{i=1}^{n} x_i y_i-\overline{x}\overline{y}\right)\Big/\sigma_x\sigma_y$$

where $\overline{x}$ and y are means of the x and y distributions, and σ_x and σ_n are their standard deviations. The program also prints these values. For purists, we hastily note this is not the most efficient way to calculate, say, a large matrix of correlation coefficients (see Cooley and Lohnes, 1962, pages 17–30) and is given only as an illustration.

Control statements—unconditional and conditional branches

The designers of FORTRAN tried to use instruction codes which would make reasonable sense to English-speaking users without extensive knowledge of the language, As a result, the commonly used unconditional branch statement GO TO (followed by a statement label) seems hardly to need explanation. It causes execution of the program to jump from the point in the sequence of instructions at which it occurs to the statement with the label specified after GO TO, missing out any other statements in between.

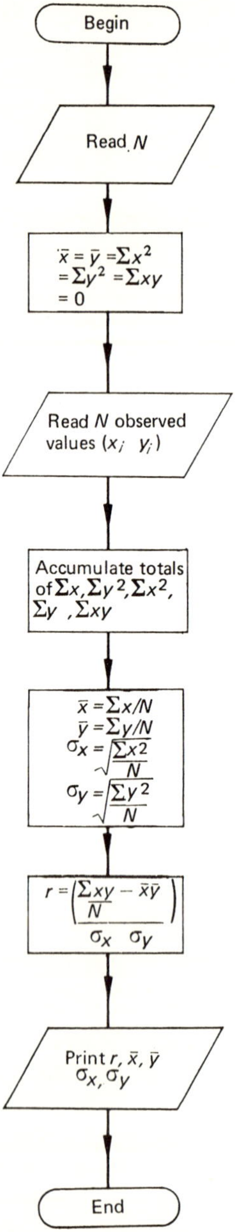

Example 7.2 Flow chart for calculation of a correlation coefficient, means and standard deviations.

```
C
C     A FORTRAN PROGRAM TO CALCULATE A CORRELATION COEFFICIENT
      DIMENSION X(100),Y(100)
      READ(1,100) N
  100 FORMAT(I3)
      XBAR=0.0
      YBAR=0.0
      SXSQ=0.0
      SYSQ=0.0
      Z=N
      READ(1,101) (X(I),Y(I),I=1,N)
  101 FORMAT(2F10.5)
      DO 10 I=1,N
      XBAR=XBAR+X(I)
      YBAR=YBAR+Y(I)
      SXSQ=SXSQ+X(I)**2
      SYSQ=SYSQ+Y(I)**2
   10 SXY=SXY+X(I)*Y(I)
      XBAR=XBAR/Z
      YBAR=YBAR/Z
      STDX=SQRT(SXSQ/Z-XBAR**2)
      STDY=SQRT(SYSQ/Z-YBAR**2)
      R=(SXY/Z-XBAR*YBAR)/(STDX*STDY)
      WRITE(2,102) R,XBAR,YBAR,STDX,STDY
  102 FORMAT(1H1,25HCORRELATION COEFFICIENT =,F20.5//8X,18HMEAN OF X VAL
     1UES =,F20.5//8X,18HMEAN OF Y VALUES =,F20.5//1X,25HSTANDARD DEVIAT
     2ION OF X =,F20.5//1X,25HSTANDARD DEVIATION OF Y =,F20.5)
      STOP
      END
```

Example 7.2 Calculation of a correlation coefficient, means and standard deviations.

EXAMPLE INPUT DATA

Columns 1–6	Columns 10–15
10	
8·3	8·9
4·2	5·2
1·9	1·8
11·4	12·4
22·6	22·1
15·4	18·7
19·7	18·6
12·9	12·3
10·8	11·1
2·9	2·7

PRINTOUT OF RESULTS

```
CORRELATION COEFFICIENT =        0.98408
      MEAN OF X VALUES =        11.01000
      MEAN OF Y VALUES =        11.38000
STANDARD DEVIATION OF X =        6.59825
STANDARD DEVIATION OF Y =        6.58829
```

One of its possible uses is as a substitute for DO loops in programs similar to the first example in this chapter, which are intended to perform the same set of operations on each of a varying number of input data records. It is quite possible to control those repetitions in such a program by supplying a control value for a DO loop as data at the start of a run, so that the program terminates when the stated number of input records have been processed. It may be more convenient, instead, to arrange for each input card to be scanned for the presence of a set terminating instruction or value, and leave the program to continue reading and processing cards until it finally locates this special code. The form of the program could then be, for example,

```
1  READ (1,100) N, etc.
   ............
   ............
   GOTO 1
2  STOP
   END
```

with a conditional branch statement to check whether the value of N indicates a jump down to the statement labelled 2, to stop an otherwise 'infinite' looping process. This kind of branching in a program, to take place only when certain conditions are satisfied and otherwise to be ignored, is achieved by means of conditional IF statements, which may be of two kinds.

Arithmetic IF

```
     e.g. IF(X) 10,11,12
10        IF (X*Y/Z) 13,14,15
```

The effect of this kind of conditional statement is to test the value of the variable or arithmetic expression in brackets after IF. Control in the program passes to the statement bearing one of the three labels listed after the parentheses, according to whether the value is negative, i.e. less than zero, actually equal to zero, or positive, i.e. greater than zero. Arithmetic IF statements are used, for the sake of brevity, in the two final examples in this chapter.

Logical IF

The general form of this statement is

IF (logical variable or expression) GOTO *l*

If the logical expression is true, control passes to the statement in the program with the label *l*. Otherwise, execution continues with the next statement in the program.

Up to now we have encountered only the class of operators used for arithmetic expressions, while noting that variables may also be defined to contain logical values, assigned as .TRUE. or .FALSE. There is a corresponding class of logical relations which are used in the construction of logical expressions, that is, expressions which when evaluated take logical values, by comparing arithmetic values.

These relations are .LT. = 'is less than'
.LE. = 'is less than or equal to'
.EQ. = 'is equal to'
.NE. = 'is not equal to'
.GE. = 'is greater than or equal to'
.GT. = 'is greater than'

Note that these full-stops, like the stops in logical constants, are part of the relational expression itself, not punctuation, and are a consequence of the construction of the language with a very limited character set.

These relations can be used to compare variables array elements or constants of the same type, but mixed type expressions involving REAL and INTEGER variables are not allowed in standard FORTRAN.

If the relationship stated is satisfied, the logical expression takes the value .TRUE. and the remainder of the statement is carried out.

```
IF (X .EQ. 1.0 E-10) GOTO 10
```

will result in a branch to the statement labelled 10 if the value of the real variable X is to be regarded as zero, with an accuracy of 10^{-10}.

```
IF (I. EQ. 1) GOTO 10
```

transfers control if I is currently 1, while

```
IF (LOGIC) GOTO 20
```

depends on the value currently assigned to the variable LOGIC, which must have been declared as of type LOGICAL at the beginning of the program.

More complicated logical expressions can be formed by the creation of compounded conditions using the logical operators

.AND.
.OR.
.NOT.

There is not sufficient space here to describe their use fully but we may briefly note their effects, which will come as no surprise to anyone familiar with similar operations in symbolic logic or their equivalent in the theory of sets.

.NOT. A	is .TRUE. when A is .FALSE., and .FALSE. when A is .TRUE.
A .AND. B	is .TRUE. only if both A and B are .TRUE., and otherwise .FALSE.
A .OR. B	is .TRUE. if either A or B is .TRUE., and .FALSE. only when both are .FALSE.

.NOT. operations are always evaluated before the others, and parentheses may be used, as in arithmetic statements, to override the normal order of evaluation and obtain the meaning required.

Instead of a GOTO, Logical IF conditions may be followed by an arithmetic IF in which the GOTO is implied,

```
IF (A.LE.B) IF(A) 10,11,12
```

to provide a greater range of conditions to be satisfied in a single statement.

They may, in addition, be followed by a call statement for a subroutine to the main program. The definition and use of subroutines in FORTRAN is discussed a little later.

Example 7.3

To illustrate the use of array subscripts and logical operations, the next example program deals with a basic problem of file organisation which is an essential preliminary or component in many kinds of calculation. This is to identify a series of values in ascending or descending order numerically, and may be required for subsequent scaling of values by the largest number, or, as in the present example, in order to assign a rank order to the various items. A similar method could be used to sort and rearrange items into ascending or

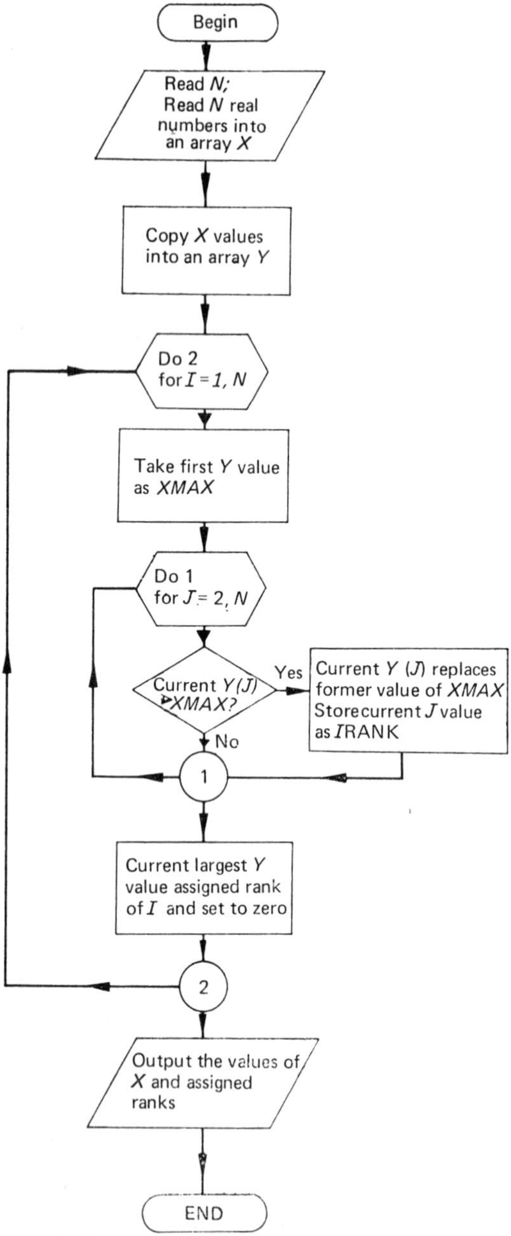

Example 7.3 Flow chart for ranking data values.

```
C
C      A PROGRAM TO ASSIGN RANKS TO A SERIES OF REAL VALUES
C
       INTEGER RANK
       DIMENSION X(100),RANK(100),Y(100)
       READ(1,100) N
  100  FORMAT(I3)
       READ(1,101) (X(I),I=1,N)
  101  FORMAT(F6.3)
C
C      THE WORKING ARRAY Y AVOIDS THE LOSS OF THE ORIGINAL VALUES
       DO 1 I=1,N
  1    Y(I) = X(I)
       DO 3 I=1,N
       XMAX = Y(1)
       IRANK = 1
       DO 2 J=2,N
       IF(Y(J) .LT.XMAX) GO TO 2
       IRANK = J
       XMAX = Y(J)
   2   CONTINUE
       RANK(IRANK) = I
   3   Y(IRANK) = 0.0
       WRITE(2,102)
  102  FORMAT(1H1,5HVALUE,5X,4HRANK)
       WRITE(2,103) (X(I),RANK(I),I=1,N)
  103  FORMAT(1H ,F6.3,4X,I3)
       STOP
       END
```

```
VALUE     RANK
 8,300      7
 4,200      8
 1,900     10
11,400      5
22,600      1
15,400      3
19,700      2
12,300      4
10,300      6
 2,900      9
```

Example 7.3 A program to assign ranks to a series of real values.

descending values, and is illustrated in the course of the matrix inversion routine given as part of the last example of this chapter. In that example, a two-dimensional array of numbers is actually rearranged systematically to make its structure fit the needs of the numerical method applied. Here, we are concerned only with knowing the rank to be assigned to a given element in a single-dimensional array, leaving the actual observations in the same order as before. One use of such a procedure will be discussed in a later example in this chapter, in which the main program given below is used as a subprogram in calculating a rank order correlation coefficient. To simplify matters a little, it is assumed that the values to be ranked are all different. This avoids the problem of tied ranks, in which some suitable convention has to be applied to derive a rank value appropriate to a series of equal observations. The method most commonly required for statistical purposes, termed the mid-rank method, assigns each observation a rank equal to the arithmetic mean of the ranks which would have been assigned had there been no scores. The reader is left to consider how this modification might be introduced into the example program, and whether other applications might require an alternative formulation in the case of ties. If the logical processes are expressed first as a modification to the flow chart, it becomes a simple matter to amend the FORTRAN instructions.

The flow chart explains the method employed. If you have difficulty in following the effect of subscript changes, try working through the program using some simple numbers of your own.

Subprograms and program structure

Chapter 3 dealt briefly with the commonly used device in high level languages of defining a subprogram which is called whenever a frequently repeated calculation is required by the main program. In FORTRAN, subprograms may be either functions, which are virtually specially defined equivalents of the standard functions we have already encountered, or they may be subroutines. In either case they are incorporated into a complete set of program instructions in a modular fashion. Every program consists of one main program unit, containing among other things statements calling functions or subroutines into use when needed. An END line marks the end of this initial program unit, which may be followed by any number of units defining the additional facilities needed. Each subprogram begins with a statement identifying it as SUBROUTINE, or a FUNCTION of a particular type, and a distinct name, chosen according to the normal rules for the language. Somewhere in each subprogram will be at least one RETURN statement, transferring control of execution back to the main program, or possibly a STOP statement. The latter might be used if a subroutine acts as an error check in the operation of the program and halts with an appropriate message when an error is found. Some compilers require identification of the beginning of the main program too, with an appropriate statement serving only to name the main program segment. This modular structure can be summarised in a diagram (where some hypothetical subprogram names are included for illustration only):

```
             ┌ ........
             │ Main program instructions
MAIN PROGRAM ┤ ........
             │ STOP
             └ END
             ┌ REAL FUNCTION TRIG (X,Y)
             │ ........
SUBPROGRAM   ┤ ........
             │ RETURN
             └ END
             ┌ SUBROUTINE FILE
             │ ........
SUBPROGRAM   ┤ ........
             │ RETURN
             └ END
             ┌ SUBROUTINE ERR (J)
             │ .....
SUBPROGRAM   ┤ STOP
             │ .....
             │ RETURN
             └ END
```

Within each program unit the order of statements must begin with declarations of type and array declarations where these are appropriate. However, such declarations may be in any convenient order.

One effect of this modular structure in FORTRAN is that names of variables or arrays, or any other names supplied in a program unit, have a defined meaning only in the program unit in which they are declared. This is also true of statement labels, which need be unique only within the program unit in which they occur. The result is that the same name used in different program segments refers to entirely different storage locations and can therefore never be assumed to have the same value. Variables bearing the same name in different segments can equally well be declared of different types.

Unless values are transferred between program units by explicit instructions, some of which are dealt with in a moment, each program unit is thus entirely self-contained in its effects.

Functions

A function subprogram is used to calculate and return a single value to the section of the program calling it. The type of values which can be returned to the main program from it depend on the way in which the function itself is *declared.* Function declarations resemble variable declarations, and functions may be of any of the types permitted for variables and constants.

Functions may be defined in two ways. The first is as a subprogram, beginning with a FUNCTION statement. The type of the function defined may be stated explicitly or implied by the name given to the function.

For example:
```
INTEGER FUNCTION FUN (X,Y,Z)
FUNCTION ROOT (A,B,C)
FUNCTION Z (Q)
```

The list in parentheses consists of *dummy* arguments corresponding in type and number to the real arguments used each time the function is called. Function subprograms are written in terms of these dummy arguments, and each time the unit is called, actual arguments are substituted in calculating the value.

As an example, the following function evaluates the positive root of a quadratic equation, $o=ax^2+bx+c$ by the formula

$$x=\frac{-b+\sqrt{b^2-4ac}}{2a}$$

(We may assume a previous check on the value of b^2-4ac to avoid a negative or zero argument in SQRT)

```
FUNCTION FUN (A,B,C)
ROOT=SQRT (B**2-4.0*A*C)
FUN=(ROOT-B)/(2.0*A)
RETURN
END
```

Function references may be used as arguments in arithmetic or logical expressions, so that a statement elsewhere of the kind

P=Q-FUN (E,F,G)

where Q, E, F and G are all defined variables, will assign to P the value of Q minus the positive root of

$$o = Ex^2 + FX + G$$

The actual arguments used in a function reference may be expressions as well as variable or array element names. However, actual arrays given as arguments corresponding to dummy arrays must also have the same number of dimensions as the dummy arrays. It is not enough for them to have the same number of elements, stored in the same order.

Functions may also be defined for *a particular program unit only*, as single statements. The form then is

Statement Function Name (dummy argument list)	=	expression in terms of dummy arguments

The type of a statement function is taken from its name, which should be chosen or declared as necessary. The example above could be written, in the same program unit, in statement function form

```
FUN (A,B,C)=(SQRT(B**2-4.0*A*C)-B)/(2.0*A)
.............
P=Q-FUN (E,F,G)
```

The function FUN could not then be defined for use in any other unit of the program.

As will be seen from the examples given, function references may be used as arguments in arithmetic expressions. They may be used in a similar way in logical expressions too.

Subroutines

Subroutines are subject to the same kind of rules regarding dummy arguments, but may be used to return a number of values to the program unit which contains a call on the subroutine.

The number and type of values returned depend upon the number and type of the dummy arguments used, and the subroutine itself is not of any particular type. The next example program uses modified versions of Examples 7.2 and 7.3 as subroutines, which should be carefully compared with their original forms. Here we must confine ourselves to an outline of the uses of dummy arguments, and especially dummy arrays.

The list of real arguments specified in a CALL to a subroutine,

e.g. CALL TRANSP (X,Y,10)

will all be substituted for the corresponding dummy arguments defined in the subroutine itself, and any variables may be returned with modified values when the subroutine is executed. Names may be used, types declared and arrays dimensioned without regard to their meanings in other program units. Only the names in the dummy argument list need correspond exactly to the real arguments supplied in the CALL statement.

Arrays used as dummy arguments may be defined within dummy array bounds, the real dimension being supplied by a call statement. This facility for using dynamic array bounds helps avoid unnecessary work when performing routine operations on actual arrays of different sizes. The actual arrays must, of course, be given actual bounds in declarations at the head of the main program unit or the program unit using the real arguments, and the dummy array bounds must not be allowed to exceed the actual dimensions declared.

We can illustrate these points with a subroutine to transpose rows and columns of a square matrix of degree N.

```
      SUBROUTINE TRANSP (A,B,N)
      DIMENSION A(N,N),B(N,N)
      DO 10 I=I,N
      DO 10 J=1,N
   10 B(I,J)=A(J,I)
      RETURN
      END
```

If the argument N were omitted, and the arrays declared with fixed bounds, only matrices of fixed size could be transposed correctly by a statement such as

CALL TRANSP (X,Y,4)

Execution of the main program could continue with the array Y containing the transpose of X, and the previous contents of Y obliterated.

Finally, as the reader may have guessed, all of the foregoing discussion of the use of dynamic arrays in subroutines also applies to dummy arrays declared in function segments. Here too dummy arguments may be used to dimension arrays, provided that the corresponding real arrays have received real dimensions effective in the program units containing references to the function.

Example 7.4

In this example we make use of the methods of the preceding two examples to illustrate the construction of a program using subroutines to evaluate some quantities. First we calculate a simple correlation coefficient, using the method of Example 7.2. Then we use the ranking method of Example 7.3 to produce rank orders of the same two distributions of observed values, and calculate the

INPUT DATA

```
 10
   8.3       8.9
   4.2       5.2
   1.9       1.8
 11.4       12.4
 22.6       22.1
 15.4       18.7
 19.7       18.6
 12.3       12.9
 10.3       11.1
  2.9        2.7
```

EXAMPLE PRINTOUT

```
R=        0,985261 N=    10

RHO =      0,987879 N=      10

T =    18,000339
```

```
C
C       A PROGRAM TO ILLUSTRATE THE USE
C       OF SUBROUTINES
C
      DIMENSION X(100),Y(100),XR(100),YR(100)
      READ(1,100) N
 100  FORMAT(I3)
      READ(1,101) (X(I),Y(I),I=1,N)
 101  FORMAT(2F10.5)
      R=0.0
      Z=N
      CALL CORREL(N,X,Y,R)
      WRITE(2,102) R,N
 102  FORMAT(1H1,2HR=,F14.6,3H N=,I5)
      CALL ORDER(N,X,XR)
      CALL ORDER(N,Y,YR)
      CALL CORREL(N,XR,YR,R)
      T=R*SQRT((Z-2.0)/(1.0-R**2))
      WRITE(2,103) R,N,T
 103  FORMAT(1H0,5HRHO =,F12.6,3H N=,I6//4H T =,F12.6)
      STOP
      END
```

```
      SUBROUTINE ORDER(N,X,RANK)
      DIMENSION X(N),RANK(N)
      DO 11 I=1,N
      XMAX=X(1)
      IRANK=1
      DO 10 J=2,N
      IF(X(J).LT.XMAX)  GO TO 10
      IRANK=J
      XMAX=X(J)
 10   CONTINUE
      RANK(IRANK)=I
 11   X(IRANK)  =0.0
      RETURN
      END
```

```
      SUBROUTINE CORREL(N,X,Y,R)
      DIMENSION X(N),Y(N)
      XBAR=0.0
      YBAR=0.0
      SXSQ=0.0
      SYSQ=0.0
      SXY=0.0
      Z=N
      DO 10 I=1,N
      XBAR=XBAR+X(I)
      YBAR=YBAR+Y(I)
      SXSQ=SXSQ+X(I)**2
      SYSQ=SYSQ+Y(I)**2
 10   SXY=SXY+X(I)*Y(I)
      XBAR=XBAR/Z
      YBAR=YBAR/Z
      STDX=SQRT(SXSQ/Z-XBAR**2)
      STDY=SQRT(SYSQ/Z-YBAR**2)
      R=(SXY/Z-XBAR*YBAR)/(STDX*STDY)
      RETURN
      END
```

Example 7.4 Program illustrating the use of subroutines.

correlation of the rank values, to give us another measure of correlation, Spearman's rank order correlation coefficient. The program also calculates and outputs a significance statistic t for the latter, which should be evaluated with $N-2$ degrees of freedom for N pairs of observed values. (On the methods employed, see any good text on social statistics, for example, Blalock, 1960, Chapter 17, and Siegel, 1956, pages 202–213.)

The subroutines given here would be particularly useful if a large number of these statistics were required for a large number of variables, in which case input data might be stored in an array, and extracted a pair of variables at a time for the calculations to be performed.

Additional features of FORTRAN

Standard FORTRAN defines two additional statements for use mainly with magnetic tape devices. These are part of the language itself, unlike most arrangements for incorporating backing store units, which are dependent on the type of machine used or the methods in use at a particular computer installation. Since they are used in one of our two final example programs, we must note that these are

```
    ENDFILE c
and REWIND  c
```

where c is the progress channel number of the appropriate peripheral unit. ENDFILE writes an end of file marker on the output, and is used to indicate the end of data in a file. REWIND positions the peripheral unit so that the next input record to be read is the first record in the file. There is no way of telling in Standard FORTRAN when an end-of-file marker has been read, but trying to read beyond one will normally result in an error and halt the program.

Various implementations of the language will define additional different ways of programming input and output using other peripheral units.

In an abbreviated introduction, we have had to omit descriptions of some other features of the language which expand the facilities we have dealt with, or provide alternative, more efficient means of performing the same functions. To avoid what might otherwise be a misleading impression of the flexibility of FORTRAN IV, we must briefly mention some of these omissions. Any extended treatment of the language will explain these features in full.

For many numerical calculations, double precision arithmetic may be useful to reduce the effects of rounding errors on results. Complex numbers are also handled in a special type of variable, but are very unlikely to occur in social science applications. A more significant set of facilities not considered in this chapter provides for the transfer of values between program units in blocks of storage which are common to desired units instead of as actual and dummy arguments. It is also possible to assign two or more values to the same storage unit in a program, either to save storage space or to have the convenience of calling the same location by different names at different times.

Several types of FORMAT descriptions are available, in addition to those we have mentioned, which handle output in different ways, and many implementations permit a 'free-format' input or output method, in which values are separated simply by spaces, a method which saves time in data preparation. Also it is often possible on particular compilers to specify text in FORMAT statements in string quotes, for example

```
      WRITE (2,100)
100   FORMAT ('TABLE HEADING FOR PROBLEM')
```

instead of in H-format, which removes a lot of the work of preparing table headings for print-out.

We have not discussed methods of handling text, although this is often not very difficult. The reason is that different implementations of the language have their own particular ways of facilitating the comparison of character strings, for example, by a set of standard subroutines automatically included in a program on computation. It may appear quite simple to use arithmetic operators on text constants, particularly for comparison for equality, but it is possible to cause arithmetic overflow in this way without knowledge of the internal machine codes for characters and their decimal equivalents. Because these codes, and arrangements for storing text data, vary between machines, it is not possible to give any general rules for text handling.

More concise and complicated branching structures than those we have illustrated can be constructed using variants of the unconditional GOTO statement. The Assigned GOTO statement is followed by an index in the form of an integer variable name, which may be assigned different values in the course of execution:

$$\text{GOTO } i(l_1,l_2, \ldots l_n)$$

There follows a set of actual statement labels, one of which must correspond numerically to the value of the integer index, assigned by a special statement of the form

$$\text{ASSIGN } l \text{ to } i$$

The Assigned GOTO causes a branch to one of the series of statement labels specified, depending on the value currently assigned to i.

An alternative computed GOTO also uses a list of statement labels

$$\text{GOTO } (l_1,l_2, \ldots l_n),i$$

and branches to the first, second, up to nth label in the list, according to the numerical value of the integer variable i, which must range between 1 and n.

We have also omitted discussion of the full range of standard functions always available in FORTRAN, to which can be added the many different sets of 'library' procedures which can be called into use in a program written for a particular installation, in the same way as standard functions. Many common procedures in numerical work, including some of the kind we have used as illustrations in this chapter, may be available in the form of functions or subroutines and need no further specification by the user beyond a function reference or subroutine call. For many numerical calculations, all that may be required of the programmer fortunate enough to have access to a good subprogram library of this kind is to write a suitable main program to use the routines available, and the necessary input and output statements to provide data and obtain results. Alternatively the user may wish to develop his own library of routines to serve as building blocks for an extensive repertoire of calculations. This is one of the benefits of the modular structure of FORTRAN. (See Veldman, 1967, for a discussion of this approach, with many illustrations.)

Two final examples

We conclude this chapter with two larger annotated examples for further study. All language features used have been discussed in detail, so that a careful reading of the preceding pages should yield an explanation of any features which are not understood. As before, if in doubt about the effect of a set of statements, try some simple hypothetical figures and work through the various stages of the calculations until it becomes clear.

Example 7.5

This example appears rather more complicated than any so far encountered, but actually is concerned with a very simple data processing problem. The intrinsic functions used have all been described earlier in this chapter. For the sake of illustration, a magnetic tape file is used temporarily for storing some initial data for later use, although in practice it is unlikely that the storage and retrieval of data of this kind would take place in the same run on the computer.

The use of computer systems as an aid in the rapid analysis of election results has become a commonplace feature of political journalism in Britain. As counting of votes continues in the majority of constituencies, a few early results are examined and the trend of voting disclosed is extrapolated to produce 'predictions' of the likely overall result. The rather simplified example given here shows how part of the process can be carried out on a fairly small computer. The program reads in the results of the previous election in the contested constituencies and stores them temporarily in a given format on a magnetic tape file. Constituencies are identified by unique serial numbers and input in ascending numerical order. This is important since the magnetic tape medium is really best suited only to serial processing of data, and avoids continual rewinding of the tape. Substitution of a random-access backing store medium would eliminate this need, but requires a more elaborate search of the storage file to locate the data needed for each constituency.

As a few results of current voting become available, they are matched by the program against the previous election in the appropriate constituency, and the results are accumulated to estimate the

```
C      A PROGRAM TO COMPARE TWO ELECTION RESULTS WHEN DATA FOR THE SECOND
C      MAY BE INCOMPLETE.  THE BASE RESULTS (ELECTION ONE) ARE STORED ON A
C      MAGNETIC TAPE FILE. ALL SERIAL NUMBERS MUST BE INPUT IN STRICT ASCENDING O
C      ORDER
       DIMENSION ACCUM(5,2),SEATS(4,2),LABELS(4),VOTERS(2),PARTY(4),
      1VOTES(4,2),TOTAL(2),PCENT(4,2),DIFF(5),TRNOUT(2),AMAX(2,2),
      2AMAJ(2),PMAJ(2),DATE(2)
C      WRITE RESULTS FOR ELECTION ONE TO A TAPE FILE,CHECKING THAT
C      SEQUENCE IS CORRECT TO AVOID LATER ERRORS
C
    2  READ(1,100)N
  100  FORMAT(I3)
       WRITE(2,101) N
  101  FORMAT(1H1,10X,25HELECTION ANALYSIS PROGRAM//1X,I5,32H CONSTITUENC
      1Y RESULTS CONSIDERED)
       NX=0
       DO 3 I=1,N
       READ(1,102) NO,NAME,DATE(1),VOTERS(1),((PARTY(J),VOTES(J,1)),
      1J=1,4)
  102  FORMAT(I3,1X,A4,1X,A4,1X,F6.0,1X,A4,1X,F6.0,1X,A4,1X,F6.0,1X,A4,1X
      1,F6.0,1X,A4,1X,F6.0,1X,A4,1X,F6.0)
       IF(NO.LE.NX)  GOTO 4
       WRITE(3,102)NO,NAME,DATE(1),VOTERS(1),((PARTY(J),VOTES(J,1)),
      1J=1,4)
       NX=NO
    3  CONTINUE
       ENDFILE 3
       REWIND 3
       GO TO 5
    4  WRITE(2,103) NO,NAME
  103  FORMAT(1H0,13HCONSTITUENCY ,I3,1X,A4,16H OUT OF SEQUENCE)
       STOP
C
C      READ ROW LABELS FOR FINAL SUMMARY TABLE
    5   READ(1,104) (LABELS(I),I=1,4)
  104  FORMAT(4A4)
C
C      SOME VALUES SET TO ZERO INITIALLY FOR LATER USE
       DO 6 I=1,4
       DO 6 J=1,2
       ACCUM(I,J)=0.0
    6  SEATS(I,J)=0.0
       AVSWNG=0.0
       ASWING=-100.0
       BSWING=+100.0
       Z=0.0
C
C      READ NO. OF RESULTS TO BE SUPPLIED FOR ELECTION TWO
       READ(1,99) ZLIMIT
   99  FORMAT(F3.0)
    7  READ(1,102) NO2,NAME,DATE(2),VOTERS(2),(PARTY(I),VOTES(I,2),I=1,4)
    8  READ(3,102) NO1,NAME,DATE(1),VOTERS(1),(PARTY(J),VOTES(J,1),J=1,4)
       IF(NO1-NO2) 8,9,7
C
C      WRITE TABLE HEADINGS FOR CONSTITUENCY RESULT
    9  WRITE(2,105) NO1,NAME
  105  FORMAT(1H1,16HCONSTITUENCY NO ,I3,4X,A4)
       WRITE(2,106)
  106  FORMAT(1H0,80H----------------------------------------------------
      1-----------------------------)
       WRITE(2,107)  DATE(1),DATE(2)
  107  FORMAT(1H0,16X,A4,16X,A4,10X,18HPERCENT DIFFERENCE)
       WRITE(2,108)
  108  FORMAT(1H0,25X,1H%,19X,1H%,12X,1H%)
C
C      CALCULATE AND PRINT PERCENTAGES FOR ALL PARTIES CONTESTING EACH
C      ELECTION, CHANGES IN VOTE DISTRIBUTIONS, TURNOUTS AND CHANGES
C      IN ELECTORATE
C
       TOTAL(1)=0.0
       TOTAL(2)=0.0
       DO 10 I=1,4
       TOTAL(1)=TOTAL(1)+VOTES(I,1)
   10    TOTAL(2)=TOTAL(2)+VOTES(I,2)
       DO 11 J=1,4
       PCENT(J,1)=VOTES(J,1)/TOTAL(1)*100.0
       PCENT(J,2)=VOTES(J,2)/TOTAL(2)*100.0
   11  DIFF(J) = PCENT(J,2) - PCENT(J,1)
       TRNOUT(1)=TOTAL(1)/VOTERS(1)*100.0
       TRNOUT(2)=TOTAL(2)/VOTERS(2)*100.0
       DIFF(5)= TRNOUT(2) - TRNOUT(1)
       DO 12 I=1,4
       IF(VOTES(I,1).EQ.0.0.AND.VOTES(I,2).EQ.0.0)  GOTO 12
       WRITE(2,109) PARTY(I),VOTES(I,1),PCENT(I,1),VOTES(I,2),PCENT(I,2),
      1DIFF(I)
  109  FORMAT(1H ,A4,F14.0,F10.2,F10.0,F10.2,F12.2)
   12  CONTINUE
       Y=VOTERS(2)-VOTERS(1)
       CHANGE=(Y/VOTERS(1))*100.0
       WRITE(2,110) VOTERS(1),VOTERS(2),Y,CHANGE,TRNOUT(1),TRNOUT(2),
      1DIFF(5)
```

```
 110   FORMAT(1H0,10HELECTORATE,F8.0,12X,F8.0,2X,10HDIFFERENCE,F6.0,2X,
      1F5.2,1H%//8H TURNOUT,3X,F8.2,12X,F8.2,2X,10HDIFFERENCE,F6.2,2X,
      21H%)
       WRITE(2,106)
C
C      ACCUMULATE PARTY VOTES FOR FINAL SUMMARY OF RESULTS
       DO 13 I=1,4
       DO 13 J=1,2
 13    ACCUM(I,J)=ACCUM(I,J)+VOTES(I,J)
       ACCUM(5,1)=ACCUM(5,1)+VOTERS(1)
       ACCUM(5,2)=ACCUM(5,2)+VOTERS(2)
C
C      CALCULATE AND PRINT MAJORITIES IN EACH ELECTION. ACCUMULATE TOTALS OF
C      SEATS HELD BY EACH PARTY
       DO 15 J=1,2
       AMAX(1,J)=AMAX1(VOTES(1,J),VOTES(2,J),VOTES(3,J),VOTES(4,J))
       DO 14 I=1,4
       IF(VOTES(I,J).NE.  AMAX(1,J)) GOTO 14
       VOTES(I,J)=0.0
       SEATS(I,J)=SEATS(I,J)+1.0
  14     CONTINUE
       AMAX(2,J)=AMAX1(VOTES(1,J),VOTES(2,J),VOTES(3,J),VOTES(4,J))
       AMAJ(J)=AMAX(1,J)-AMAX(2,J)
 15    PMAJ(J)=AMAJ(J)/TOTAL(J)*100.0
       WRITE(2,111) (DATE(I),AMAJ(I),PMAJ(I),I=1,2)
 111   FORMAT(1H0,8HMAJORITY,8X,A4,F10.0,F7.2,1H%,4X,A4,F10.0,F7.2,1H%)
       WRITE(2,106)
C
C      CALCULATE SWING BETWEEN FIRST TWO PARTIES IN INOUT DATA,PRINT
C      AND ADD TO ACCUMULATOR VARIABLES IN PROGRAM
       SWING=PCENT(1,2)-PCENT(1,1)+PCENT(2,1)-PCENT(2,2)
       SWING=SWING*0.5
       IF(ASWING.LT.SWING)  ASWING=SWING
       IF(BSWING.GT.SWING)  BSWING=SWING
       AVSWNG=AVSWNG+SWING
       WRITE(2,112)  SWING,PARTY(1),PARTY(2)
 112   FORMAT(1H0,12HSIMPLE SWING ,F6.2,5H% TO ,A4,6H FROM ,A4)
       Z=Z+1.0
       IF(Z - ZLIMIT) 7,16,16
  16   IF(Z.EQ.0.0)  GOTO 17
C
C      CALCULATE AND PRINT SUMMARY TABLE OF ALL RESULTS PROCESED
       WRITE(2,113)
 113   FORMAT(1H1,25X,7HSUMMARY)
       WRITE(2,106)
       AVSWNG=AVSWNG/Z

       WRITE(2,114)  AVSWNG,BSWING,ASWING
 114   FORMAT(1H0,35HMEAN SIMPLE SWING FOR MAJOR PARTIES,F10.2,2X,5HRANGE
      1,F6.2,3H TO,F6.2)
       WRITE(2,106)
 17    WRITE(2,115)
 115   FORMAT(1H0,23HTOTAL VOTE ELECTION ONE,10X,12HELECTION TWO,6X,18HPE
      1RCENT DIFFERENCE)
       WRITE(2,108)
       TOTAL(1)=0.0
       TOTAL(2)=0.0
       DO 18 I=1,4
       TOTAL(1)=TOTAL(1)+ACCUM(I,1)
  18    TOTAL(2)=TOTAL(2)+ACCUM(I,2)
       DO 19 J=1,4
       PCENT(J,1)=ACCUM(J,1)/TOTAL(1)*100.0
       PCENT(J,2)=ACCUM(J,2)/TOTAL(2)*100.0
 19    DIFF(J) = PCENT(J,2) - PCENT(J,1)
       WRITE(2,116) (LABELS(I),ACCUM(I,1),PCENT(I,1),ACCUM(I,2),PCENT(I,2
      1),DIFF(I),I=1,4)
 116   FORMAT(1H ,A4,F14.0,F10.2,F10.0,F10.2,F12.2)
       WRITE(2,106)
       PCENT(1,1) = TOTAL(1)/ACCUM(5,1)*100.0
       PCENT(1,2) = TOTAL(2)/ACCUM(5,2)*100.0
       DIFF(1)=PCENT(1,2)-PCENT(1,1)
       WRITE(2,117) ACCUM(5,1),ACCUM(5,2)
 117   FORMAT(1H0,16HTOTAL ELECTORATE,F10.0,10X,F10.0)
       WRITE(2,118)  PCENT(1,1),PCENT(1,2),DIFF(1)
  118  FORMAT(1H0,7HTURNOUT,F18.2,1H%,F19.2,1H%,9X,F4.2,1H%)
       WRITE(2,119)
 119   FORMAT(1H0,10HSEATS HELD,3X,12HELECTION ONE,9X,12HELECTION TWO,5X,
      110HDIFFERENCE)
       WRITE(2,106)
       DO 20 I=1,4
       DO 20  J=1,2
 20    PCENT(I,J)=SEATS(I,J)/Z*100.0
       DO 21 I=1,4
       DIFF(I)=PCENT(I,2)-PCENT(I,1)
 21    WRITE(2,120) LABELS(I),SEATS(I,1),PCENT(I,1),SEATS(I,2),PCENT(I,2)
      1,DIFF(I)
 120   FORMAT(1H0,A4,F14.0,F10.2,1H%,F10.0,F10.2,1H%,F10.2,1H%)
       WRITE(2,106)
       STOP
       END
```

PRINTOUT: CONSTITUENCY RESULT

```
CONSTITUENCY NO    5     CONS

------------------------------------------------------------------------------

               1960                    1970              PERCENT DIFFERENCE

                          %                       %             %
CON.         760.       2.06       1269.        4.21          2.14
LAB.       13540.      36.76      11430.       37.89          1.12
LIB.       22530.      61.17      17470.       57.91         -3.27

ELECTORATE  55000.                58000.   DIFFERENCE 3000.     5.45%

TURNOUT      66.96                 52.02   DIFFERENCE-14.95   %

------------------------------------------------------------------------------

MAJORITY          1960      8990.  24.41%     1970      6040.   20.02%

------------------------------------------------------------------------------

SIMPLE SWING   0.51% TO CON. FROM LAB.
```

SUMMARY TABLE

```
                           SUMMARY

------------------------------------------------------------------------------

MEAN SIMPLE SWING FOR MAJOR PARTIES        3.43   RANGE-12.91 TO 17.55

------------------------------------------------------------------------------

TOTAL VOTE ELECTION ONE             ELECTION TWO        PERCENT DIFFERENCE

                          %                      %              %
CON         48770.      35.15     44999.       36.09           0.94
LAB         58963.      42.49     54800.       43.95           1.45
LIB         31022.      22.36     24901.       19.97          -2.39
OTHR            0.       0.00         0.        0.00           0.00

------------------------------------------------------------------------------

TOTAL ELECTORATE     185930.              195500.

TURNOUT                 74.63%              63.79%            *-10.84%

SEATS HELD    ELECTION ONE           ELECTION TWO        DIFFERENCE

------------------------------------------------------------------------------

CON              1.       25.00%        2.       50.00%      25.00%

LAB              2.       50.00%        1.       25.00%     -25.00%

LIB              1.       25.00%        1.       25.00%       0.00%

OTHR             0.        0.00%        0.        0.00%       0.00%

------------------------------------------------------------------------------
```

Example 7.5 A program to compare two election results when data for the second may be incomplete.

average national swing. The second stage in 'prediction', not given here, projects the consequences of a swing of this magnitude in terms of gains and losses for the major parties when all the results have been counted.

Although more useful measures can be employed, and are necessary to obtain projections of the performance of more than two parties, the definition of the 'swing' used here is simply the most common one of half of the absolute value of one party's loss plus the gain of the other, expressed in percentages of the total turnout of voters. (For a fuller account see Bartholomew and Bassett, 1971, pages 25–31 and 112–114; and Butler, 1963.)

An extension of the method illustrated which the authors have operated uses a remote access console and a time-sharing system to control the program and communicate the new results, but this does not affect the program itself and requires only that channel numbers should be associated with the appropriate peripheral units. In the example, program channel three must be thought of as associated with a magnetic tape unit, and the other channels with any suitable input and output peripherals.

No flow chart is given for this or the final example program, but with the aid of the annotations, given as comment in the programs themselves, the reader who has grasped the essentials of the language can easily follow the processes involved. Again, if in difficulty, try some simple numbers in the calculations as indicated. In addition to the ENDFILE and REWIND statements, the program makes use of the standard intrinsic function AMAX1 to find the largest of its string of arguments, instead of containing explicit FORTRAN instructions for this process.

Example 7.6

A final, more complex example is included for the benefit of readers with a reasonable degree of statistical or mathematical knowledge. To understand it fully requires some explanation of the methods employed, although the language and structural features are well within the grasp of anyone who has followed the present chapter with care. In fact, it illustrates clearly the power and flexibility of a high level language which employs only a very restricted vocabulary and grammar, and a limited number of simple statements.

A common problem in describing statistical associations between observed variables is to find a convenient means of expressing a functional relationship, as an aid to interpolation or prediction of future observations. The example given here uses least-squares approximation to fit a polynomial of a given degree, that is, an expression of the form

$$y = c_1 + c_2x + c_3x^2 + \dots c_{n+1}x^n$$

```
C      A PROGRAM TO FIT A POLYNOMIAL OF GIVEN DEGREE TO A MAXIMUM OF
C      100 DATA POINTS USING THE LEAST SQUARES METHOD
C
       REAL LHS
       DIMENSION X(100),Y(100),COEFF(11),LHS(11,11)
        READ(1,100) N,NOBS,(X(I),Y(I),I=1,NOBS)
 100   FORMAT(2I3/(2F10.5))
C
C      THE NUMBER OF POINTS AND THE OBSERVATIONS ARE READ AS DATA,
C      SUBROUTINE CURVFT CALCULATES THE POLYNOMIAL COEFFICIENTS
C      OF DEGREE N
C
       N=N+1
       CALL CURVFT(N,NOBS,X,Y,COEFF,LHS)
       WRITE(2,101)
 101   FORMAT(1H1,21HORDER      COEFFICIENT)
       DO 1 I=1,N
       J=I-1
 1     WRITE(2,102) J,COEFF(I)
 102   FORMAT(I5,5X,F12.6)
       STOP
       END


       SUBROUTINE CURVFT(N,NOBS,X,Y,COEFF,LHS)
       REAL LHS
       DIMENSION PX(100),X(NOBS),Y(NOBS),LHS(N,N),RHS(11),
      1COEFF(N)
       N2=(N-1)**2
C
C      TWO ARRAYS ARE ESTABLISHED HOLDING LEFT AND RIGHT HAND SIDES
C      OF THE SET OF NORMAL EQUATIONS
C
       DO 1 I=1,N2
       PX(I)  = 0.0
       DO 1 J= 1,NOBS
 1     PX(I) = PX(I) + X(J)**I
C
C      SUMS OF POWERS OF THE INDEPENDENT VARIABLE X ARE REGROUPED AS
C      L.H.S. COEFFICIENTS
       DO 2 I=1,N
       DO 2 J= 1,N
       K=I+J-2
       IF(K.LE.0) GO TO 3
       LHS(I,J) = PX(K)
       GO TO 2
 3     LHS(I,J) = NOBS
 2     CONTINUE
C
C       R.H.S COEFFICIENTS ARE CALCULATED
       RHS(1) = 0.0
       DO 4 J=1,NOBS
 4     RHS(1) = RHS(1) + Y(J)
       DO 5 I=2,N
       RHS(I) = 0.0
       DO 5 J=1,NOBS
 5     RHS(I) = RHS(I) + Y(J)*X(J)**(I-1)
C
C      SUBROUTINE MATINV INVERTS THE MATRIX LHS
       CALL MATINV(N,LHS)
       DO 6 I=1,N
       COEFF(I) = 0.0
       DO 6 J=1,N
 6     COEFF(I) = COEFF(I) + LHS(I,J)*RHS(J)
       RETURN
       END
```

```
      SUBROUTINE MATINV (N,X)
C
C     COMPUTES THE INVERSE OF A REAL SQUARE MATRIX X OF DEGREE N
C     BY THE GAUSS JORDAN METHOD. THE INVERSE REPLACES THE ORIGINAL
C     MATRIX.
C
      DIMENSION X(N,N),KP(11),KR(11),KC(11)
      DO 1 I=1,N
    1 KP(I) = 0
      DO 9 I=1,N
C
C     PIVOT ELEMENT IS LOCATED
      PIVOT = 0.0
      DO 4 J=1,N
      IF(KP(J).EQ.1) GOTO 4
      DO 3 K= 1, N
      IF(KP(K)-1) 2,3,37
    2 IF(PIVOT .GE. ABS(X(J,K))) GO TO 3
      IR = J
      IC = K
      PIVOT = ABS(X(J,K))
    3 CONTINUE
    4 CONTINUE
      KP(IC) = KP(IC) + 1
      IF(IR .EQ. IC) GO TO 6
C
C     IF THE PIVOT ELEMENT IS NOT ON THE DIAGONAL OF THE MATRIX,
C     ROWS ARE REARRANGED UNTIL IT IS
      DO 5 L=1,N
      HOLD = X(IR,L)
      X(IR,L) = X(IC,L)
    5 X(IC,L) = HOLD
    6 KR(I) = IR
      KC(I) = IR
      PIVOT = X(IC,IC)
      X(IC,IC) = 1.0
C
C     THE PIVOT ROW IS DIVIDED BY THE PIVOT ELEMENT
      DO 7 L= 1,N
    7 X(IC,L) = X(IC,L) / PIVOT
      DO 9 M=1,N
      IF(M.EQ.IC) GO TO 9
      FACTOR = X(M,IC)
      X(M,IC) = 0.0
C
C     NON-PIVOT ROWS ARE REDUCED
      DO 8 L =1,N
    8 X(M,L) = X(M,L) - X(IC,L)*FACTOR
    9 CONTINUE
C
C     WHEN THE REDUCTION PROCESS IS COMPLETE, COLUMNS ARE REARRANGED
C     TO GIVE THE INVERSE OF THE ORIGINAL MATRIX
      DO 11 I=1,N
      J= N-I +1
      IF(KR(J) .EQ. KC(J))  GO TO 11
      L = KC(J)
      K = KR(J)
      DO 10 M = 1,N
      HOLD = X(M,K)
      X(M,K) = X(M,L)
   10 X(M,L) = HOLD
   11 CONTINUE
   37 RETURN
      END
```

PROGRAMMER: | DEPARTMENT: | CONTRACT:
DATE: | PAGE: OF

Statement number

```
 2  12
   1.0      3.0
   2.0      7.0
   3.0     13.0
   4.0     21.0
   5.0     31.0
   6.0     43.0
   7.0     57.0
   8.0     73.0
   9.0     91.0
  10.0    111.0
  11.0    133.0
  12.0    157.0
```

```
ORDER      COEFFICIENT
  0          1.000000
  1          1.000000
  2          1.000000
```

Example 7.6 A program to fit a polynomial of given degree to a maximum of 100 data points using the least squares method.

to a set of observed values. The method consists, basically, of minimising the expression

$$\sum_{i=1}^{N} (y_i - c_1 - c_2x_i - c_3x_i^2 \ldots - c_{n+1}x_i^n)^2$$

where n is the degree of polynomial to be fitted to a set of N observations on x and y. Differentiating the above expression with respect to the coefficients c_i and equating the results to zero establishes a set of $n+1$ equations (termed *normal equations*) which are solved to obtain the required polynomial coefficients.

The program given here sets up normal equations for the derivation of coefficients of polynomials of a specified degree not exceeding ten, and for a maximum of 100 observations. The main program calls a subroutine CURVFT which makes use of a subroutine for matrix inversion as part of the process of solving the normal equations. Other means of solving simultaneous equations could be used (see Calderbank, Appendix 1, pages 72–75) but the procedure for matrix inversion may be of interest in itself to some readers familiar with the questions of matrix algebra. Very roughly it is the matrix equivalent of the reciprocal of a single coefficient, when solving an equation of the kind

$$ax = y$$

In matrix algebra if

$$\mathbf{A}\mathbf{x} = \mathbf{y}$$

$$\text{then} \quad \mathbf{x} = \mathbf{A}^{-1}\mathbf{y}$$

where **A** is a matrix of coefficients, and **x** and **y** are vectors (see, for example, Sterling and Pollack (1968) pages 603–616). The inverse is constructed within the same storage locations as are reserved for the original matrix, resulting in a considerable saving of store for large matrices, at the expense of erasing the original method. Three working arrays are used to keep track of the rearrangement of the matrix involved in the Gauss-Jordan method of pivotal condensation. (See Cooley and Lohnes, pages 191–193.) The least-squares method and curvefitting are fully discussed in, for example, Burford (1968) pages 300–320, and Sterling and Pollack (1968), pages 382–388.

Appendix

In Example 7.3, subroutine ORDER is given as a brief and very simple approach to the problem of ranking data values. It is, in fact, an inefficient routine, since it makes $N(N-1)$ comparisons when it is called, irrespective of the initial order of the array of values. It would do this even if the values were already in a perfect rank order. Figure 3.8 gives an Algol version which uses a more efficient sorting method, but which rearranges the original array of data. This method is capable of recognising when an array is fully ordered, and can vary in its running time according to the degree of disorder in the original set of values. Two further FORTRAN subroutines are given here as an Appendix. Their careful study will develop further awareness of the concept of efficiency in programming methods. The first provides for tied rank values and, while substantially similar to the simpler subroutine ORDER, it is substantially quicker when a number of tied values do in fact occur in the data. The second example is more

```
      SUBROUTINE RANK(X,R,N)
C
C       AN ALTERNATIVE FORTRAN SUBROUTINE
C       TO PRODUCE RANKING OF A
C       SET OF DATA OBSERVATIONS.
C
      DIMENSION X(N),R(N)
      DO 1 I=1,N
 1    R(I) = 0.0
      DO 10 I=1,N
      IF(R(I))  2,2,10
 2    HIGHER = 0.0
      EQUAL = 0.0
      P=X(I)
      DO 5  J=1,N
      IF( P - X(J) )  3,4,5
C
C       THE RANKS ARE IN THIS CASE RETURNED AS A REAL ARRAY,
C       FOR EACH VALUE, A COUNT IS MADE OF ALL VALUES WHICH ARE
C       LARGER OR EQUAL.  IF THERE ARE OTHER EQUAL VALUES, THE RANK IS
C       ASSIGNED BY THE 'MID-RANK' METHOD.
C       E.G.  IF THREE VALUES ARE TIED AT THE 5-TH RANK, THEY ARE
C       EACH GIVEN A RANK OF 6.
C       TWO VALUES TIED AT THE 3-RD RANK WOULD EACH BE GIVEN A
C       RANK OF 3.5
C
 3    HIGHER = HIGHER + 1.0
      GO TO 5
 4    EQUAL = EQUAL + 1.0
      R(J) = - 1.0
 5    CONTINUE
      IF (EQUAL .GT. 1.0)  GO TO 7
      R(I) = HIGHER + 1.0
      GO TO 10
 7    Q = HIGHER + (EQUAL + 1.0) / 2.0
      DO 8 J=1,N
      IF ( R(J) .GE. 0.0) GO TO 8
      R(J) = Q
 8    CONTINUE
 10   CONTINUE
      RETURN
      END
```

```
      IF ( J .GE. P) GO TO 31
      IF ( J .LE. 1) GO TO 32
      F(K)  = I + 1
      G(K) = N
      N = I - 1
      K = K +1
      GO TO 60
 32   M = I + 1
      GO TO 60
 31   IF ( P.LE. 1 ) GO TO 33
      F(K) = M
      G(K) = I - 1
      M = I + 1
      K = K + 1
      GO TO 60
 33   N = I - 1
 60   CONTINUE
      SIZE = N - M + 1
      IF ( 2 - SIZE ) 12 ,12,13
 100  CONTINUE
C
C       THE ARRAY R NOW CONTAINS THE REFERENCE SUBSCRIPTS OF A RE-ORDERED
C       ACCORDING TO THE MAGNITUDES OF THE CORRESPONDING ELEMENTS IN A,
C       THESE ARE NOW TRANSLATED INTO RANK VALUES.
C
      DO 61  I = 1, NA
      G(R(I)) = I
 61   CONTINUE
      RETURN
      END
```

```
      SUBROUTINE KEYSORT(A,R,NA,F,G)
      INTEGER P,RI,RJ,RM,RN,SIZE,R,F,G
      DIMENSION A(NA),R(NA),F(NA),G(NA)
C
C       SORTS THE NUMBERS IN AN INTEGER ARRAY OF RANKS ACCORDING TO
C       THE MAGNITUDE OF ELEMENTS IN THE ARRAY A.
C       ONCE THE RANK OF ELEMENT  D   IS DETERMINED,  THE ELEMENTS OF
C       A ARE PARTITIONED INTO THREE SUBSETS,  D  ITSELF, AND ELEMENTS
C       LARGER AND SMALLER THAN D,  EACH OF WHICH IS SIMILARLY TREATED
C       IN TURN.
C       D   IS CHOSEN AS THE APPROXIMATE MIDDLE ELEMENT OF THE SET
C       AT EACH ITERATION.  THE ARRAYS F AND G ARE USED AS STACKS
C       TO STORE THE BOUNDS OF SUBSETS, AND USE A STACK POINTER K.
C       THE CHOICE OF D IS ARBITRARY, BUT AFFECTS THE EFFICIENCY
C       OF THE SUBROUTINE, DEPENDING ON THE INITIAL ORDER OF A.
C       THE MIDDLE ELEMENT OF A IS THE BEST TO CHOOSE AS THE BASIS FOR
C       PARTITIONING IF THE ORDER OF ELEMENTS IS NEARLY RANDOM.
C
C       TO AVOID THE USE OF FURTHER STORAGE, THE RESULTS
C       OF THE INDIRECT RE-ORDERING PROCESS ARE CONVERTED
C       AT THE END TO RETURN THE RANKS IN THE ARRAY G.
C       AN INDIRECT METHOD AVOIDS ANY RE-ORDERING OF THE ORIGINAL ARRAY.
C
C
      M= 1
      N = NA
      SIZE = NA
  9   IF (SIZE - 2)  100,10,10
 10   K=1
C       INITIALISE THE RANKS.
      DO 11 I = 1,NA
 11   R(I) = I
 12    IF( SIZE .GT.  2)  GO TO 20
C       DEAL WITH SUBSETS OF ORDER 2 SEPARATELY.
C
C
      RM = R(M)
      RN = R(N)
      IF (A(RM) .GE. A(RN))  GO TO 13
      R(M) = RN
      R(N) = RM
C       EXTRACT THE BOUNDS OF THE NEXT SUBSET
 13   K = K - 1
      IF ( K .EQ. 0)  GO TO 100
      M = F(K)
      N = G(K)
      GO TO 60
 20   I = M
      J = N
C       CHOOSE THE MIDDLE ELEMENT AS  D.
      P = (I+J) / 2
      RM = R(P)
      R(P) = R(M)
      D = A(RM)
 21   IF (I - J) 22,30,22
C       J INDEXES A HIGH TO LOW SCAN.
 22   RJ = R(J)
      IF (A(RJ) .LE. D) GO TO 24
      R(I) = RJ
      I = I + 1
 26   IF ( I - J)  27,30,27
 27   RI = R(I)
C       I INDEXES A LOW TO HIGH SCAN.
      IF (A(RI) .GE. D) GO TO 25
      R(J) = RI
      J = J - 1
      GO TO 21
 25   I = I + 1
      GO TO 26
 24   J = J - 1
      GO TO 21
C       I IS NOW THE RANK OF D, REFERENCED BY RM, AND R(I) IS VACANT, SO
 30   R(I) = RM
      J = I - M
      P = N - I
C       CHOOSE THE SMALLER SUBSET FOR TREATMENT, STORING THE BOUNDS
C       OF THE LARGER SUBSET,  UNLESS THE SMALLER SUBSET HAS ONLY ONE
C       ELEMENT IN WHICH CASE DEAL WITH THE LARGER SUBSET IMMEDIATELY.
C
```

. . . .

complicated, and is based on a similar algorithm to the program given in Fig. 5.5. The example is a FORTRAN version of an algorithm given by J. Boothroyd (1967), and uses more storage than the other methods in return for a substantially shorter average run-time. The latter depends upon the degree of randomness in the order of the data to be ranked.

Subroutine	Data Set	
	(1)	(2)
RANK	66.78 seconds	21.27 seconds
ORDER	62.88 seconds	63.30 seconds
KEYSORT	1.56 seconds	1.65 seconds

The timings for the three subroutines illustrate clearly their relative inefficiency and the interaction between different algorithms and the data submitted. They were obtained from the University of Southampton's ICL 1907 computer for (1) 1000 randomly generated numbers between 0 and 1·0 and (2) a set of 1000 observed data values containing many ties and nearly random in order of magnitude.

References

D. J. Bartholomew and E. E. Bassett (1971) *Let's Look at the Figures: the Quantitative Approach to Human Affairs*, Harmondsworth, Penguin.

J. Boothroyd, Algorithm 26, *Computer Journal* **10** (1967), pages 308–309.

R. L. Burford (1968) *Statistics: A Computer Approach*, Columbus, Merrill.

D. E. Butler (1963) *The Electoral System in Britain since 1918*, 2nd ed., Oxford, Clarendon Press.

W. W. Cooley and P. R. Lohnes (1962), *Multivariate Procedures for the Behavioral Sciences*, New York, John Wiley.

A. C. Day (1972) *FORTRAN Techniques*, Cambridge University Press.

National Computing Centre Limited (1970) *Standard FORTRAN Programming Manual*, Computer Standard Series, N.C.C., Manchester.

S. Siegel (1956), *Nonparametric Statistics for the Behavioral Sciences*, New York, London, McGraw-Hill.

T. D. Sterling and S. V. Pollack (1968) *Introduction to Statistical Data Processing*, Englewood Cliffs, N.J., Prentice-Hall.

D. J. Veldman (1967), *FORTRAN Programming for the Behavioral Sciences*, New York, Holt, Rhinehart and Winston.

Further reading

Practice in writing programs for a particular machine is essential to learning any programming language. For reference, the manuals describing any particular implementation of FORTRAN are essential, but any of the following courses may be useful for further reading on facilities not covered in this chapter.

V. J. Calderbank (1969) *A Course on Programming in FORTRAN IV*, London, Chapman and Hall.

D. D. McCracken (1961) *A Guide to FORTRAN Programming*, New York, John Wiley.

E. James, F. O'Brien, P. Whitehead (1970) *A FORTRAN Programming Course*, London, Prentice-Hall.

Veldman (1967) and Cooley and Lohnes (1962) contain many useful routines for statistical analysis, as well as an introduction to more advanced techniques. Day (1972) draws together brief and simple descriptions of advanced uses of the language, particularly for non-numerical work, otherwise to be found in various theoretical journals.

8 Prospects and privacy

The major emphasis of this book has been on the mechanics of computing and some of the areas of application, skills and problems which the social science user is likely to encounter. However, particularly in the social sciences, it is of crucial importance to discuss the societal context within which the computer has developed. In Chapter 1 we dealt with some of the intellectual and emotional consequences of the advent of computers. In this conclusion two inter-linked areas will be explored, first some likely machine and software developments, and second the implications of these developments in the area of individual privacy. In many ways a certain long-term reciprocity can be seen between these two areas. Machine and software developments both influence and are influenced by social reactions.

Hardware and software prospects

Looking ahead, in hardware terms, it seems likely that the trend towards smaller, faster computers with higher capacity and cheaper memories will continue, although the basic functional definitions of Chapter 2 will still summarise most systems quite adequately.

Automated production of L.S.I. logic circuits will help to reduce the price of minicomputers too, but we think that most social scientists will continue to need the resources of a large computing centre for applications involving substantial storage needs.

Some computer scientists are sceptical about the general applicability of the idea of parallel processing. Nevertheless, some combination of parallel with sequential execution of instructions offers one way of achieving very significant reductions in run times (Slotnick, 1971). If it were possible, for example, for the computer to recognise in some way that the FORTRAN loop

```
   DO 10 I=1,1000
10 A(I)=1.0
```

need take only as long as a single assignment statement, or if a programmer could write parallel instructions, then the time taken to run a program could be greatly reduced without changing the storage needed. Another hardware idea, for some time of experimental status, provides for the addressing of storage locations not by name or position but by their content. The importance of this so-called associative memory lies in the ability to search the memory by content and in parallel, in approximately the same access time as for a single element in a conventional store. The wider use of hardware stacks for dynamic push-down storage would also produce considerable time savings in the manipulation of data structures for which provision is currently made by software.

Mass storage developments using several new technologies are likely to remove serious problems of information accumulation reasonably economically. Various experimental laser devices can already store up to 10^8 bits on a square inch of film, while holographic memories promise high resolution and access speeds at low cost. Holography is also being applied to the construction of 3-dimensional displays, and offers a simpler 'rotation' of the image with true parallax effects. Bell Telephone Laboratories have recently developed a storage tube which uses an infra-red laser to produce opacity in a liquid crystal sandwiched between glass sheets. This or similar photochromic displays could provide a cathode ray tube replacement with no need for continuous refreshing of the image. In peripherals, however, the likely emphasis for the next few years will be on improved reliability and performance of existing devices, until they can pass what one recent writer calls the 'coffee and sugar doughnut' test. 'An operator must be able to spill coffee through a sugar doughnut directly into the works of the device' (Tomash, 1971, page 67). As it is, reasonably fast and precise line-printers have already taken a number of years and considerable investment to develop.

However, hardware costs at present represent only about 25% of the total cost of an average commercial data processing installation. Most of the dramatic increases in computing speeds have not been the result of improved software techniques, and the reduction of unit costs by faster operation has involved much increased overall capital costs of equipment. Only by improving the efficiency of operating systems in multi-processing or extensive time-sharing among users is it possible to approach an economic use of modern hardware, and even some computer professionals doubt whether this can be done in very large computing systems. Certainly neither is cheap to develop for general purpose use.

The high overall development costs of hardware and software seem to indicate the continued use of general-purpose facilities, by software means, rather than pressure for special-purpose machines peculiar to the social sciences. They also place an ever greater responsibility on social scientists to be efficient in their use of expensive equipment. To some extent, of course, this will be eased by improvements in general-purpose software. Existing applications of read-only memories and special micro-programs to handle basic system functions will probably become widespread. We can expect continued improvement in compilers and operating systems, with an extension of the virtual storage concept noted earlier in this book. By improving the machine code generated by higher level languages, and removing the need to spend time programming the use of backing store, a programmer's job can be stripped to its problem-solving essentials.

General hardware and software improvements will, we hope, contribute to greater ease of use and economy in interactive computing. It is undoubtedly true that, notwithstanding the developments of the past decade or so, this kind of operation is still very expensive when compared with batch processing. Many earlier optimistic forecasts of a 'computer utility' for a wide range of operations on any kind of data base have proved ill-founded. Nevertheless, the more spectacular and immediate results of on-line operation will continue to generate pressure for its development and dissemination. At present most widespread on-line systems have concentrated on a *data communication* service, rather than a *data analysis* service, sidestepping some of the more acute problems of linking terminals to central computers. Services dealing with, for example, stock prices, are usually merely interrogatory, dealing with simple queries generated locally. The real difficulties come with the flexibility of operations which would be required in a system truly described as a computer utility, and the large number of remote terminals which it would support.

Packaged programs are unlikely to provide all the facilities a user needs, and for certain purposes will only be developed adequately from within the social sciences. General software development may make this task much simpler for an unskilled user. At the same time, however, the professionals' field is becoming more specialised and inaccessible, so that a social scientist interested in more advanced computing needs some ability to program for himself, and must be able to communicate with computer experts to benefit from their research and advice. Some programming must be regarded in the same way as some statistical knowledge, as among the basic tools of empirical social science.

Although we have introduced programming in this book by means of FORTRAN, it does seem that this type of language is not necessarily the best tool for applications much beyond the scope of our third chapter. The near-universality of FORTRAN compilers has to be weighed against the relative inefficiency of trying to perform every task by extensions to a language designed for second-generation computers. Efficiency considerations also suggest that, except for rather simple purposes, English-type languages are a rather cumbersome means of communicating with computers.

For some operations, we need languages capable of handling complex data structures as easily as numbers. Any powerful special-purpose social science language would also need to be capable of self-extension, in which case it would probably be as difficult to learn as any general-purpose language, which hardly justifies the idea of a special-purpose definition in practice. With the possible exception of simulation aids, any improvement in general computing skills in the social sciences seems likely to take place by the adoption and promotion of advanced functional languages like POP2, rather than by a special-purpose or natural-language approach (compare Figs. 5.3 and 5.5).

We can also hope that the standard of documentation of programs suitable for use in the social sciences will improve, and that with it a more rapid dissemination of work will help improvements to take place in a cumulative way. Journals in the more mathematical social sciences already take note of computing systems and publish methods for the solution of common problems in the form of algorithms in Algol or Fortran. The journal *Computers and the Humanities* and some occasional publications (for example, Mitchell *et al.*, 1973) are beginning to meet a similar need for information in less mathematical fields. The major difficulty lies in the exchange of complete programs or methods which are too large for publication as complete algorithms, which, of course, includes many simulation aids and the processes for special language systems. For preference, these are exchanged between users in a machine-readable form. For efficiency, such programs may contain sections of assembler-level code, which is specific to a type of computer.

Communicating software at this level cannot be machine independent and currently such systems require laborious translation for another manufacturer's equipment. The difficulty is akin to the so-called '$m \times n$ compiler problem', this being the number of different compilers required to process m different languages on n different machines. The use of standardised high level languages for which compilers are widely available is one common way around the problem, at a cost of lowered efficiency. The other is to increase the use of some of the compiling techniques described in Chapter 3, increasing the amount of basic software written in efficient high level languages. Being realistic, we do not expect manufacturers to standardise their machine codes. All this reinforces our recommendation that social scientists should not use esoteric computer languages.

Briefly, then, we expect the continued use of general-purpose digital computers using software, at least partly provided from within the social sciences, to prove most fruitful.

Computers and privacy

For these reasons there is both cause to rely on the computer's speed, storage capacity and accuracy and to be cautious about the uses to which these assets might be put. In recent years, one of the most controversial areas, which emphasises both these aspects, has been that of data banks and rights to privacy. Indeed, this point of contact with computers has been for many the crucial test of the ultimate benefits of the computer age. Data banks have particular importance for the social sciences, where social research itself may soon progress as much through the centralised storage and retrieval of individual or aggregated information, as through other methods.

A. F. Westin (Westin, 1971, pages 158 ff) has suggested that there are three recognisable stages to the storage and retrieval of information by computer systems. The first stage recognisable in the late 1950's and early 1960's was the computerisation of individual files by small and large concerns. This usually consisted in merely making existing files machine-readable, and using them in exactly the same way, although rather more easily, than they had been previously used. The second stage, evident from the late 1960's, was the formation of data banks which tended to be developed on the basis of a particular *type of use*, rather than on the files of a *particular firm*. This might mean that several firms, or institutions, concerned with the same type of information, would pool that information. In the social sciences, the most obvious examples are the survey analysis data banks, where many types of institutions such as governments, universities, and polling organisations have contributed information on similar areas (Land, 1971). This might be seen as similar to the process of forming general archives, but commercial or government data banks usually have facilities for updating individual files, either at the data banks themselves, or by remote line links. The third stage, which Westin sees as the main recent growth area, has been the expansion of data banks to cover a wide-ranging field of activities, in which files on individuals would contain comprehensive information and be available to a number of different agencies through an efficient computer system. This latter stage is the main point of issue for those concerned with the use and abuse of data banks. It is felt that the synthesising of many different aspects of an individual's personal history from many different sources, which would then be available to varied (and perhaps unscrupulous) users, would seriously undermine the privacy of the individual. At worst, this could lead to the perpetuation of unknown and unchallengeable inaccuracies of detail, thus giving the potential for absolute control to those with access to this information (Younger Report, 1972, Chapter 20; Warner and Stone, 1970).

A number of conflicting, and sometimes confusing, issues arise out of this analysis of data banks. It is fair to say that the advent of the computer has not *caused* the problems for which it is blamed, but has produced a sharpening of the conflict of interests which has always been present. The issue of privacy has always been a potentially explosive one, but previously one which has largely centred on an individual's conflict with a particular institution.

With the advent of computers two main points seem to arise. One is the question of what should be private to an individual, which is an essentially *political* question. The other is the question of security of information, once that information is obtained, which is a largely *technical* question. Of course, these two sometimes overlap, particularly where information is considered legitimately stored for one purpose, but not for another, and a decision is needed as to who should have access. However, it seems important to separate the two areas, since computer professionals sometimes consider the issues to be largely technical ones concerned with software security, on-line passwords, and aggregating individual information, and those outside the computer field may consider the issues as largely political. Given evidence of efficient security of individual information some of the political decisions needed might prove less contentious, except for those who maintain that the very existence of any form of data bank violates individual privacy.

Many social scientists are concerned with information about individuals which is of an even more sensitive kind than that in which government agencies or businesses have a direct interest. This arises from the nature of much fundamental research. A great deal of social and behavioural research also, by its very nature, raises issues of obtaining proper consent from its subjects for what would normally be regarded as a violation of their privacy (Warner and Stone, 1970, pages 128–129; Sjoberg, 1967). However, as a group, social researchers have shown remarkably little concern as yet for the way in which deposition of individual data with data banks may violate the conditions of confidentiality under which the information was acquired.

The problem of privacy has scarcely arisen in social science data banks, which at present receive remarkably little use. Nevertheless, as social scientists become more generally proficient at information handling by computer, an increased demand on resources is easily foreseen.

There are a number of practical steps which could considerably reduce the risk to individual privacy, while not damaging the main purpose of data banks in social science. The first of these is to try to ensure through efficient security systems the protection of such individual information as is collected. One of the major fears has been the prospect of amalgamation of many individual pieces of information, which by themselves constitute only a limited and disjointed personal picture, but together present a relatively complete data set on one individual. There are two possible answers to these problems. First, that *separate* data banks should exist for each organisation, which should do no more than provide in machine-readable form data already in existence, with access confined only to the organisation itself respecting individual confidentiality. Second, that there could be a data bank amalgamating information, but it would do so on an *aggregate* and not on an *individual* basis. Means should be found of aggregating information on such a scale that it would still be useful for social and economic planning purposes, but it would be impossible to identify individuals within the data set. Various aggregation procedures have been discussed, but there is an extremely critical balance between the data being useful for planning or research purposes and keeping individual information protected.

Feige and Watts (1970) discuss specific procedures for what is called the 'partial aggregation' of data. The utility of this process depends largely on the statistical analyses which are to follow the aggregation. If, for example, a standard regression procedure is to be used, with a known independent variable, then the data can be aggregated to minimise bias in this case. However, if the process of aggregation is a general one, where no *a priori* statistical operations are known (for example, in a situation where future users and uses are unknown in detail) then the inbuilt errors can be considerable. The crucial technique to counteract these errors could be to allow for *flexible* aggregation, on the basis of different regression models, and independent variables, or on the individual proclivities of researchers. In this latter case 'trade-offs' could be catered for in which a researcher would specify the maximum acceptable within-group variation for one variable, trading off this variation against that of another. If aggregation procedures could be adopted which are flexible, as most currently are not, then at least a measure of utility could be salvaged from what is generally a statistically destructive operation.

1. Collection of data subject to confidentiality of use
2. Coding of information on individuals, removing obvious identification such as name and address
3. Analysis of data for research purposes, while the researcher holds the coding key and details of individuals
4. Consideration of the desirable degree of individual protection in reporting results before publication of the analysis
5. Consideration of individual protection before the release of coded data for use by other social scientists. (This may require aggregation of the raw data by suitable geographic areas or other dimensions of classification.)

Fig. 8.1 Recommended stages in data processing.

The opposite problem may arise, however, if the aggregation procedures are too flexible. For example, many researchers are concerned with particular categories of individuals (occupational groupings such as doctors, or academics, etc.) with reliance on a small sample and/or a small population. For information in these small surveys to be useful, it may need to be analysed to the stage where it is possible to identify individuals. The point might be reached where a data bank is requested to supply only computed analyses of data, and not individual data cards or other individually coded values. For example, a researcher could specify that particularly sensitive data could be released only in the form of a standard analysis chosen from a range available at the data bank, or in the form of a matrix of correlations or factor loadings. Thus in order to preserve individual security, it might be necessary to sacrifice extremely detailed geographical analyses on the smallest census data areas, or analyses which dealt with very small aggregates in the reprocessing of data already gathered and stored. We are suggesting that these considerations should, in the manner of Fig. 8.1, be considered as part of the normal research practice of a socially responsible social scientist.

Even if aggregation techniques are used, the data concerning individuals are usually still stored, and therefore technically available for analysis. In this context a number of security problems need to be resolved. These include those who have access to the software of the computer; the assurance that maintenance engineers do not facilitate illicit operations or transmissions; the separation of access to data from access to programs, the security of checking and monitoring programs and the use of passwords. Each of these involves considerable technical expertise and money to put into operation. At present the greatest security naturally exists at military installations, where the priorities for such systems are high, but costs are in the region of 10–30% of the total. It may be that, as an increasingly high priority is given to the question of privacy, users and manufacturers would be prepared to incorporate more elaborate security devices. However, the main impetus is much more likely to come from concern over industrial espionage and sabotage, than from the commercially unimportant question of privacy. In the last analysis, the holding of individual records and their security is a complex question of losses and gains, losses in terms of individual privacy, and gains in terms of planning for social benefits and the acquisition of knowledge. The main danger is that there may be only one party to the decision—the computer user—for the individual subject is unaware and powerless in this situation.

References

E. L. Feige and H. W. Watts (1970) 'Protection of Privacy through Micro-aggregation' in R. L. Bisco (Editor) *Data Bases, Computers, and the Social Sciences*, New York, John Wiley, pages 261–272.

F. Land (1971) 'Survey Archive Data Banks', *Social Science Research Council News Letter* **13**, pages 15–18.

J. C. Mitchell, J. Thompson, G. Thorn and D. Weir (1973) *Computerguide 3: Programs for Social Scientists* (*Social Data Analysis Programs in the U.K.*), Manchester, National Computing Centre.

G. Sjoberg (Editor) (1967) *Ethics, Politics and Social Research*, Cambridge, Mass., Shenkman; 1969 edition: London, Routledge and Kegan Paul.

D. L. Slotnick, 'The Fastest Computer', *Scientific American*, February, 1971; repr. in R. R. Fenichel and J. Weizenbaum (Editors), *Computers and Computation*, San Francisco, W. H. Freeman.

E. Tomash, 'Marketing in the 70's—Peripherals and People' *in* F. Gruenberger (Editor) (1971) *Expanding Use of Computers in the 70's: Markets, Needs and Technology*, Englewood Cliffs, N.J., Prentice-Hall.

M. Warner and M. Stone (1970) *The Data Bank Society*, London, Allen & Unwin.

A. F. Westin, 'Civil Liberties and Computerized Data Systems' in M. Greenberger (Editor) (1971) *Computers, Communications and the Public Interest—Towards a Computer Utility*, New York, John Hopkins Press.

Younger Report—*Report of the Committee on Privacy*, Cmd. 5012, HMSO, London, 1972.

Further reading

Questions of computers and privacy are extensively discussed in

A. F. Westin (1967) *Privacy and Freedom*, New York, Athenaeum; 1970 edition: London, Bodley Head,

Warner and Stone (1970) *The Data Bank Society*, George Allen & Unwin,

J. Martin and A. R. D. Norman (1970) *The Computerized Society*, Englewood Cliffs, N.J., Prentice-Hall,

and The Younger Report.

The papers edited by Gruenberger (1971) are a useful corrective to some of the more euphoric forecasts of the future of computing.

Index